Foreword

This is a research report of great significance; the first to look in depth at women's experiences of concealed pregnancy in Ireland.

It aimed to create an understanding of the social, emotional, psychological and practical factors contributing to a woman's decision to conceal her pregnancy. It documents the services that are in place for a woman trying to cope with a concealed pregnancy.

The women's stories reveal the emotional toll concealment places on a woman. The accounts of healthcare professionals highlight the challenges they face in supporting women with a concealed, denied or undetected pregnancy. It outlines the problems for everyone when a woman presents to them for care in an advanced stage of pregnancy. These accounts give many examples of how healthcare professionals respond successfully to these challenges in the course of their daily work.

Concealed pregnancy has wide-ranging implications for the woman, her social network and the professional services she comes into contact with. It is my hope that the findings from this study will allow the Crisis Pregnancy Agency, along with its partner organisations, to standardise the response to a woman in this situation and will assist health and support services in developing/delivering the best quality care to women. It is also my hope that the programme of cultural change embarked upon by the Crisis Pregnancy Agency, along with the education, advice and contraceptive services we provide for, will improve understanding of sexuality issues. I hope that these services will also help parents, teachers and the general public to support women in crisis, and thereby remove the impediments that force a woman to conceal her pregnancy.

I would like to thank, first of all, the author of the study, Catherine Conlon, of the Women's Education, Research and Resource Centre (WERRC), UCD.

I would like to thank and acknowledge the input of the Agency's research staff, Dr. Stephanie O'Keeffe, Madeleine O'Carroll and Mary Smith. I would also like acknowledge the key role HSE West had in commissioning the research in partnership with the CPA, and to thank the hospitals that facilitated the research, and the health professionals in HSE West and HSE Dublin Mid-Leinster who gave so generously of their valuable time to participate in this study.

Most importantly of all, sincere thanks and appreciation is due to the women who participated in this sensitive report. We recognise their courage in sharing their experiences. Their contribution has helped to make this research rich in insights that will guide the development of a national policy and framework of services, which will respond in the best possible way to concealed pregnancy in medical, social, counselling and support services settings throughout Ireland.

Olive Braiden
Chairperson,
Crisis Pregnancy Agency

About the authors

Catherine Conlon, Research Co-ordinator, Women's Education, Research and Resource Centre (WERRC), UCD.

Catherine Conlon graduated with an MA in Women's Studies from UCD in 1994 and has since worked as a social researcher both within the university sector at Trinity College Dublin (Department of Sociology) and now within WERRC, University College Dublin, as well as in the public sector as Research Officer at the National Council on Ageing and Older People. She is Research Co-ordinator at WERRC, working on a range of projects in the areas of social policy, gender and equality, gender and health, and women's adult education. She is co-author of *Women and Crisis Pregnancy* (1998) with Evelyn Mahon and Lucy Dillon and author of *Mixed Methods Research of Crisis Pregnancy Counselling and Support Services* (2005).

Acknowledgments

I am honoured to have met the women who shared the experiences of their pregnancy with me during this research. Their bravery in participating in the study challenges us to acknowledge how concealed pregnancy continues to be a feature of our society. In particular they challenge us to realise how aspects of our society can converge to create a situation where a woman finds the realisation of pregnancy unimaginable to face. I warmly thank you all and hope this report does justice to your stories.

I received crucial help and support from the Social Work and Counselling Support Service Departments of the hospitals where the research was conducted, which was vital to the success of the study. I wish to extend my sincerest thanks for the unerring commitment and dedication shown by you all to this work.

We in WERRC have been very pleased to undertake this research on behalf of the Crisis Pregnancy Agency and HSE West and commend their vision in commissioning this piece of work. Many thanks to all of the members of the Research Advisory group for their invaluable help and support throughout the research process.

I am as ever indebted to the members of our in-house research advisory group who were a crucial resource to me throughout the research – Ursula Barry, Ailbhe Smyth, Maeve Casey and Patrica Kennedy.

Finally thanks to my colleagues Sarah Murphy and Joan O'Connor, who acted as Research Assistants on the section of the case study dealing with professionals and whose statistical know how compensated for my aversion to number crunching. Thanks also for dealing with queries arising while I took leave to give birth to my delightful little girl Aoibhe (sister of the equally delightful Jane).

The views expressed in this report are those of the authors and do not necessarily reflect the views or policies of the sponsors

TABLE OF CONTENTS

P/O NO:
ACCESSION NO: KHO3080
SHELFMARK: Opus Women's Health ②

LIST OF TABLES

LIST OF FIGURES

Executive summary

Background

This study arose out of interested and concerned observations of social work and crisis pregnancy counselling and support staff attached to the antenatal and maternity departments of an Irish rural-based general hospital. Staff noted a recurring incidence in social work caseloads of women attending for antenatal care later than recommended guidelines, often having made no or limited disclosure of the pregnancy to significant others. These cases were considered to come within the staff's understanding of 'concealed pregnancies'. Discussions with colleagues in other areas of the antenatal and maternity services indicated particular issues, concerns and challenges arising in meeting the needs of women in such circumstances. This led to a research initiative, in partnership with the Crisis Pregnancy Agency, to gain a deeper understanding of concealed pregnancy. A primary objective of the research would be to generate recommendations to guide and inform the planning and development of a national policy and framework of services responding to concealed pregnancy in medical, social, counselling and support services settings throughout Ireland.

Defining 'concealed pregnancy'

A review of the international and national literature indicated that concealed pregnancy is not a thing of the past but rather remains a feature of contemporary western societies. Meanwhile, no specific research has been conducted on this issue to date in Ireland, and only very limited research has been conducted internationally. The scope of the literature is lacking, with very few studies concentrating on concealed pregnancy in the absence of neonaticide[1] and psychiatric disorders. Data on the incidence of concealed pregnancy was inadequate, both internationally and in Ireland. In the Irish setting, data sources were limited to maternity hospital annual reports and references to pregnancies as 'concealed' in a few Irish obstetric studies, usually looking at the issue of babies born before arrival at hospital and/or to 'unbooked[2]' women.

Generating a consistent definition of pregnancy denial and concealment from the literature was a difficult task. Definitions that existed tended to be ambiguous and often failed to incorporate fully the range of physiological, cultural, social and psychological dimensions of the phenomenon. As such, our definitions and questions were tentative and intended to be the subject of on-going review and modification as our understandings came to be informed by emerging research findings.

In conceptualising the research at the outset, concealed pregnancy was defined as a situation where a woman presents for antenatal care past twenty weeks' gestation, without having availed of antenatal care or without disclosing the pregnancy to her social network.

Research methodology

A case-study approach was followed for this study, reflecting both the sensitive nature of the topic under inquiry and the exploratory nature of the research in light of the dearth

---

1 Neonaticide usually refers to the killing of a child during the first 24 hours of life. Infanticide usually refers to the killing of a child during the first year of life (Craig 2004).

2 This is a term applied in Irish maternity clinics and hospitals to women who have not attended for ante-natal care prior to arriving at the hospital to give birth.

of previous work in this area. A case-study approach entails assembling data relating to the research question from a range of sources to generate insights from a multiplicity of perspectives with the aim of achieving an in-depth understanding.

The data sources generated for the research were as follows:

- Documentary analysis of case-notes relating to women presenting with a concealed pregnancy generated by maternity social work and crisis pregnancy support services
- In-depth interviews with women who concealed their pregnancy
- Interviews with health professionals who come in contact with women who have concealed pregnancy.

Typologies of concealed pregnancy

Based on the review of literature, three typologies of the process resulting in a pregnancy being concealed have been advanced:

'Unconscious denial' – A woman has no subjective awareness of being pregnant throughout the majority of the pregnancy or even up to a totally unexpected sudden delivery.

'Conscious denial' – The fact of the pregnancy is recognised by the woman but she continues to deny it to herself and others, thereby cognitively realising the pregnancy but not displaying emotions associated with pregnancy.

'Concealment of pregnancy' – A woman acknowledges the pregnancy to herself but hides it from others and does not present for antenatal care at least until after twenty weeks' gestation, up to the point of delivery or in some cases not at all.

These typologies were assessed against our analysis to assess the extent to which they fit with the accounts of women who participated in this research.

Our analysis indicated that the term 'undetected pregnancy' was a better fit with the accounts of women who reported no subjective awareness of being pregnant until advanced pregnancy or even labour than 'unconscious denial'. The evidence generated in this research indicates that this was an outcome of failure to detect the pregnancy on the part of physicians women were attending rather than the outcome of a psychological process of denial on the part of the woman.

The second typology – 'conscious denial' – did fit well with the accounts of women who recognised the fact of the pregnancy but continued to deny it to themselves and others. All expressed a sense of feeling detached from the pregnancy and of having a very different relationship to the pregnancy, their growing 'bump', foetal movements and scan pictures of the foetus than would be expected. Their accounts indicate that this was a coping mechanism they invoked because the reality of the pregnancy was unimaginable to them, generated anxiety or pain, as well as being a very real threat to how they had anticipated the trajectory of their lives and that of their families.

The final typology of concealment also seemed to fit well with the accounts of women who described acknowledging the pregnancy themselves but concealing it from others. Concealment was a coping strategy. For some women it served to allow them manage their own sense that the pregnancy was a personal crisis. Others concealed the pregnancy to cope with anticipated disapproval, to retain control over the outcome of the pregnancy or because external stressors in the woman's life led them to the view that the pregnancy was incompatible with their situation. Women concealing the pregnancy often engage in a process of adaptation to the pregnancy and the prospect of motherhood, including displaying emotions associated with pregnancy, engaging with the foetus or making preparations to care for the baby after delivery.

Factors and processes involved in undetected, denied and concealed pregnancy

The factors identified by women as to why their pregnancy went undetected or why they entered into a process of either denying or concealing the pregnancy could be categorised under the headings of physiological, social/cultural and psychological factors.

Physiological factors

Factors arising under the physiological heading can generally be explained as the symptoms of pregnancy being inconsistent or under-pronounced for women in this study group. This set of factors operated either to contribute to the pregnancy going undetected or to facilitate denial or concealment of pregnancy. They included:

- Missed periods prior to pregnancy or having bleeding during pregnancy.
- Absence of symptoms associated with pregnancy, or only having mild symptoms. For example, not experiencing morning sickness, changes in body shape or feelings of tiredness.

It is important to bear in mind that women not expecting to become pregnant may not be alert to these indicators of pregnancy.

In the cases of undetected pregnancy the women explained how there were significant unusual features in their pregnancies that led to inconsistencies between their pregnancy experience and the usual symptoms in pregnancy.

Social/cultural factors

For women who denied or concealed their pregnancy the social contexts in which they became pregnant made it difficult for them to accept the pregnancy. These included:

- Viewing their situation as unconventional, including being unmarried but particularly being without a partner at all.
- Concerns over parents' reaction.
- Their own life-chances or those of their families being threatened by them becoming a parent now.

In this context concealment allowed them retain control over the outcome of the pregnancy.

Psychological/social factors

Psychological factors, which were often a response to social factors, also featured in women's accounts and included:

- A belief by the woman that pregnancy was inconsistent with her self-image to the extent that she cast from her mind the possibility that any of the symptoms she noted could be caused by pregnancy.

- External stressors, such as illness in the family or difficulties in the woman's relationship. These were key factors in cases where women concealed the pregnancy.
- The concealment taking on a momentum of its own, whereby women passed a point where it seemed reasonable for them to tell their families and communities.

Some women found sexuality issues particularly difficult to deal with openly, and this learned behaviour was a factor in the difficulty they experienced in disclosing the pregnancy.

Processes entailed in concealing pregnancy

Women described a range of processes by which their pregnancies proceeded while being undetected, denied or concealed. Issues relevant to the pregnancy going undetected include:

- Having an irregular menstrual cycle so that missed periods did not indicate pregnancy.
- Encountering unusual symptoms during pregnancy.
- Deferring to the expertise of their GP in the face of suggestions by others that they might be pregnant.

The process of consciously denying pregnancy entailed:

- Believing that the pregnancy would never become established and not contemplating having to take on parenting a child as an outcome.
- Managing their own thought processes in line with the belief that they were not pregnant up to advanced pregnancy, including blocking out the possibility of pregnancy by keeping busy both physically and mentally with their jobs, college and housework.
- Drinking to forget, in some cases.

Women who were consciously denying the pregnancy were also engaged in a process of concealment and employed strategies similar to the concealed pregnancy group. The strategies women employed to conceal their pregnancy involved a fine balance of taking action so as to hide the pregnancy while at the same time not appearing to look or act any differently in any aspect of their lives to avoid raising any suspicions that they might be pregnant. Actions they took to hide the pregnancy involved:

- Wearing concealing clothing.
- Isolating themselves from family and friends so as to go unnoticed.
- Trying to contain the development of the pregnancy by exercising and dieting.
- Planning to place baby for adoption and, in the case of three women, even hiding the signs of labour.

The process of concealment was complex and there was consensus among the women on the intensity of the time, effort and stress entailed in keeping the pregnancy concealed.

Implications of concealed pregnancy

A range of implications of concealing their pregnancy were recounted by women in relation to impacts on the well-being of the woman and the baby, as well as other emotional and social impacts.

The first set of implications related to how a concealed pregnancy impeded women's participation in the full range of antenatal care set down by current practices in the medical management of pregnancy. Women highlighted concerns this raised for the well-being, (or, in medical terms, 'outcomes') for the baby:

- Difficulties in determining estimated date of delivery.
- No opportunity to detect foetal anomaly or other complications.
- Risks associated with unassisted birth.

Women described a set of consequences arising from not having adapted to the pregnancy. They were concerned that they had put their own well-being and that of the child at risk during pregnancy. Many described how the concealment process meant they had not adjusted their lifestyle to accommodate the pregnancy in accordance with widely held practices, such as stopping smoking or drinking, avoiding physical work, or starting a healthy eating regime. They also described feeling unprepared for labour.

Concealment of pregnancy placed a heavy emotional toll on women, including intense distress and upset, even to the point that some experienced suicidal-like feelings. Throughout the pregnancy and birth women often described an intense feeling of isolation.

The aftermath of concealment included women feeling judged for concealing the pregnancy at all. Women also described how concealment of the pregnancy impacted on their personal relationships. They had to deal with misgivings and in some cases recriminations among partners, parents, siblings and friends for not having sought their confidence earlier. The sense of stigma women felt while pregnant persisted after the baby was born and continued to impact negatively on their confidence in public spaces.

Women's accounts of contact with medical and support services

Our analysis included a focus on the extent to which women concealing their pregnancy had contact with medical, social, counselling and support services during their pregnancy. This related to contacts directly dealing with the concealed pregnancy and contacts during the time when the woman was pregnant but the pregnancy was undisclosed or undetected. There was a high tendency among women to present to GPs during a concealed pregnancy. Women gave mixed views on how well GPs responded to their needs; however, GPs were evaluated positively when they acknowledged the emotional toll of concealment, were supportive, understanding and non-judgemental and facilitated a quick referral on for antenatal care.

Women were more likely to attend a crisis pregnancy counselling service where there was one attached to the antenatal or maternity service they eventually attended. Those who attended counselling cited the following as benefits of the service:

- It provided an outlet to talk after a long period of keeping the pregnancy concealed
- It allowed women to address aspects of the pregnancy that would otherwise have been kept silent
- It helped women make an informed decision
- It offered information and advice on practical supports and services.

Women were referred to Medical Social Work Departments of the hospital they attended for antenatal care and/or the birth of their baby. They cited continuity of care resulting from on-going contact as a particularly positive feature of this service. Women contemplating placing their baby for adoption were put in contact with either health-board social workers or adoption-agency social workers. They gave high praise for the level of information on and preparation for adoption they received as well as constant reassurance that they were doing 'a good thing'. The follow-on care provided to the women was also greatly appreciated, in particular, introductions to foster-care staff and facilitating meetings between the woman and her baby during fostering.

When attending antenatal outpatient departments, women appreciated efforts by staff not to single them out for special attention or treatment due to the late stage of their presentation. Regardless of how staff responded to women, many described feeling very self-conscious while in the public space of the clinic. The role of antenatal education was welcomed by many women in preparing them for childbirth, particularly when offered on a one-to-one consultation basis.

Women gave strong praise for the midwifery and nursing staff of the maternity departments they attended, citing instances of individual midwives taking the initiative to talk with and comfort them when they experienced emotional upset or trauma after delivery. Again, women tended to appreciate not being singled out for any special treatment, and most preferred being accommodated in a ward with other women to having special accommodation arrangements made for them.

Health professionals' perspectives on challenges and practices entailed in responding to undetected, denied or concealed pregnancy.

The issue of concealed pregnancy has not been addressed in any structured, systematic or integrated way to date in healthcare settings. While there was evidence that caregivers have provided a response tailored to the individual needs and circumstances of women who present with a concealed pregnancy, these are usually implemented on an ad-hoc basis, and in some instances are dependent on the level of experience, goodwill and sensitivity of individuals.

The accounts of the health professionals who participated in the study demonstrated that there was agreement on the specific challenges they experience when a woman presents in an advanced stage of pregnancy. Challenges in relation to the medical management of such pregnancies arose out of:

- not knowing a woman's medical history
- difficulties in establishing how long a condition may have been present or the severity of its impact (e.g. blood pressure)
- staff time-pressures and workload
- issues surrounding management of labour and delivery
- presentation 'out of hours'
- concerns about a woman's medical aftercare in the case of an unassisted birth.

In relation to the counselling, emotional and support needs of women, challenges cited included:

- difficulties in trying to engage women who conceal their pregnancy until advanced pregnancy
- development of rapport and building a relationship of trust sufficient to sustain on-going contact with the service
- time-pressures and the intensive nature of response required
- managing the contact between mother and baby
- managing contact between a woman and her family members
- presentation 'out of hours'
- lack of facilities
- tension between maintaining a woman's right to confidentiality and lack of knowledge on caregivers' part of background details of a woman's pregnancy and her exposure to risk
- tensions in providing support to a woman contemplating adoption
- responding to the specific needs of migrant women.

Health professionals' accounts revealed evidence of good practices that have developed organically in response to women who present late in pregnancy; these can be drawn on in the development of a national framework for the management of concealed pregnancy.

Recommendations

A very detailed set of recommendations has been formulated out of this research to guide and inform the planning and development of a national policy and framework of services responding to concealed pregnancy in medical, social, and counselling and support service settings throughout Ireland. The recommendations address the role of the Crisis Pregnancy Agency as a planning and co-ordinating body, the Health Service Executive and the various medical, social and counselling professionals identified through the research as partners in caring for women with a concealed pregnancy.

Recommendations to the Crisis Pregnancy Agency outline actions relating to influencing cultural change, education and awareness raising, provision of skills training for 'frontline' professional caregivers, facilitating information sharing among practitioners and building competency among 'Key Contacts' at health service, community and family levels.

Recommendations to the Health Service Executive address the issues of data collection on concealed pregnancy in the future, providing resources to GPs to screen for pregnancy, increasing coverage of social work services and reviewing policy on foster care placement.

Detailed recommendations arising from issues and, in particular, good practice identified by women and health professionals in interviews are also addressed to the following professional groups:

Counselling Agencies (Non-Governmental and Health Service Organisations)

General Practitioners

Hospital Managers

Outpatient (Antenatal) Nurse Managers

Medical Social Workers

Antenatal Educators

Maternity Department Nurse Managers

Community/Adoption Agency Social Workers.

1.0 Concealed pregnancy as a response to crisis pregnancy: a historical overview

1.1   Background to the study

This study arose out of interested and concerned observations of social work and crisis pregnancy counselling and support staff attached to the antenatal and maternity departments of a rural-based general hospital. Staff noted a recurring incidence in social work caseloads of women attending for antenatal care later than recommended guidelines, often having made no or limited disclosure of the pregnancy to significant others. These cases were considered to come within the staff's understanding of 'concealed pregnancies'. Discussions with colleagues in other areas of the antenatal and maternity services indicated particular issues, concerns and challenges arising in meeting the needs of women in such circumstances.

Concealed pregnancy is a matter of keen interest and concern to the Agency in its wider remit of addressing the issue of 'crisis pregnancy'. Thus a partnership was forged between the hospital based Social Work Service, key personnel involved in counselling services funded by the Agency, and the Crisis Pregnancy Agency itself, for the purposes of undertaking a dedicated initiative in the area of concealed pregnancy. A central aspect of the initiative was to commission research into the factors contributing to and processes entailed in a woman concealing her pregnancy. A primary objective of the research would be to generate recommendations from this research to guide and inform the planning and development of a national policy and framework of services responding to concealed pregnancy in medical, social, counselling and support services settings throughout Ireland.

1.2   Parameters of the research

In conceptualising the research, concealed pregnancy was defined as a situation where a woman presents for antenatal care past twenty weeks' gestation, who has not availed of antenatal care and has not disclosed the pregnancy to her social network. Staff initiating the research had observed that some women presented as late as 36-38 weeks, and occasionally a woman was in labour when she first presented to the hospital.

Meanwhile, no specific research had been conducted on this issue to date in Ireland, and only very limited research had been conducted internationally. Therefore, our definitions and questions were tentative and intended to be the subject of on-going review and modification as our understandings came to be informed by emerging research findings.

To establish the prevalence of concealed pregnancy in the Irish context, references to concealed pregnancy in maternity hospital annual reports, where cited, were reviewed for the period 1995 to 2003. The National Maternity Hospital (NMH) was the only maternity hospital or department reporting statistics on concealed pregnancy regularly as part of the Medical Social Workers report. The NMH reported 7 concealed pregnancies in 1995 (1 in every 946 births), 18 in 1997 (1 in every 420 births), 24 in 1998 (1 in every 326 births), 15 in 2000 (1 in every 523 births) and 12 in 2001 (1 in every 678 births). For the years that are missing, we can only presume that data wasn't recorded.

Looking at the international context Wessel, Endrikat and Buscher (2003) produced the only comprehensive study on concealed pregnancy. The authors estimate that in

Germany one in every 475 births are concealed. Vallone and Hoffman (2003) note that data on the prevalence of concealed pregnancy in the United States is unknown. Wessel et al. (2003) argue that the commonly held view of denied pregnancies as exotic and rare events is not valid. In their view denial and concealment of pregnancy is not a thing of the past but very much of the moment.

1.3   Aims and objectives of the research

The overall aim of this study was to generate an understanding of the factors contributing to and processes entailed in the concealment of pregnancy by a woman until the pregnancy is well advanced, sometimes up to the point of delivery. The specific objectives of the research were:

- To generate an understanding of the social, emotional, psychological and practical factors contributing to women's concealment of pregnancy. This should allow the development of typologies of women experiencing concealed pregnancy and refinement of the definition of concealed pregnancy.
- To document the main kinds and levels of service provision that exist for women with concealed pregnancy.
- To examine the nature of contacts women concealing a pregnancy make with healthcare professionals or support services.
- To assess how much women with concealed pregnancies know about the support services available, particularly those associated with crisis pregnancy.
- To identify any barriers (both formal and informal) perceived by women with concealed pregnancies to accessing antenatal and other support services.
- To outline any other issues, themes or thought-patterns articulated by women with concealed pregnancy.
- To establish a blueprint for the development of a national framework for the management of concealed pregnancy in Ireland to apply across the range of services, from antenatal care to other support services.

1.4   Pregnancy and motherhood in the Irish cultural context

In considering concealment of pregnancy it is important to place this in the context of the cultural meanings attaching to pregnancy and motherhood in Ireland generally. Women's response to and management of pregnancy in the Irish context takes place against a background whereby highly proscribed sexual morality – particularly through the control of women's bodies and sexuality – has been central to cultural expressions of Irishness (Inglis 2003). Gray and Ryan's (1997) analysis of representations of womanhood in Irish identity illustrate how, at the foundation of the state in the 1920s, the family was placed at the centre of Irish culture and the nation came to be increasingly symbolised by Irish motherhood. Women's behaviour was linked with the dignity and integrity of the nation. The images of women and mothers emanating from such symbolism incorporated messages about appropriate lifestyles of women and young girls and in particular the appropriate context for motherhood culminating in strict dictates prescribing women's sexual behaviour. While they acknowledge the massive socio-economic changes that have occurred in Ireland since then, they demonstrate continuities in the use of such symbols and representations of women in contemporary Ireland. In particular, the designation of the traditional nuclear, marriage-based family, with the mother at its centre, as the core unit of Irish society has endured. Thus pregnancy outside the designated context of the institution of marriage has been heavily censured. Deviancy, stigma, shame and condemnation have all attached to non-marital pregnancy and in turn shape the options facing single pregnant women. Significantly, Mahon, Conlon and Dillon (1998), writing in the late 1990s, demonstrated that stigma attaching to non-marital pregnancy still shapes women's decision-making when faced with a crisis pregnancy.

Mahon et al. (1998), in a seminal work on women and crisis pregnancy in Ireland, outline strategies invoked by Irish women in response to a crisis pregnancy and how these have changed over time. Up to the 1950s the dominant response of women was to conceal the pregnancy by disappearing from their community either by emigrating or, in many cases, entering institutions during the pregnancy, giving birth and placing the baby for adoption. At the beginning of the twentieth century a substantial proportion of residents of workhouses were unmarried mothers. In 1906 Mother and Baby Homes were established under the auspices of voluntary organisations. O'Hare, Dean, Walsh, and McLoughlin (1985) and Flanagan and Richardson (1992) provide detailed accounts of these homes. Magdalene homes were the first form of these homes. They were run by orders of Irish nuns, particularly the Good Shepherd Sisters. Women resident there performed menial, manual work in return for their board and keep. Some never returned to their communities, and stayed in the home all their lives. Accounts of conditions in these homes depict them as harsh, cruel places, where women's civil rights and liberties were continuously abused and withheld. Inglis (2003) describes them as part of the institutional Church's strategy for shaming and containing women who transgressed their moral rules and regulations. Over time other voluntary organisations established Mother and Baby homes as places where women resided during pregnancy and childbirth. Women were facilitated in placing their baby for adoption and then returned to their communities. These services have been subject to much reform and restructuring in recent decades, so that residential support services for women during their pregnancy are retained without being associated with connotations of shame and stigma.

Another strategy of managing a non-marital pregnancy was to marry before the child was born. Mahon et al. (1998) illustrate how vital statistics from the 1957 census provide evidence that pre-marital conceptions were a greater feature of Irish life at this time that non-marital birth statistics would suggest. However, women who became pregnant were encouraged to marry their partners. These statistics suggest that the rise in non-marital births since then can be partly explained by an unwillingness by women to enter marriage under these conditions.

The introduction of the Adoption Act in 1952 led to greater numbers of Irish women resolving a non-marital pregnancy by placing their baby for adoption, often preceded by concealment of the pregnancy (Flanagan and Richardson 1992, Mc Cashin 1995). The proportion of non-marital births placed for adoption was very high between the passing of the Act and the introduction of social welfare supports for unmarried mothers in 1973 and the legalisation of abortion in Britain in 1967. In 1967 97% of non-marital births were adopted. The proportion fell in subsequent years to number 71% by 1971, 30% by 1980 and 7% by 1990. By 2002, just 0.5% of births outside marriage were placed for adoption.

After the legalisation of abortion in Britain in 1967 this option also featured among the response of unmarried women to pregnancy. The high level of secrecy and silence surrounding Irish women's abortion experiences suggests that this represents an option that allows for concealment of the pregnancy (Mahon et al. 1998). Recent research by the Crisis Pregnancy Agency (2005) suggests that the number of Irish women travelling to Britain for abortions has steadily increased over the last three decades. In 2003, 6,320 women giving addresses in the Republic of Ireland had abortions in clinics in Britain (Crisis Pregnancy Agency 2005:23).

Since the 1970s most women faced with a crisis pregnancy have chosen to withstand the stigma of becoming an unmarried mother, parenting their child while continuing to live among their community. The emergence of more liberal, tolerant attitudes during the last three decades of the twentieth century, combined with specific welfare provision for single lone mothers has seen the incidence of non-marital motherhood grow steadily (Mahon et al. 1998). The percentage of non-marital births has risen from 3.7% in 1975 to 9.1% in 1985 and further to 32% in 2000. Significantly, analysis of recent patterns of family formation in Ireland indicate that these trends point to changing patterns of family formation away from a dominant marriage-based model to incorporate a range of family forms; statistics on non-marital births can no longer be conflated with crisis pregnancy or lone parenthood (Fahey and Russell 2001, Murphy-Lawless et al. 2004).

1.5   Concealed pregnancy as a cultural phenomenon in Irish society

Inglis (2003) characterises concealment of pregnancy followed by giving birth in secret and then abandoning, killing or allowing the baby to die as a final response to crisis pregnancy. Guilbride (2004) discusses court cases dealing with infanticide[3] in Ireland from the 1920s, when the State was founded, through to the 1950s. Evidence is presented that the incidence of infanticide was far greater than the number of cases brought before the courts. The author details how during this period almost every woman who appeared before the courts on a charge of infanticide was classified as poor or destitute and was unmarried. In many cases while the charge brought was of infanticide, the sentence handed down was of concealment of the birth. The great majority of the women were sentenced to periods of detention in Magdalene homes, while some were sentenced to state prisons. Guilbride (2004) describes how the Infanticide Act of 1949 re-categorised the crime as one equivalent to manslaughter on the grounds of mental disturbance in the wake of giving birth. Following the passing of the Act, mental hospitals replaced Magdalene homes as the usual place of detention for women found guilty under the Act.

In more recent Irish history, the issue of infanticide came to the fore in 1984 when the body of a baby who had died from stab wounds was found on a beach in Co. Kerry (for a detailed account see McCafferty 1985, O'Halloran 1985, Hayes 1985 and Inglis 2003). During the Garda investigation a young woman, Joanne Hayes, from a rural village in the county was identified as having presented to hospital and reported that she had had a miscarriage; the doctors believed she had given birth. After Garda questioning of herself and her family, the woman and her family all confessed that the baby found had been born to the woman at her family home, that she had killed it and her family had assisted her in disposing of the body. In fact, the woman had given birth at her home following a concealed pregnancy, the baby had died and she had concealed the body on the family farm. The charges against the woman were dropped following incontrovertible evidence

---

3 Infanticide usually refers to the killing of a child during the first year of life (Craig 2004).

that she was not the mother of the baby found on the beach. However, a state Tribunal of Inquiry was launched to discover how the woman and her family could have made such confessions. The proceedings of the Tribunal entailed intense scrutiny of the woman, her private and sexual life and her family life, all under the gaze of the public. The circumstances that gave rise to the concealment of her pregnancy up to the stage of unassisted delivery of a child that did not survive were graphically described and have since been subjected to analysis by journalists, authors and academics.

Earlier that same year of 1984 a fifteen-year-old girl, Ann Lovett, had gone to a grotto in a secluded area of the Catholic church in her town to give birth, having concealed her pregnancy. Both the girl and her newborn baby were later found dead. Again, intense media attention was given to the case. The abhorrence expressed at the plight of the young girl generated a pervasive sense that it should never happen again. However, there continue to be reports in the media of bodies of newborn infants found or newborn infants anonymously left in public places.

As part of this research a search was conducted of the archive of one of the Irish broadsheet newspapers, 'The Irish Times', for the ten-year period 1996-2005. This was done to sensitise ourselves to the prevalence of cases of bodies of newborn infants discovered or live babies found in Ireland in our more recent past. In the ten-year period analysed, a total of 24 newborn babies (live and deceased) were found. Eighteen cases of the discovery of bodies of newborn infants were reported during the ten-year period, compared with six reports of live babies found (see Appendix 1). The majority of newborn babies' bodies were discovered in rural areas whereas the majority of live newborn babies were found in cities. This is not claimed to represent a complete and accurate picture of the prevalence of new-borns found during this time period given our reliance on a single source.

A brief content analysis of these reports provides some insight into current policies and positions on how the discovery of newborn babies, either alive or dead, is responded to. There appears to be a policy to identify the mother in cases of the discovery of an infant, regardless of their status. Two approaches are taken. Firstly a public appeal to the mother, and, in some cases, to anyone who may have known or suspected a woman to be concealing a pregnancy, to come forward. The second approach is a police inquiry. A number of the cases included reports of house-to-house inquiries being carried out by teams of Gardai/police in the area where the baby was found. Contacts with hospitals, doctors and women's groups were also reported as methods of inquiry used.

The focus of appeals has tended to emphasise concern for the mother, assurances of compassionate treatment and appropriate help, as well as confidentiality. In some cases the appeal also focuses on parents' duty or entitlement to name the child and provide an appropriate burial service. In cases of live babies found, appeals to the mother are made immediately and then, if unsuccessful, periodic appeals continue to be made. The appeals again tend to emphasise concern for the mother's wellbeing, as well as reports on the baby – including any names given to the child, its age and accounts of how the baby is being cared for. A photograph of the baby usually accompanies the appeal. The requirement for the mother to give her signed consent for any permanent placement of the baby for adoption is a primary concern in such cases.

In cases where a body is found, reports over the past ten years indicate a policy of no criminal charges being brought. In most cases where mothers were identified no arrest was made. There was the only one case among those reviewed where 'arrest' was cited in news reports. A report from the coroners' court in 2003 on the death of a baby whose body was found on a beach in Dublin and whose mother remained unidentified provides an important insight into the issue of adjudicating on infanticide. In this case the City Coroner advised the jury that while formally this was a case of unlawful death, a verdict of "death due to want of attention at birth" was appropriate (IT 2003). When asked by a jury member as to possible alternative verdicts, the coroner discussed the issue of infanticide. He advised that a verdict of infanticide speaks of more active involvement. In this case he stated that it was most likely a matter of death by passivity due to a lack of care and sustenance, which he believed to be qualitatively different from infanticide. The jury returned a verdict in line with the coroner's suggestion.

1.6   Overview of context for research

This portrayal of the extent to which concealed pregnancy has featured among women's 'management' of a pregnancy in Ireland to date serves to locate this research against the background of how the issue has been treated in public discourse currently and in recent Irish history. These events have shaped our cultural understanding of women who conceal their pregnancies and the circumstances under which those pregnancies come to an end. To date we have come to know of women who conceal their pregnancies and their fates through these stories and media reports. It is against this background that the current research is located. As well as fulfilling the central objective of the research to develop a framework of recommendations for appropriate management of concealed pregnancy in health and social services, this research also strives to generate a better understanding of the social and cultural factors and processes entailed in the concealment of pregnancy. Revising our cultural understanding and attitudes is central to the process of generating social change towards a milieu in which women are better positioned to cope with the realisation that they are pregnant.

1.7   Overview of the report

Chapter 1 provides an historical overview of the extent to which concealed pregnancy has featured among women's strategies to manage a crisis pregnancy.

Chapter 2 provides an account of the methodological approach taken in this study.

Chapter 3 presents a review and critique of the Irish and international literature on concealed and denied pregnancy. The typologies of pregnancy concealment and denial proposed across all of the literature reviewed are synthesised in the review. A critical assessment of the scope of literature in this area is also presented.

Chapter 4 provides an analysis of the documentary data, as well as a profile of research participants in the study.

Chapters 5, 6, 7 and 8 present an analysis of qualitative interviews with women who concealed their pregnancy who participated in the research.

Chapter 5 sets out the typologies of pregnancy denial and concealment observed in this research and assesses the extent to which they fit with the typologies generated through a review of the literature. Women's responses to their pregnancy are characterised and described to explicate these typologies. This chapter concludes with a presentation of a refinement of the definition of concealed pregnancy as generated by the research.

Chapter 6 presents an analysis of the factors that gave rise to concealed pregnancy among the women studied, together with a description of the processes entailed in the concealment of pregnancy. In literature reviewed, explanations of why women conceal pregnancy involved a range of social, cultural, psychological and physiological factors. The factors identified in the analysis of women's qualitative accounts could also be categorised under the headings of physiological, social/cultural and psychological factors.

Chapter 7 turns to look at the outcomes of concealed pregnancy. The outcomes are considered in two ways. Firstly the consideration women gave to their options as regards abortion, adoption and motherhood are discussed, and the decisions women ultimately made are outlined. The second way in which 'outcomes' are discussed relates to the meaning of this term from a medical perspective. In that context 'outcomes' of a pregnancy relate to the various indicators of wellbeing in the baby and the woman during pregnancy and after birth. In our analysis such 'outcomes' are considered as implications of the processes entailed in the concealment of a pregnancy. A broad set of outcomes or implications is considered, incorporating physiological, social and emotional dimensions.

Chapter 8 documents the contact women concealing their pregnancy had with medical and support services during their pregnancy. A range of services are discussed, including general practitioners, crisis pregnancy counselling and support services, social work services, antenatal outpatient departments, hospital maternity departments and other hospital departments to which women presented.

Chapter 9 presents findings from interviews conducted with members of the health profession with whom women have contact during pregnancy. This included midwives, nurses, doctors, antenatal and parentcraft educators, hospital administrative staff, social workers and crisis pregnancy counsellors. The challenges faced by these professionals when a woman presents with a concealed pregnancy are discussed first. This is followed by a discussion of the practices initiated by healthcare workers across these disciplines in response to the particular needs of women concealing a pregnancy.

Chapter 10 presents the principal conclusions emerging from the study.

Chapter 11 presents a set of recommendations to guide and inform the planning and development of a framework of services responding to concealed pregnancy in medical, social, counselling and support services settings throughout the health services on a national basis.

2.0 Research methodology

2.1 Research approach

A case-study approach was followed for this study. This approach suited both the sensitive nature of the topic under inquiry and the exploratory nature of the research, given the dearth of previous work in this area. A case-study approach entails assembling data relating to the research question from a range of sources to generate insights from a multiplicity of perspectives with the aim of achieving an in-depth understanding.

The data sources generated for the research were as follows:

- Documentary analysis of case-notes generated by maternity social work and crisis pregnancy support services relating to women presenting with a concealed pregnancy.
- In-depth interviews with women who concealed their pregnancy.
- Interviews with health professionals who come in contact with women who have a concealed pregnancy.

2.2 Advisory group

The project partners who commissioned the research established an advisory group to oversee the conduct of the research. The group comprised social workers, crisis pregnancy counsellors, antenatal educators and health researchers.

2.3 Selection of study sites

This research evolved out of the interested observations of social work practitioners attached to the maternity services of one general hospital in the West of Ireland. This was selected as one of the sites for the case study. It represented a setting where there was already an understanding of the area of inquiry and where co-operation of staff necessary to facilitate the assembly of the data had already been established. For a second site a dedicated maternity hospital in the capital city, Dublin, was selected to generate an urban sample to complement the rural setting of the first site. A pre-existing relationship had been forged between some members of the advisory group and a representative of the social work department of one of the three possible hospitals in Dublin. The openness of the entire department of that hospital to be involved in the study secured it as the second study site.

2.4 Data collection and analysis

It was decided to select a specific timeframe as the basis for selecting cases for inclusion in the research in the two study sites. The preceding eighteen-month period was selected, spanning July 2003 to December 2004. This yielded the following population of cases for inclusion in the study:

Table 2.1 Population of study group x site of study (n)

Study site	Population of cases
Rural-based general hospital	31
Dublin based maternity hospital	20
Total	51

On the basis of these returns the prevalence of late presentations to hospital due to concealed pregnancy in both hospitals can be calculated. In the reference period the number of births in the rural hospital was 2,562 and the number in the city hospital was 12,505. In the rural hospital the prevalence of concealed pregnancy was 2.5:1,000 or 2.5 late presentations in every 1,000 births or 1 late presentation in every 403 births. In the city hospital the prevalence of concealed pregnancy was 1.6:1,000 or 1.6 late presentations in every 1,000 births or 1 late presentation in every 625 births. Thus the incidence of late presentation was higher in the rural-based hospital than in the city hospital. For a comparison with the international context the study by Wessel et al. (2003) is the only comprehensive study on concealed pregnancy and they estimate that in Germany 1 in every 475 births is concealed.

2.4.1   Documentary data

Documentary data in the form of case-notes generated by the medical social work team was the first data-set analysed for this research. The data related to all women presenting with a concealed pregnancy in the eighteen-month timeframe selected. For ethical and confidentiality reasons coding of the case-notes was carried out by the Medical Social Workers of the hospitals involved.

A template was developed to facilitate standardised coding of all case-notes of the study group. The development of the template was informed by:

- a review of literature relating to concealment of pregnancy
- the aims and objectives of the research
- consultation with medical social workers recording the information and review of forms and protocols in use by the service.

The template comprised primarily closed, quantitative categories, with a small number of open-ended qualitative categories included. The template is reproduced in Appendix 2. All social workers involved in coding case-notes were given a training session on completing the template by the researchers.

Analysis of the data generated from this source was carried out using the statistical data analysis package SPSS.

2.4.2   In-depth interviews with women

The researcher conducted once-off, in-depth, unstructured interviews with a sub-set of the population of 51 women in contact with the medical social workers across both hospitals between July 2003 and December 2004. These interviews served to generate a deeper insight into their experiences and world view.

A purposeful sampling approach was determined to be most appropriate for the selection of interview participants. The core objective of purposeful sampling is the selection of information-rich cases to study in depth. Information-rich cases are those from which one can learn a great deal about issues of central importance to the purpose of the research. In this approach sampling decisions are directed by a desire to include a range of variations of the phenomenon in the study. The aim is to have representative coverage of variables likely to be important in understanding how diverse factors converge as a whole. In applying this sampling procedure our understanding of the phenomenon of concealed pregnancy was informed by:

- a review of the literature
- briefings from professionals informed by their experience of working in the area
- analysis of documentary data, as discussed above.

Once the sample was selected, each woman was contacted in the first instance by telephone by a social worker. Where possible this was the social worker with whom she had had direct contact while in the hospital. She was given an explanation of the research and was asked to consider giving her consent to allow her name and contact details to be released to the researcher. An information sheet was posted out to all women who indicated a willingness to consider having their details released [See Appendix 3]. The information sheet also acted as a consent form to having the details released. Two copies of the form were enclosed – one for retention by the woman and one that could be signed and returned to the social worker to indicate the woman was willing to consent to her details being released. A stamped addressed envelope marked 'confidential' was enclosed, which the woman could use to return the consent form.

After three days a follow-up call was made asking each woman if they found the information clear, inviting any questions she may have and asking her to return the consent form within the next three days.

Once women returned the consent form complete with signed consent their contact details – comprising name, address and telephone numbers – were passed on to the researcher. The researcher called each woman to introduce herself and to describe the study again. The researcher offered the woman an opportunity to discuss the study by telephone or face-to-face. Once it was established that women were fully informed of what the study entailed and they had indicated their consent to participate, an arrangement was made for the interview to take place, at a time and place convenient for the woman. Before proceeding with the interview, women were taken through a consent form by the researcher [See Appendix 4]. Once women indicated they were fully informed about all aspects of the study and gave their signed consent to participate, the interviews were conducted. All interviews were conducted by the principal researcher.

The interviews were entirely unstructured. Women were invited to recount their experience following their own narrative, having regard to the focus of the study. Participants determined the duration and scope of the interview. This meant that in some cases women did not discuss particular aspects of their experience, either because they did not want to discuss it or did not themselves consider it to be relevant. At the end of each interview women were asked if they would like to be contacted again by the researcher by telephone about a week later to see if they had anything further they wanted to add or any questions they wanted to ask. A small number of women replied that they had discussed everything and did not wish to be contacted again. The majority of women expressed a desire to be contacted. When contacted again no participant added further to their interview; rather the focus of the follow-up contact was on how the woman felt following the interview and reiteration by the researcher that the participant could contact her at any time.

Given the sensitivity of the topic, participants often became emotional and upset during the retelling of their experience. This was acknowledged and discussed by the researcher and women were given time to release these feelings and recover. Postponement of the interview was offered to women who became upset, but none took this up. Also, women were all offered access to a counsellor attached to the study to help them deal with the emotions raised by the interview. No woman took up the offer of contacting the study's counsellor.

The sample size aspired to for the qualitative interview component of the study was twenty participants: ten from each hospital. In the rural hospital the population numbered 31 women. It was considered unethical to contact one woman due to her personal circumstances. Contact was made with all 30 remaining women in order to generate a final sample of ten participants. In the Dublin hospital the population numbered twenty. In two cases it was considered unethical to contact the women due to personal circumstances. Of the remaining eighteen only three agreed to be interviewed[4].

Table 2.2 Details of qualitative interview participants (n)

Study site	No. of interview participants
Rural-based general hospital	10
Dublin based maternity hospital	3
Total	13

In all cases women agreed for the interviews to be taped. Eleven interviews were transcribed in full while two were analysed in audio format. Interviews were analysed using the qualitative data analysis software NUD*IST. The primary analytical procedure was coding for key themes for the purposes of generating an understanding of the dimensions of each theme across the entire data set. Themes were identified having regard to the findings from the documentary analysis of the case-notes, the research aims and objectives, and a review of literature on concealment of pregnancy. Furthermore, following a grounded theory approach to qualitative data analysis, new themes that emerged inductively from this research were sought out and explored in an attempt to discover further insights into factors shaping women's concealment of pregnancy.

In presenting the analysis of interviews with women, all those interviewed are identified using pseudonyms so as to protect their identity.

2.4.3 Interviews with health professionals

Data collection was also conducted with health professionals who come into contact with women concealing their pregnancies in both the hospital and community settings within the health service administrative areas where the hospitals are located. The purpose of this element was:

- to hear about the challenges encountered by caregivers in meeting the needs of a woman with a concealed pregnancy
- to hear of innovative practices already developed in response to the needs of this group
- to get health professionals' feedback on emerging recommendations based on analysis of interviews with women.

4 Of the remaining fifteen, six women were not contactable at all, three women did not reply to three or more contact attempts while six women refused to participate.

A combination of focus groups and one-to-one interviews were used in this stage of the research.

The following health professionals were targeted for participation in the study:

- Midwives
- Nursing staff in antenatal/maternity settings
- Administrative staff in antenatal/maternity settings
- Antenatal educators
- Staff of accident and emergency departments
- Medical social workers
- Consultant obstetricians
- Health board/HSE social workers
- Crisis pregnancy services counsellors
- Adoption agency social workers
- General practitioners.

General practitioners were the only group who could not be successfully recruited for the study. Initially members of the advisory group identified a list of GPs known to them through professional contacts in relation to crisis pregnancy. While five were contacted for participation, only one practice – based in the West – agreed to take part in a focus-group meeting. A second strategy was to ask the Irish College of General Practitioners to facilitate us in alerting members to the research and asking those who had encountered concealed pregnancy in practice if they would be willing to participate. However, difficulties in implementing such a strategy together with a very limited timeframe imposed by the study schedule meant this was not possible. In the event only one GP practice participated in the study. This meant it was not possible to include the perspective of general practitioners in the research.

Each focus group involved 4-10 participants and lasted one and a half to two hours. Individual interviews lasted 30 minutes to one hour and the interview schedule was the same as in the focus groups. A standardised structured topic guide addressing the issues of challenges, innovative practices and recommendations was followed in all interviews.

Table 2.3 Details of focus groups with health professionals (n)

Professional group	Rural hospital area	City hospital area	Total
Managers, midwives, nurses, care assistants and antenatal educators of antenatal outpatient departments	1	1	2
Managers, midwives and nurses of maternity and accident and emergency departments	1	1	2
Hospital based social workers, community social workers, adoption agency social workers	1	1	2
Counsellors of crisis pregnancy counselling and support services	1	1	2

Table 2.4 Details of one-to-one interviews with health professionals (n)

Professional group	Rural hospital area	City hospital area	Total
Hospital-based consultant obstetricians and gynaecologists	2	2	4

2.5   Data handling and storage

All data generated by this research in the form of completed templates, taped interviews and their transcripts were stored in a secure facility at WERRC's offices at UCD. Tapes and hard copies of completed templates and transcripts will be destroyed 12 months after publication of the research. Data sets entered into SPSS and NUD*IST will be archived securely on the University College Dublin computer server.

2.6   Access negotiation and ethical issues

Ethical approval for this research was secured from the Research Ethics Committee of both hospitals in which the study was conducted.

3.0 Review of published literature on concealed pregnancy

3.1 Scope of the review

For a review of literature on the topic of concealed pregnancy literature searches were conducted on electronic databases (including Social Science Citation Index, Psychlit and Medline) and the catalogues of University College Dublin, as well as those of other universities in the Republic of Ireland using IRIS, the Consortium of Irish University and Research Libraries web-based catalogue. Searches were conducted using key words or phrases such as 'concealed pregnancy', 'denial of pregnancy' and 'neonaticide[5]'. Bibliographies of collected literature were also scanned for further references. The results of these searches illustrated that national and international research in this area is sparse, consisting primarily of a small number of individual psychiatric case-reports cited in psychiatric/psychology journals and studies of pregnancy denial and concealment preceding neonaticide. Given the scarcity of references we extended the timeframe of our literature search to cover a 25-year period: 1980 to 2005.

Much of the literature identified relates to pregnancy denial and concealed pregnancy in cases of mental illness and crimes such as neonaticide. Very little literature focuses solely on pregnancy denial and concealed pregnancy from a social point of view. Wessel et al.'s (2003) study of 24 obstetric facilities (including hospitals and midwives' practices) in Berlin is currently the only large-scale study into denial and concealment of pregnancy.

In this review definitions of 'concealed pregnancy' and 'denied pregnancy' will be considered and the factors attributed to concealment or denial of pregnancy in studies reviewed. Findings regarding the prevalence of this phenomenon in Ireland and internationally will be reported. The focus will then extend to compiling a social profile of women who conceal and/or deny their pregnancy from existing literature. Finally, outcomes reported from denied or concealed pregnancies will be documented.

3.2 Defining concealed pregnancy and pregnancy denial

Finding a universal definition of concealed pregnancy and pregnancy denial was problematic. Definitions that do exist can be ambiguous and incorporate physiological, social and psychological dimensions of the phenomenon. Sadler (2002) argues that there is no universal definition of a concealed pregnancy and its definition depends largely on the researcher carrying out the study. The same can also be said of pregnancy denial, for which there is no fixed definition. Quite often the literature makes reference to the terms 'concealed pregnancy', 'denied pregnancy' and 'pregnancy denial' without clarifying exactly what is being referred to. It poses a considerable problem when research does not differentiate between the process entailed in denial of pregnancy and that entailed in concealment of pregnancy.

Wessel et al. (2003) define pregnancy denial as 'the subjective lack of awareness of being pregnant' (2003:29). Concealment, on the other hand, is the activity of keeping something secret. Terming 'concealment' as an activity implies that there is some form of awareness of the pregnancy. Denial and concealment of pregnancy are widely considered to be coping mechanisms invoked by women when pregnant unexpectedly. In examining the literature, there was great difficulty in trying to compile a concrete definition of 'concealed

5 Neonaticide usually refers to the killing of a child during the first 24 hours of life. Infanticide usually refers to the killing of a child during the first year of life (Craig 2004).

pregnancy and 'pregnancy denial'. For the purpose of this review, the following stream of definition has been constructed to represent that present in the literature:

Figure 3.1: Stream of definition for pregnancy denial and concealed pregnancy, based on a review of the literature

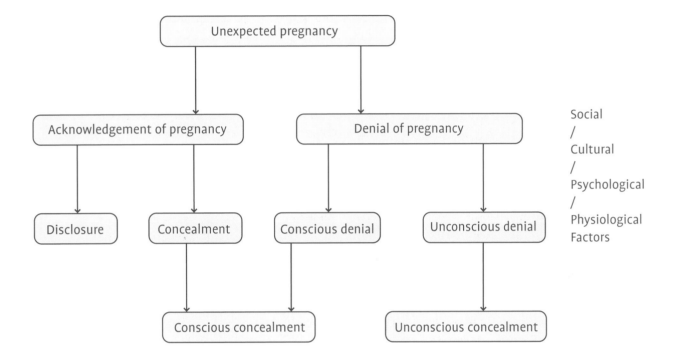

In the above diagram, it is shown that in the event of an unexpected pregnancy a woman has two possible responses: to acknowledge or deny the pregnancy. If she acknowledges it she may choose to disclose or conceal it. If she denies the pregnancy this may be unconscious denial – where the woman shows no signs of awareness – or conscious denial both to herself and others, implying some form of awareness (Miller 2003, Dulit 2000). Regardless of the antecedents, the outcome for all women is that the pregnancy is concealed.

3.2.1   *Unconscious denial*

This refers to where a woman has no subjective awareness of being pregnant throughout the majority of the pregnancy, or even up to a totally unexpected sudden delivery. Spielvogel and Hohner (1995), Brezinka, Huter, Biebl and Kinzl (1994) and Miller (1991) make the distinction between psychotic and non-psychotic unconscious denial of pregnancy. While all acknowledge that unconscious denial of pregnancy in a mentally ill woman may be part of a woman's psychosis, they highlight that it is not only psychotic women who experience unconscious pregnancy denial. Women with no mental health problems can be prone to unconscious pregnancy denial under extreme stress. Unconscious denial, Bonnet (1993) argues, can stem from the fact that the idea of pregnancy can be so unimaginable to the woman, this then results in denial when pregnancy occurs. Miller (2003) terms unconscious denial as 'pervasive denial' and argues that the lack of psychological awareness of pregnancy can often mimic itself in a lack of physical signs of pregnancy. Dulit (2000) uses the term 'true denial' to describe unconscious denial of pregnancy whereby pregnancy is denied at all levels – physiological, psychological and social. Maldonado-Duran, Lartigue and Feintuch (2000) describe unconscious denial of pregnancy as 'total denial' whereby the woman continues to deny her pregnancy to herself and others, contrary to all evidence.

In explaining unconscious denial of pregnancy, Vallone & Hoffman (2003) assert that for these women, pregnancy 'simply is not in the realm of their possibility' (2003:227). Finnegan, McKinstry and Erlick Robinson (1982) argue that it is possible for women to unconsciously deny a pregnancy and consequently unconsciously conceal a pregnancy from themselves and others through a process of rationalisation of symptoms e.g. weight gain being attributed to 'getting fat', or, as Craig (1997) reports, thinking the delivery was a 'bowel movement'.

3.2.2   Conscious denial

Conscious denial of pregnancy implies some form of awareness. Spinelli (2001) argues that to deny something, prior knowledge of the fact must exist. Dulit (2000) characterises conscious denial of pregnancy as where the fact of the pregnancy is recognised but the woman continues to deny it to herself and others. Miller (2003) uses the term 'affective denial' to describe conscious denial of pregnancy. Here women cognitively realise they are pregnant but do not display emotions associated with pregnancy.

Finnegan et al. (1982) refer to how others may collude in the denial of pregnancy. In their case-report on three cases of pregnancy denial, one woman had visited two separate doctors who did not pick up on her pregnancy, while in the case of another woman, her interpreter refused to accept the pregnancy even after the baby was born.

Green and Manohan (1990) argue that the line between conscious and unconscious denial of pregnancy isn't fixed. Haapsalo and Petaja (1999) note that sometimes there is intermittent acknowledgement of pregnancy but that it is quickly denied again. Several studies also highlight the fact that a woman may be in denial because she simply does not know she is pregnant (Wessel et al. 2003, Finnegan et al. 1982, Maldonado-Duran et al. 2000). This is quite common in the early stages of pregnancy and falls into the 'grey area' category between conscious and unconscious denial of pregnancy.

3.2.3   Concealment of pregnancy

It is argued that for concealment to occur, some knowledge of the pregnancy must be present (Wessel et al. 2003, Spinelli 2001, Treacy, Byrne and O'Donovan 2002). Concealment is characterised by a woman acknowledging the pregnancy to herself but hiding it from others. Concealment is also considered to be a coping strategy. In medical terms, concealment is classed as failure to present for antenatal care until after twenty weeks' gestation (Wessel et al. 2003, Treacy et al. 2002).

According to Craig, reasons for concealment of pregnancy are often related to social factors, such as stigma of lone motherhood or religious beliefs regarding abortion. It is reported that many women who conceal their pregnancies are prone to social isolation in order to keep their pregnancy a secret (Craig 1997, Finnegan et al. 1982). Yet, Drescher-Burke, Krall and Penick (2004) argue that the majority of women who conceal pregnancy and go on to commit neonaticide reside at home with their family. Relationships with her family and the father of the baby are also important factors in determining whether a woman conceals her pregnancy or not (Spinelli 2001, Bonnet 1993, Vallone and Hoffman 2003). Research also indicates that perceptions of stigma over having an illegitimate child or being a lone mother may make a woman more prone to conceal her pregnancy (Wessel et al. 2003, Saunders 1989, Craig 1997). Saunders (1989) argues that until the cultural stigma of having an illegitimate child is 'modified', more women will feel forced to conceal their pregnancies. The literature also signifies that a woman's religious beliefs with respect to pre-marital sex have a role to play in whether she conceals her pregnancy or not (Wessel et al. 2003, Craig, 1997, Saunders 1989, Finnegan et al. 1982). Wessel et al. (2003) note that a 'strict religious upbringing', especially in the case of teenagers, may be a reason for concealment of pregnancy (2003:29). Craig (1997) found the majority of neonaticidal women who conceal their pregnancy to be living in rural areas. Mahon et al. (1998) note how keeping pregnancy secret from others allows women to maintain control over their decision-making.

3.2.4   *Critique of definitions in the literature*

Generating a consistent definition of pregnancy denial and concealment was a difficult task. Each definition varied according to the particular research study. Much of the literature focused on neonaticide and subsequent denial and concealment of pregnancy, with Wessel et al. (2003) providing the only study focusing on concealed pregnancy more broadly. Notably, the authors argue that there is no single dynamic underlying concealed pregnancy: explanations defy easy conceptualisation or referral to a particular theoretical model. Rather, they argue that each case should be examined on its own merits.

3.3   Typologies of concealed and denied pregnancy presented in literature

The table below has attempted to piece together definitions of concealed and denied pregnancy to form a more holistic view of concealed pregnancy and pregnancy denial. In presenting this table we set out the state of development of definitions of pregnancy denial and concealment in the literature reviewed. As our primary research progressed, the typologies set out here were tested to consider whether they fit with the factors and processes entailed with pregnancy denial or concealment we observed.

Table 3.1 Typologies of pregnancy denial and concealment as presented in literature

	Unconscious denial	Conscious denial	Concealment
Alternative terms applied	Passive denial; true denial; total denial	Affective denial	Ignored pregnancy
Definition	– No sign of subjective awareness contrary to all evidence – Neither psychological awareness nor physical signs displayed – Denied at all levels – psychological, social and physiological – Failure to verify pregnancy or adjust lifestyle/attire	– Some form of subjective awareness – Cognitive realisation of pregnancy but no display of normal associated emotions – Intermittent acknowledgement followed by denial – No planning for baby	– Knowledge of pregnancy by woman but attempts by all means to prevent disclosure to others
Explanations	– May be associated with psychosis – observed also in non-psychotic women **Non-psychotic related explanations:** – Outcome of extreme external stress – Idea of pregnancy is unimaginable to woman due to inconsistency with social roles and self-concepts – Lack of psychological awareness can mimic itself in lack of physical signs – Ignorance of anatomical and physiological information on pregnancy and childbirth – Rationalisation of symptoms – Conflicted/inhibited sexuality in response to strict religious/parental prohibition relating to sexuality – Feeling conflicted about the prospect of becoming a parent – Young age/adolescence – Anxiety generated by pregnancy in women who deny pregnancy is so great that powerful defences are called into action in form of denial and rationalisation – Social isolation	– Idea of pregnancy is unimaginable to woman due to inconsistency with social roles and self-concepts – In substance users tendency to cope by denying an unacceptable reality – Young age/adolescence – The somatic changes associated with pregnancy may give rise fears of death or disfigurement – Conflicted/inhibited sexuality in response to strict religious/parental prohibition relating to sexuality – Feeling conflicted about the prospect of becoming a parent – Anxiety generated by pregnancy in women who deny pregnancy is so great that powerful defences are called into action in form of denial and rationalisation	– Young age / adolescence are significant risk factors – There may be some collusion by others e.g. failure of Dr. to recognise symptoms, collusion of friend/partner – Fear or guilt over sexual activities exacerbated by family, religious or social censure – Embarrassment at having allowed the pregnancy to occur – Strategy to retain control over management of the pregnancy and decisions about the outcome **Explanations specific to adolescence:** – In adolescents psychological development predisposes them to delay decisions and fail to consider long-term repercussions – Embarrassed, anxious, confused and unfamiliar with the healthcare system

Explanations specific to adolescence:
– In adolescents psychological development predisposes them to delay decisions and fail to consider long-term repercussions
– Embarrassed, anxious, confused and unfamiliar with the healthcare system

Adapted from: Drescher-Burke et al. (2004), Vallone and Hoffman (2003), Wessel et al. (2003), (2002a) and (2002b), Treacy et al. (2002), Spinelli (2001), Craig (1997), Spielvogel and Hohner (1995) Green and Manohan (1990), Foster and Jenkins (1987), Finnegan et al. (1982), Spillane, Khalil and Turner (1996).

3.4   Prevalence of concealed pregnancy

Research on the prevalence of concealed pregnancy in Ireland and internationally is limited. The study by Wessel et al. (2003) is the only comprehensive study on concealed pregnancy. The authors estimate that in Germany 1 in every 475 births is concealed. They further estimate that in 1 out of every 2455 births the pregnancy was denied throughout the pregnancy, such that the foetus was born without any preceding subjective awareness of pregnancy on the part of the woman. Vallone and Hoffman (2003) note that data on the prevalence of concealed pregnancy in the United States is unknown. The majority of the literature available centred on neonaticidal women and women suffering from psychiatric problems (such as eating disorders) who concealed their pregnancy. The focus tended to rely on a psychiatric evaluation of concealed pregnancy as opposed to a social evaluation.

Data on the incidence of concealed pregnancy in Ireland is scarce, and limited to maternity hospital annual reports and references to pregnancies as 'concealed' in a few Irish obstetric studies, usually looking at the issue of babies born before arrival at hospital and/or to 'unbooked' women[6].

For the purpose of this study, references to concealed pregnancy in maternity hospital annual reports were reviewed for the period 1995 to 2003. Annual reports of hospital obstetric activity are published for the National Maternity Hospital, Coombe Women's Hospital and the Rotunda Maternity Hospital only. Information on maternity services outside Dublin is limited to Health Board/HSE Annual Reports; these make no reference to concealed pregnancy. Hospital reports were found to be inconsistent in the terminology used and in the reporting of concealment of pregnancy.

The National Maternity Hospital reported 7 concealed pregnancies in 1995 (1 in every 946 births), 18 in 1997 (1 in every 420 births), 24 in 1998 (1 in every 326 births), 15 in 2000 (1 in every 523 births) and 12 in 2001 (1 in every 678 births). For the years that are missing, we can only presume that data wasn't recorded. The Coombe Women's Hospital made no reference to concealed pregnancy in its annual reports between 1995 and 2003. The Rotunda Maternity Hospital made one reference in 2001 to a woman who had a concealed pregnancy in its section on 'neonatal deaths' and, again, in 2003, one woman was described as having a concealed pregnancy in the 'neonatal deaths' section of the report.

As stated above, in Irish research concealed pregnancies have featured in studies of women who arrive to a hospital in labour without having previously attended or booked there. These are termed 'unbooked women'. Treacy et al. (2002), in their study of unbooked women in the Rotunda Hospital between January 1998 and December 1999, note that fifteen of the women studied had concealed pregnancies. Spillane et al. (1996), in their study of babies born before arrival at the Coombe Women's Hospital over a four-year period (1988-1991), found that fourteen women had neither booked nor attended for antenatal care. Of this group they note that five of the women studied had concealed their pregnancy. Treacy et al. (2002) estimated that for the two-year period 1 in every 768 pregnancies was concealed. Spillane et al. (1996) estimated that for the four-year period

---

6 There are a range of reasons why a woman would be 'unbooked' other than concealment of pregnancy, including transfer from another hospital.

they studied, 1 in every 6889 pregnancies was concealed. There is a stark difference between the above ratios of concealed pregnancies to births per year; this is primarily related to differences in the criteria used to categorise 'concealed pregnancy'.

It is clear that at present the information-recording and reporting systems of maternity hospitals do not allow for any reliable conclusions to be drawn on the incidence of deliveries in hospital following a concealed pregnancy. This indicates a need for more accurate methods of collecting data and keeping records of women relating to concealment of pregnancy. No primary research taking concealed pregnancy as its primary focus has been carried out in the Irish context. Meanwhile, where research reports have referred to concealed pregnancy the definitions being followed are unclear. Therefore, we have a few pieces of the puzzle, but most are missing.

Wessel et al. (2003) argue that the commonly held view of denied pregnancies as exotic and rare events is no longer valid. Concealed pregnancy is not a thing of the past but very much of the moment. However, a lack of rigorous data-collection and record-keeping may put women with concealed pregnancies at risk of being overlooked.

3.5   Social profile of women whose pregnancy is concealed

Compiling a social profile of women whose pregnancy is concealed proved to be difficult, primarily due to lack of data. The literature most often consisted of a psychiatric evaluation of concealment as a factor in neonaticide and unconscious pregnancy denial, and it was too limited to extract a social profile of women. Within data relating to Ireland sporadic information reported by the National Maternity Hospital, Dublin, allowed for some limited age-profiling of women who presented with a concealed pregnancy. In 1998, the mean age of a woman with a concealed pregnancy in the National Maternity Hospital was 22.1 years, within an age range of 17–42 years (National Maternity Hospital 1999). In 2000, the mean age for women with a concealed pregnancy was 23.2 years, within an age range of 17-31 years (National Maternity Hospital 2001). In 2001, the mean age for women with a concealed pregnancy was 22.8 years, within an age range of 20–31 years. However, this data is inconsistent in its reporting and cannot be held to be conclusive.

The study group of Spillane et al. (1996), discussed above, included fourteen women who had neither booked nor attended antenatal care when they delivered their baby before arrival at hospital. The study provides the following general profile of the fourteen women: single, unemployed and younger first-time mothers. In five of the fourteen cases the pregnancy had been concealed.

From the international literature, Wessel et al. (2003) provide the most comprehensive profile from a study that featured the largest study group (N=65) of all those reviewed. The age of the group ranged between 15 and 44 years old, with a median of 27 years. Almost 60% had a close partner. Over half of the women had at least one previous pregnancy with only one-third never having been pregnant before. 45% lived with their partner and less than 10% lived with their parents with the remainder living alone.

With most of the literature focusing on concealment as an antecedent to neonaticide, very little attention is given to the social aspects of concealed pregnancy, such that it is difficult to conclude a holistic social profile of women with a concealed pregnancy. Yet again, Irish research is lacking, and what limited international research does exist pays little attention to educational level, socio-economic status and social support networks.

3.6   Implications of denial and concealment of pregnancy

One focus of interest regarding concealment or denial of pregnancy is the extent to which it poses risks for the mother and her expected child. Some studies have focused on the stress associated with denying or concealing a pregnancy and associated negative psychological outcomes. Foster and Jenkins (1987) note how a teenager developed anorexia while trying to conceal her pregnancy from her family. Sable and Wilkinson (2000) note how stress is often associated with poor pregnancy outcomes for the baby also. In the Irish context two studies have shown that low birth weight, delivering pre-term, neonatal death and risk of maternal mortality are more common in women who conceal pregnancy (Treacy et al. 2002, Geary et al. 1997). Wessel et al. (2003) compared the outcomes of the deliveries/newborns of their study group of women (who concealed their pregnancy) with those of all deliveries in the city in which the study took place during the reference year. They found a statistically significant worse outcome for newborns delivered following denial of pregnancy in relation low birth weight, recording as 'small for gestational age' and transfer to neonatal units. The risk of these outcomes was elevated for the study group by 2.0 to 3.4 fold. However, when incidence of prematurity was compared with that among deliveries in one particular hospital in the reference year no statistically significant difference was observed.

Treacy et al. (2002) and Geary et al. (1997), working in an Irish context, associated these poorer outcomes with the absence of antenatal care. Wessel et al. (2003) challenge this view, arguing that obstetric care is not an independent variable in determining the outcome of a concealed pregnancy. They conclude that the primary reason for the worsened foetal outcome is the absence of adaptation to pregnancy by the women simply because they did not know about or acknowledge being pregnant (Wessel et al. 2003: 34). They also note references in other studies to retrospective feelings of intense embarrassment and guilt for putting a baby at risk among women who had concealed a pregnancy.

This discussion of outcomes for women with a concealed pregnancy is brief and indicates that more research is needed, particularly at the psychological and social levels.

3.7   Recommendations for reducing the incidence of denied or concealed pregnancies

Some researchers have argued that more lenient abortion laws would help alleviate concealed pregnancy (Resnick 1970 (in Drescher-Burke 2004), Saunders 1989). The promotion of adoption and alternatives to adoption are also suggested by some researchers (Spinelli 2001, Bonnet 1993). In France, the law allows for a woman to enter a hospital anonymously, have a hospital-assisted delivery and immediately surrender her baby for adoption without revealing her identity. In Germany, Belgium, Italy, Hungary and South Africa 'baby chutes' or 'baby boxes' are provided by voluntary organisations, where women can place newborns into care anonymously. 'Project Cuddle' in the United States is aimed at reducing concealed pregnancies and abandoned newborns through helping women at risk of concealment to connect with resources such as health centres, adoption agencies and legal representatives (Vallone and Hoffman 2003).

Across most studies recommendations to address pregnancy concealment have been targeted at professionals as opposed to women. Principal among them is the recommendation to increase awareness of concealed pregnancy on the part of primary healthcare providers, maternity and other health service providers (Bonnet 1993, Roussot, Buchmann, McIntyre and Russell 1998, Green and Manohan 1990, Wessel et al. 2003). The role of health professionals beyond antenatal and maternity settings in connecting women with pregnancy-related services has been emphasised. Roussot et al. (1998) argue that GPs – as the first point of contact – are key in connecting pregnant women with antenatal services. Spielvogel and Hohner (1995) argue that conscious denial of pregnancy is consistent with responses of substance users to unacceptable realities, and they recommend that healthcare workers in this area should actively inquire about sexual activity and a possible pregnancy. They also identify young age as a significant risk factor for pregnancy denial and concealment. They advocate that healthcare givers working with young women should actively question them about sexual activity and review the benefits of early pregnancy testing (Spielvogel and Hohner 1995). Spielvogel and Hohner (1995) further consider women with a history of sexual and physical assault to be at risk of pregnancy denial in an attempt to avoid re-emergence of related traumas the physical act of pregnancy may induce. They therefore recommend that a sexual and physical assault history be taken as part of every woman's antenatal intake visit.

Identification of risk and education are also to the fore in the literature's recommendations for dealing with concealed pregnancy. Strategies on how to deal with concealed pregnancy are recommended for those in contact with women who may be concealing their pregnancy (teachers, family members, students, teachers, work colleagues, health service providers, etc). This is considered a principal means of avoiding collusion of significant others with the concealment, which still leaves women alone and vulnerable. Education and outreach programmes dealing with family planning, concealed pregnancy and neonaticide – aimed at women (particularly during teenage years), schools, parents and health service providers – are also recommended (Spinelli 2001, Saunders 1989, Drescher-Burke et al. 2004, Vallone and Hoffman 2003). It is recommended that parents, teachers and other key youth workers should be educated to take an assertive, non-judgemental approach to checking out suspicions of pregnancy and given resources for assistance (Vallone and Hoffman 2003).

Spielvogel and Hohner (1995) recommend that once a pregnancy is disclosed – either in advanced pregnancy or at point of delivery – caregivers should be understanding and provide reassurance. Informing women of others who have had similar experiences and putting in place accelerated education and parenting programmes, in keeping with those delivered to all women in antenatal care, are examples of good practice in this regard (Spielvogel and Hohner 1995). The authors further recommend that presentation of a woman with a concealed pregnancy in a particular therapeutic environment (e.g. for substance use) should be met with a comprehensive, non-judgemental response that integrates obstetric care with the other appropriate therapeutic treatments, such as psychiatric care and substance-use treatment.

3.8   Critique of literature on pregnancy denial and concealment

This review of the international and national literature indicates that concealed pregnancy is not a thing of the past but rather remains a feature of contemporary western societies.

However, the scope of the literature is lacking, with very few studies concentrating on concealed pregnancy in the absence of neonaticide and psychiatric disorders.

The national and international research in this area consisted primarily of a small number of individual psychiatric case-reports cited in psychiatric/psychology journals and studies of pregnancy denial and concealment preceding neonaticide. Much of the literature identified relates to pregnancy denial and concealed pregnancy in cases of mental illness and crimes such as neonaticide. The majority of the literature available centred on neonaticidal women and women suffering from psychiatric problems (e.g. eating disorders) that concealed their pregnancy. The focus tended to rely on a psychiatric evaluation; very little literature focused on pregnancy denial and concealment from a sociological point of view. This makes it difficult to generate a holistic social profile of women who deny or conceal a pregnancy. Crucially, such a limited approach means that a central aspect to our understanding of the factors and processes entailed in pregnancy denial or concealment is missing, indicating a need for the incorporation of a sociological focus in our inquiry.

Generating a consistent definition of pregnancy denial and concealment from the literature was a difficult task. Definitions that existed could be ambiguous, and often failed to incorporate fully the range of physiological, cultural, social and psychological dimensions of the phenomenon. What was consistent about the range of definitions was the tendency to consider denial and concealment of pregnancy as coping mechanisms invoked by women when pregnant. This does not allow for cases where a pregnancy goes undetected by a woman and/or her physician. The implication of such a characterisation is to attribute the processes entailed in pregnancy denial or concealment to individual women as opposed to acknowledging the possibility that they could be attributable also to other actors, systems or factors.

Data on the incidence of concealed pregnancy was inadequate, both internationally and in Ireland. In the Irish setting data was limited to maternity hospital annual reports and references to pregnancies as 'concealed' in a few Irish obstetric studies, usually looking at the issue of babies born before arrival at hospital and/or to 'unbooked women'. However, inconsistencies in the definitions and measurements generated stark differences between the ratios reported. It is clear that at present the information-recording and reporting systems of maternity hospitals do not allow for any reliable conclusions to be drawn on the incidence of deliveries in hospital following a concealed pregnancy. Furthermore, compiling a social profile of women who conceal their pregnancy proved to be difficult primarily due to lack of data. The literature most often consisted of a psychiatric evaluation of concealment as a factor in neonaticide and unconscious pregnancy denial and was too limited to extract a social profile of women.

Finally, the primary focus of interest regarding outcomes of concealment or denial of pregnancy in the literature related to the extent to which it poses medical health risks for the mother and her expected child. This indicates a need for more research relating to outcomes of pregnancy denial and concealment, particularly at the psychological and social levels.

4.0 Analysis of documentary data and profile of study group

Analysis of documentary data

4.1   Introduction

An analysis of documentary data (in the form of social-work and medical case-notes of women who presented for antenatal care after twenty weeks' gestation to two ante-natal/maternity care settings in Ireland during 2003-2004) is presented here. The two fieldwork sites comprised a rural-based hospital in the West of Ireland and a Dublin-based maternity hospital. The total number of cases over the study timeframe of eighteen months is 51, reflecting the low incidence of concealed pregnancy cited in national and international studies as discussed earlier. Thirty-two women presented for antenatal care after twenty weeks' gestation in the rural-based hospital while the remaining nineteen women presented late to the Dublin-based maternity hospital. These case-notes were coded onto templates designed specifically for this research and analysed using SPSS.

4.2   Methodological limitations

During the course of the research, data sources and gaps in the system of data recording gave rise to certain limitations. The case-notes analysed for this research were generated for another purpose and the template was thus applied retrospectively to them in both sites. The system of data recording in both sites differed significantly and led to substantial levels of missing data in the Dublin-based maternity hospital.

4.3   Parameters of the study group

This first section of analysis of the template sets out to provide an insight into the reasons why women presented late for antenatal care without having disclosed the pregnancy to any health professional and/or significant others. Referring back to our working definitions we differentiate between denial of pregnancy and concealment of pregnancy.

Denied pregnancy:

Where the woman has no subjective awareness of being pregnant throughout the majority of the pregnancy or even up to a totally unexpected sudden delivery.

Concealed pregnancy:

Where the woman does know about her existing pregnant state, usually at a very early stage but attempts by all means to prevent discovery of the pregnancy, at least from figures of authority in her life and from healthcare professionals. At the most extreme form concealment means the woman has not disclosed the pregnancy to any of her social network. However, the definition for this study allows for some limited disclosure e.g. telling her partner or a close friend who, as she may anticipate, then colludes with her and does not impel her to disclose the pregnancy further. A one-off contact with a health professional e.g. GP or clinic nurse to perform a pregnancy test without any further contact is also within this definition.

4.3.1   Weeks' gestation at booking

Firstly the stage of pregnancy at which women presented to hospital is considered. Fifteen women were between the stages of 20 and 27 weeks' gestation when they presented to hospital for antenatal care. Another fifteen women were between the stages of 28 and 35 weeks' gestation at presentation to the hospital. Eight women presented to hospital at between 36 and 39 weeks, with three women presenting at 40 weeks and over. Two women booked for antenatal care before twenty weeks but are included in the sample as they concealed their pregnancies for the full duration from their family because of fear of their reaction. The remaining eight women had not presented to hospital for any antenatal care and arrived to the hospital in labour.

4.3.2   Reasons for late presentation

In this group of 51 women, eleven women presented late because they were not aware they were pregnant. Nine women were described as being in denial to themselves about their pregnancy. Almost two-thirds (31) of the women presented late because they were concealing the pregnancy from others. Comparing the two hospital sites, women in the rural-based hospital were much more likely to conceal their pregnancy: 71% of these women concealed, compared with 45% of those in the city-based hospital.

Figure 4.1 Reasons for late presentation

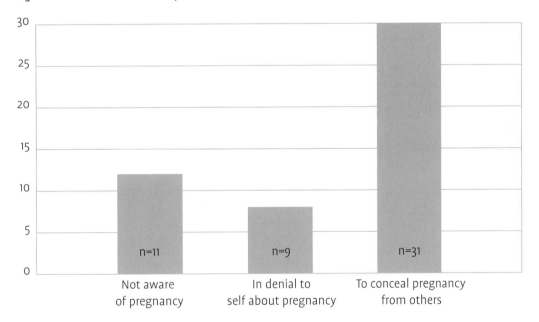

The prevalence of late presentations to hospital due to concealed pregnancy in both hospitals was calculated. In the rural hospital the prevalence of concealed pregnancy was 2.5:1,000 births, or 1 late presentation in every 403 births. In the city hospital the prevalence of concealed pregnancy was 1.6:1,000 births, or 1 late presentation in every 625 births. Thus the incidence of late presentation was higher in the rural-based hospital than in the city hospital. For a comparison with the international context, the only comprehensive study on concealed pregnancy estimates that 1 in every 475 births is concealed in Germany (Wessel et al. 2003).

4.3.3   Presentation at hospital and weeks' gestation at booking

Forty-three women presented to hospital for antenatal care, while the remaining eight women arrived in labour. Two women booked for antenatal care before twenty weeks but are included in the sample as they concealed their pregnancies for the full duration from their families because of fear of their reaction.

Table 4.1 Stage at presentation/reason for late presentation crosstabulation

Stage at presentation/ reason for late presentation crosstabulation	Not aware of pregnancy	In denial to self about pregnancy	To conceal pregnancy from others
	(n)	(n)	(n)
Prior to 20 weeks	0	0	2
20-27 weeks	3	2	10
28-35 weeks	2	3	9
36-40 weeks+	3	4	4
In labour	2	0	6
Unknown	1	0	0
Total	11	9	31

4.3.4   Time between booking and delivery

An indication of the time lapse between presentation for antenatal care and delivery was measured by subtracting the women's 'week of gestation at booking' from their 'week of gestation at delivery' as stated in their hospital charts. Almost half of the women presented to hospital less than eight weeks before giving birth.

Table 4.2 Lapse between booking and delivery

Lapse between booking and delivery	Study group	
	N	%
Arrived in labour	8	16
Less than 4 weeks	12	24
4 to 7 weeks lapse	4	8
8 to 11 weeks lapse	11	22
12 to 15 weeks lapse	8	16
16 to 19 weeks lapse	5	8
20 weeks + lapse	3	6
Total	51	

4.4 Profile of the women

4.4.1 Age

Table 4.3 Age profile of women who presented for antenatal care late in pregnancy

Age category	Total number of women (N)		Rural-based maternity hospital		Dublin- based maternity hospital	
	N	%	N	%	N	%
16 years and under	2	4	0	0	2	10
17-19 years	21	41	16	52	5	25
20-24 years	15	29	8	26	7	35
25-29 years	6	12	3	10	3	15
30-34 years	4	8	2	6	2	10
35-39 years	1	2	1	3	0	0
40-44 years	2	4	1	3	1	5
Total number	51		31		20	

Two of the women in the study group were in the age category of sixteen years and under and both had presented late to the Dublin-based maternity hospital. The majority of women who presented late (41%) were concentrated in the 17-19 year age category. However, this category was over-represented in the rural group (52%) and under-represented in the city group (25%). The converse is true for those in the 20-24 age group, who accounted for 29% of the overall group. This represented the majority (35%) of the city study group compared to 26% of the rural study group. Overall, there was a greater concentration of ages in the rural study, where 78% were aged between 17-24 compared with 60% in this age range in the city study group.

4.4.2 Area of origin

From the 51 women that information was collected on, 21 came from a rural area. Sixteen women resided in towns while the remaining fourteen women lived in the city.

Figure 4.2 Area of origin of women who presented late in pregnancy to hospital

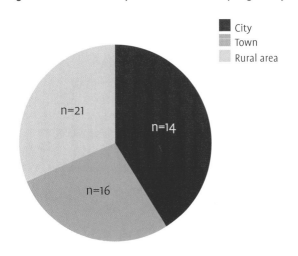

4.4.3   Nationality/ethnicity

In response to a question on nationality, 45 women described themselves as Irish. Of the remaining six women, three women came from Africa, two were from Asia and one was from the UK. All but one of the six non-national women were in the city study group.

In response to a question on ethnicity, three women were described as 'black', two women as 'Asian', while the remaining 46 women were described as 'white'.

4.4.4   Education

In the study group, one woman was described as having 'some primary level' education. The majority of women (36 women) had been educated to second level; of these, six women were described as having 'some second level', twelve women had been educated to Group-/Inter-/Junior-Certificate level, while eighteen women had attained their Leaving Certificate. One woman had completed a PLC course while a further five women had third-level education. Three women had attained a college certificate/diploma, while the remaining two had a college degree. Information relating to educational attainment was not recorded for eight of the women.

Overall, 37% had not completed their Leaving Certificate, 35% had completed their Leaving Certificate, while 12% were educated to a level higher than Leaving Certificate up to college degree.

Figure 4.3 Level of education

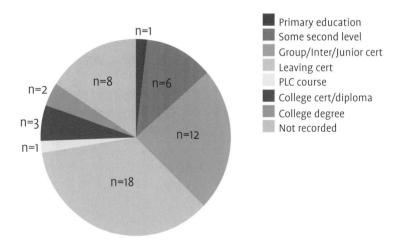

4.4.5   Current employment status

In response to a question on current employment status, seventeen women were described as students. A further eighteen women were employed either full time or part time. Seven women were classified as homemakers, while eight women were described as unemployed. This information was not recorded for the remaining woman.

Figure 4.4 Current employment status of study group

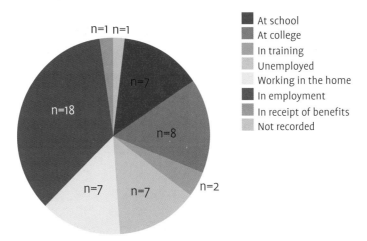

4.4.6   *Accommodation*

Twenty-seven women described themselves as 'living with parent(s)' while two women were living with a sibling. A further eight women were living with their partner/husband. Five women described their living situation as 'other'. This included a woman who was living with her grandmother and two women who lived with their children. One woman was described as 'living with friends', while in six cases the women were living alone. Information for two women was not documented.

4.4.7   *Previous pregnancies and outcomes*

For the majority of women (37 women) this was their first pregnancy. There were fourteen women who had been pregnant before. One of these women's pregnancies ended in a miscarriage. Two women who had been pregnant previously each placed a child for adoption. Thirteen of the fourteen women who had been pregnant previously had children ranging in age from one to seventeen years old.

4.4.8   *Relationship and marital status*

Regarding marital status the vast majority – 47 women – were single. Three women were married and one woman was separated. Detailing their relationship status, almost half of the women were 'not in a relationship' (24 women). Twenty women were in a long-term relationship, while four women described themselves as being in a 'casual' relationship. Information on relationship status was not recorded for three of the women.

Figure 4.5 Relationship status of women who present late in pregnancy

Relationship status

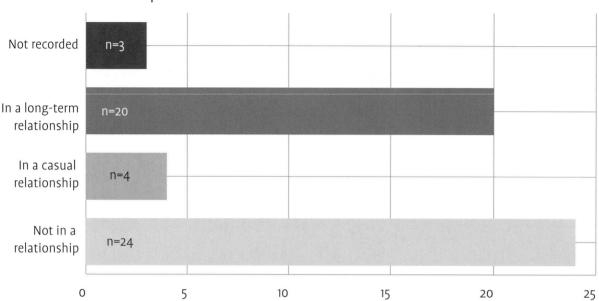

4.5   Processes entailed in late presentation

4.5.1   Factors prompting discovery of pregnancy

Twenty-three women mentioned a 'missed period' as one of the factors prompting the discovery of the pregnancy. A further 23 women reported weight gain as a factor, while eleven women mentioned morning sickness as a factor prompting discovery. Six women reported foetal movement as a factor in their discovery. Eight women in total described another's prompt as being a factor. Three women received a prompt from their mother. Another two women were prompted by a friend while a further two women received prompts from their sister. Only one woman received a prompt from their partner.

Table 4.4 Factors prompting discovery of pregnancy

Factor	Frequency of response
Missed period	23
Weight gain	23
Morning sickness	11
Foetal movement	6
Mother's prompt	3
Friend's prompt	2
Sister's prompt	2
Partner's prompt	1

4.5.2   Factors contributing to late presentation

A list of fourteen factors contributing to why women presented late for antenatal care was compiled and information on these was collected from case reports on each woman. A significant factor was the 'fear of upsetting parents', which 26 women reported as their reason for presenting late. 25 women reported 'fear of disappointing parents' as a factor in their late presentation for antenatal care. For thirteen women 'fear of parents reaction' was a factor in presenting late to hospital. Ten women reported protecting their family from stigma as a factor in late presentation. Three women hid their pregnancy because they feared being rejected by their parents.

Sixteen women presented to hospital late in pregnancy in order to 'conceal their sexual activity'. A further ten women mentioned 'to avoid stigma related to pregnancy' as one of their reasons for presenting late. Nine women presented late in order to prevent others becoming involved in their decision, while another eleven women presented late to hospital to facilitate placing the baby for adoption.

For one woman 'fear of rejection by biological father' was a factor in her late presentation, while five women presented late in pregnancy to hide their relationship with the biological father. Three women thought revealing their pregnancy would threaten their relationship with the biological father.

Table 4.5 Factors in late presentation including circumstances

Factor	Frequency of response
Fear of upsetting parents	26
Fear of disappointing parents	25
To conceal sexual activity	16
Fear of parents' reaction	13
To facilitate placing the baby for adoption	11
To protect family from stigma relating to pregnancy	10
To avoid stigma relating to pregnancy	10
To avoid others becoming involved in decision making	9
To conceal relationship with biological father	5
Pregnancy would threaten current relationship	3
Fear of rejection by parents	3
Fear of rejection by biological father	1

4.6   Role of the biological father in pregnancy

4.6.1   Nature of relationship with biological father

At the time when the pregnancy occurred, 24 women were not in a relationship with the biological father. Four women described themselves as being in a 'casual relationship' with the biological father. Twenty women were described as being in a 'long-term' relationship with the biological father. The information was not recorded for the remaining three women.

Figure 4.6 Nature of relationship with biological father

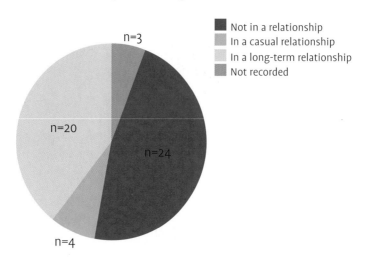

4.6.2   Current partner as biological father

When the information on the woman was recorded by the social worker/counsellor of those 24 women who were in a relationship (twenty women were in a long-term relationship while four women were in a casual relationship), nineteen women reported that their current partner was the biological father. Three women stated that their current partner was not the biological father while information for the remaining two women was not recorded.

4.6.3   Stage in pregnancy at disclosure to biological father

Nineteen women disclosed to the biological father before attending for antenatal care. Four women disclosed to the biological father after attending antenatal care and prior to delivery. Two women disclosed to the biological father after delivery. Seven women did not disclose their pregnancy to the biological father at any stage during pregnancy or after delivery. Information for the remaining women was not recorded.

4.6.4   Supportiveness of biological father during pregnancy and after delivery

In the case of eighteen women the biological father was reported to be supportive while they were pregnant. For fifteen women the biological father was described as unsupportive during pregnancy. For the remaining eighteen women it is unknown whether the biological father was supportive or not during pregnancy.

23 women anticipated that the biological father would support them after the birth, while 21 women predicted no support. Four women were unsure as to whether they would receive support or not. Information for the remaining three women was not recorded.

In the event, the biological father was reported to be supportive after delivery in 25 cases. In ten cases the biological father had been unsupportive since delivery. For the remaining sixteen women the information was not documented.

4.6.5   Biological father's presence at birth

Ten of the women stated the biological father would be present at the birth, while in another 36 cases the biological father would not be present. Information for five of the women was not recorded.

Figure 4.7 Presence of birth father at birth

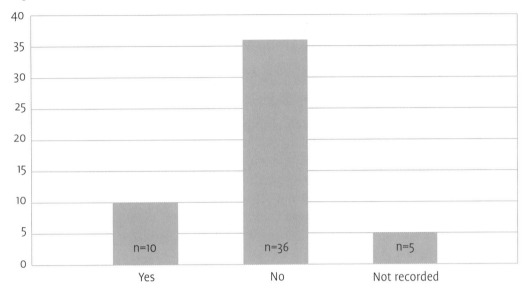

4.6.6   *Intention to record biological father's name on birth certificate*

Nine women intended to record the biological father's name on their child's birth certificate. A further ten women did not intend to record the biological father's name. At the time of coding it was known that three women did record, while two women did not record. Twenty-seven women were uncertain or did not know whether they were going to record.

Figure 4.8 Intention to record biological father's name on birth certificate

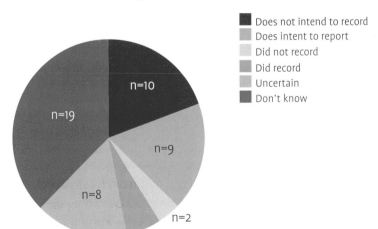

4.6.7   *Biological father's role in parenting*

Sixteen women stated that they were intending to parent with the biological father.

4.6.8   *Limited involvement of the biological father*

It is clear from the above data that the role of the biological father in pregnancies of women who present late for antenatal care is limited, while in a significant proportion of cases no partner is present at all throughout the pregnancy. Almost half of the women (24 women) in this study were not in a relationship with the biological father. The biological father was supportive during pregnancy in eighteen of the cases studies and supportive after delivery in only half of the cases. Almost one-third of the women (sixteen women) intended to parent with the support of the biological father. One-fifth of the women stated that the biological father would be present at the baby's birth and almost a quarter of the women (twelve women) intended to or did record the biological father's name on the birth certificate.

4.7   Role of family and friends in pregnancy

The family plays a significant role in the lives of women who present late in pregnancy. Over half of the women (26 women) mentioned the fear of upsetting their parents as a factor in concealing their pregnancy. Half of the women mentioned disappointing their parents as a factor in concealing their pregnancy. Fear of their parents' reaction was significant factor for over a quarter of women (thirteen women). Three women feared being rejected by their parents and so hid their pregnancy from them. Detailed below is the stage at disclosure to family, their level of support during and after pregnancy and their presence at the birth.

4.7.1   *Stage in pregnancy at disclosure to family and friends*

28 of the women disclosed to their mother before attending for antenatal care, a further six women disclosed to their mother after attending for antenatal care and before delivery, while ten women disclosed to their mother after delivery. For two women this was not applicable, as their mothers were deceased. Information for the remaining five women was not recorded.

21 women disclosed to their father before attending for antenatal care, six disclosed to their father after attending for antenatal care and before delivery while eight women disclosed to their fathers after delivery. For three women this was not applicable, as their fathers were deceased. Information for the remaining thirteen women was not recorded.

Fifteen women disclosed to their siblings before attending for antenatal care, four disclosed to siblings after attending for antenatal care and before delivery, while a further six women disclosed to their siblings after giving birth. Seven women did not have any siblings. Information for the remaining nineteen women was not recorded.

Thirteen women had disclosed to a friend before attending for antenatal care. A further seven women disclosed to friends after attending for antenatal care and before delivery. Three women disclosed to their friends after delivery. Twelve women did not disclose to friends at any stage during pregnancy and after delivery. Information for the remaining sixteen women was not recorded.

4.7.2   *Supportiveness of family and friends during pregnancy and after delivery*

27 women said that their mothers were supportive during pregnancy. 39 women stated their mothers were supportive after delivery, with six mothers described as unsupportive after delivery. This did not apply to two of the women, as their mothers were deceased. This information was not documented for the remaining four women.

22 women also said that their fathers were supportive during pregnancy. For 31 women their fathers were supportive after delivery. Five women were unsupported by their fathers since delivery. This did not apply to three of the women, as their fathers were deceased. This information was not documented for the remaining twelve women.

In the case of eighteen women, siblings were supportive during pregnancy. For 25 women their siblings were supportive after delivery. Information was not documented for the remaining eight women.

4.7.3   Presence of family and friends at birth

Twelve women stated that their mother was present at the delivery, while four women had their sister present. One woman had her friend present at the birth.

4.7.4   Attendance with other health professionals before presentation to hospital

33 women were referred to antenatal care by their GP. Seven women referred themselves to antenatal care. Another hospital department referred one woman for antenatal care. Eight women were not referred as they presented to the hospital in labour. This information was not recorded for two women.

4.8   Outcomes of pregnancy

4.8.1   Options considered for resolving pregnancy

Of the 51 women studied, 41 women considered parenting, eighteen women considered adoption while only six had considered abortion. Seven women had considered placing their baby in foster care, which they believed to be an option available to them while they came to a decision on how they would proceed and/or put in place any necessary arrangements to allow them bring the baby home. Of those 41 women who considered parenting, fourteen were from the city hospital (70% of that group) and 27 were from the rural-based hospital (87% of that group). Of the eighteen women who considered adoption, 9 were from the rural-based hospital (29% of that study group) and 9 were from the city hospital (45% of that study group). Of the six women who considered abortion, two were from the Dublin-based maternity hospital and four were from the rural-based hospital. Of the seven women who considered foster care, two were from the Dublin-based maternity hospital and five were from the rural-based hospital.

Figure 4.9 Options considered by women for resolving the pregnancy

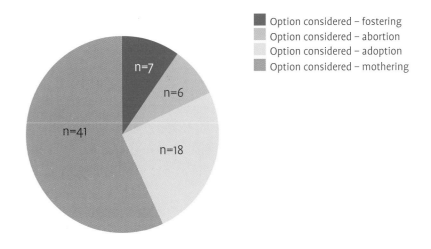

- Option considered – fostering
- Option considered – abortion
- Option considered – adoption
- Option considered – mothering

n=7

n=6

n=41

n=18

4.8.2   Decision on options at point of discharge

49 women gave birth to a single live child while in the cases of two women their babies were stillborn. Of the 49 live births, the majority of women (39 women) had decided to parent. Five women were contemplating adoption and had placed the baby in pre-adoption foster care. Two women were still considering their options and had placed their baby in temporary foster care. Two women were still considering their options and had taken their baby home. The information is unknown for the remaining woman.

4.9   Contact with antenatal and social work services

43 of the 51 women presented late to the hospital for antenatal care, with the remaining eight women arriving in labour. In examining attendance at antenatal education classes and referral to social work service, there were marked differences between the rural and Dublin-based study groups. In the table below, we can see that almost 68% (21 women) of the rural study group attended antenatal education classes, whereas none of the Dublin group attended any antenatal classes. However, 30% (6 women) of the Dublin group arrived to the hospital in labour, which contributes directly to the high percentage that did not attend.

Table 4.6 Attendance at antenatal classes

Attendance at antenatal classes	Unaware of pregnancy (N)		In denial to self of pregnancy (N)		To conceal pregnancy from others (N)	
	Rural	City	Rural	City	Rural	City
Yes	4	0	3	0	14	0
No	2	5	0	6	8	9
Total number	11		9		31	

4.9.1   Source of referral to social work service

The majority of women (47%) were referred to the hospital social work service by antenatal staff, while almost a quarter of women were referred by the maternity ward. All of the women from the rural hospital were referred by either of these routes. Routes of referral to social work services were more diverse for Dublin-based women. Three Dublin-based women self referred to the social worker, two were referred by their GP while a further two women were referred to the social work service by an outside adoption service. Information was not recorded for 35% of the Dublin study group.

Table 4.7 Source of referral to social work service

Source of referral to social worker	Unaware of pregnancy (N)		In denial to self of pregnancy (N)		To conceal pregnancy from others (N)	
	Rural	City	Rural	City	Rural	City
Antenatal staff	5	1	3	1	13	1
Self	0	1	0	2	-	0
Maternity ward	1	1	0	2	7	1
Adoption social worker	0	0	0	0	-	2
GP/hospital doctor	0	0	0	1	1	0
Medical social worker	0	0	0	0	1	0
Not recorded	0	2	0	0	0	5
Total number	11		9		31	

4.9.2   Continued contact with social-work service after discharge

Almost 57% (29 women) of the total study group continued contact with the social work service after discharge. 58% (eighteen women) of the rural-based group continued contact compared with 55% (eleven women) of the Dublin based group.

Table 4.8 Continued contact with social work service after discharge

Continuation of contact with social worker	Unaware of pregnancy (N)		In denial to self of pregnancy (N)		To conceal pregnancy from others (N)	
	Rural	City	Rural	City	Rural	City
Yes	3	3	1	4	14	4
No	3	2	2	2	8	5
Total number	11		9		31	

4.9.3   Contact with other agencies

Approximately 76% of women (n=39) had some contact with other crisis pregnancy support services and adoption services after discharge. 97% (n=30) of the rural-based group had continued contact after discharge, compared with 45% (n=9) of the Dublin-based group.

Table 4.9 Contact with other agencies

Continuation of contact with other agencies	Unaware of pregnancy (N)		In denial to self of pregnancy (N)		To conceal pregnancy from others (N)	
	Rural	City	Rural	City	Rural	City
Yes	6	0	3	4	21	5
No	0	5	0	2	1	4
Total number	11		9		31	

4.10   Summary of documentary analysis

This chapter presents an analysis of documentary data in the form of social-work and medical case-notes of women who presented for antenatal care after twenty weeks' gestation at two antenatal/maternity care settings in Ireland during an eighteen-month period in 2003-2004. The two fieldwork sites comprised a rural-based hospital in the West of Ireland and a Dublin-based maternity hospital. The total study group over the study timeframe of eighteen months was 51.

Of the 51 women, 40 presented to hospital for antenatal care past twenty weeks' gestation, two women presented prior to 20 weeks and were included in this sample as they continued to conceal their pregnancies up until delivery and eight women arrived in labour. This information was not documented for the remaining woman. Eleven women (22%) presented late because they were not aware they were pregnant, nine women (18%) presented late because they were in denial to themselves of the pregnancy while almost two-thirds of the women (n=31) presented late because they were concealing the pregnancy. Overall, the incidence of late presentation was much higher in the rural-based hospital, with 1 late presentation in every 403 births; the Dublin hospital had 1 late presentation in every 625 births. Those in the rural-based hospital were much more likely to be concealing their pregnancy – 70%, as compared with 45% of those in the Dublin-based hospital. This would suggest that concealment of pregnancy is a more rural than urban phenomenon.

Meanwhile, many more of those in the Dublin hospital (30%) presented in labour, compared with only 6% in the rural hospital.

Among those who presented late because they had not disclosed the pregnancy, a significant factor was the fear of upsetting or disappointing parents, each of which was reported by half of the women. Almost one in three did not disclose the pregnancy because they wanted to conceal their sexual activity. One in five women had not disclosed the pregnancy so as to facilitate their consideration of the option of adoption. Five women (10%) wanted to conceal their relationship with the biological father.

It appears that biological fathers play a limited role in the pregnancy of women who presented late during and after the pregnancy. A significant proportion of the study group had no partner present at all throughout the pregnancy. Regarding marital status, the vast majority – 47 women – were single. Almost half of the women (n=24) were not in a relationship with the biological father, with a further four describing the relationship as casual. Of the total study group seven women (14%) did not disclose their pregnancy to the biological father at any stage during pregnancy or after delivery. While the remaining 44 women had disclosed the pregnancy at some point to the father, he was reported to be supportive in only 25 cases. In ten cases the partner was present at the birth, while one-third (sixteen women) intended to parent with the biological father.

As regards options considered during pregnancy, 41 of the 51 women in the study group considered parenting, eighteen women considered adoption while only six considered abortion. Seven women had considered placing their baby in foster care, which they believed to be an option available to them while they come to a decision on how they would proceed. Proportionally, women from the Dublin hospital study group were more likely to consider adoption than the rural-based study group (45% city group compared with 29% of rural group) and less likely to consider parenting than the rural-based study group (70% compared with 87%). Of the 51 women in the study group, two gave birth to a stillborn baby. Of the 49 women with live births by the time their contact with the services ended, the majority of women (39 women) had decided to parent. Five women were contemplating adoption and had placed the baby in pre-adoption foster care. Four women were still considering their options between parenting and adoption of which two had placed their baby in temporary foster care while two had taken their baby home.

4.11   Profile of study group

Drawing on the analysis of the documentary data discussed above, a brief profile of the population of 51 women who presented at both hospitals during the eighteen-month timeframe selected for the study is presented here.

As regards the age of the women, the group comprised predominantly younger women, with an average age of 21 years for the 51 women and the majority (21) concentrated in the 17-19 year age category. Over one-quarter (26%) of the women were aged 25 and over, up to age 44. Overall, there was a greater concentration of ages in the rural study group where 78% were aged between 17 and 24, compared with 60% in this age range in the Dublin study group.

Six of the study group were of African or Asian origin, while the remaining 45 were Irish. The majority of women were either students (17) or in employment (18) at the time of becoming pregnant. As regards education, eighteen had not yet attained the Leaving Certificate, eighteen had completed their Leaving Certificate, six were educated to a level higher than Leaving Certificate up to College Degree[7]. For most of the women (37) this was their first pregnancy.

Analysis of women's living situations showed that 27 women were living with parent(s), while two women were living with a sibling. A further eight women were living with their partner/husband. Five women had other living situations; for example, one woman was with her grandmother, two were living with their children. One woman was living with friends. In six cases the woman was living alone. Information for two women was not documented.

Regarding marital status, the vast majority of women (47) were single. Three women were married and one woman was separated. Almost half of the women were not in any relationship (24 women). Twenty women were in a long-term relationship, while four

---

7 Information on education attainment was not available for eight women.

women described themselves as being in a 'casual' relationship. For three of the women, their relationship status was unknown.

For the majority of women (37 women) this was their first pregnancy. There were fourteen women who had been pregnant before. One of these women's pregnancies ended in a miscarriage. Two women who had been pregnant previously each placed a child for adoption. Thirteen of the fourteen women who had been pregnant previously had children ranging in age from one to seventeen years old.

All women in our study group presented to hospital at some point during this pregnancy. Two women booked for antenatal care before twenty weeks but are included in the sample as they concealed their pregnancies from their family for the full duration because of fear of their reaction. The remaining 49 women presented late – defined as after twenty weeks' gestation. Women were described as presenting late because they were not aware they were pregnant (11), they were in denial to themselves about their pregnancy (9) or were concealing the pregnancy from others (31).

Of those presenting late (after 20 weeks' gestation), fifteen women presented between twenty weeks' gestation and the end of the second trimester at 28 weeks. The remaining 34 women presented to hospital during the third trimester. Of these, eight women presented between 36 and 39 weeks and three presented at forty weeks and over. Eight women had not presented to hospital for any antenatal care and arrived to the hospital in labour. Almost half of the women presented to hospital less than eight weeks before giving birth.

5.0 Typologies of pregnancy denial and concealment

5.1   Introduction

This is the first of four chapters presenting an analysis of the qualitative interviews conducted with thirteen women recruited from the overall study group of 51 women. The chapter will set out the typologies of concealed pregnancy observed in this research. The nature of women's response to their pregnancy will be characterised and described to explicate these typologies. The format of the analysis will take the typologies generated from the review of the literature reported in Chapter 3.0 and assess the fit of these typologies with the accounts of women interviewed for this study. This will allow for a refinement of our understanding based on contemporary, Irish, qualitative, in-depth accounts of concealed pregnancy.

All women interviewed for this study agreed that excerpts of their interview could be reproduced in the study subject to steps being taken to protect their identity. Women have been given pseudonyms throughout the analysis in keeping with this agreement. In excerpts from women's interviews 'R' stands for respondent and indicates where the woman is speaking and 'I' stands for interviewer.

5.2   Typologies of concealed pregnancy

Based on the review of literature reported earlier, three typologies of the process resulting in a pregnancy being concealed have been advanced:

'Unconscious denial' – A woman has no subjective awareness of being pregnant throughout the majority of the pregnancy or even up to a totally unexpected sudden delivery.

'Conscious denial' – The fact of the pregnancy is recognised by the woman but she continues to deny it to herself and others, thereby cognitively realising the pregnancy but not displaying emotions associated with pregnancy.

'Concealment of pregnancy' – A woman acknowledges the pregnancy to herself but hides it from others and does not present for antenatal care at least until after twenty weeks' gestation, up to the point of delivery or in some cases not at all.

5.2.1   Assessing fit of 'unconscious denial'

The first typology, 'unconscious denial', fits with the accounts of three women interviewed for this study. In all three cases the women had no subjective awareness of being pregnant throughout the majority of the pregnancy. They became aware of their pregnancy at 30 weeks, 36 weeks and 39 weeks respectively. In all cases, upon confirmation of pregnancy by a physician, they immediately disclosed their pregnancy to their significant others and embarked on the process of attending antenatal care. However, when we examine the factors that gave rise to their lack of awareness, the common pattern among the women was failure to detect the pregnancy on the part of medical physicians they attended.

An abridged version of one of the women's account of 'having no subjective awareness of being pregnant throughout the majority of the pregnancy' is presented below. The accounts of the other two women are presented in a similar format in Appendix 5.

LISA

R: I went to the doctor and the doctor would say it's cystitis, but he kept telling me it was this and I'd come home and he'd give me antibiotics. I'd come home and I'd get nowhere so maybe two weeks down the line I'd go back down to him... I was on the [contraceptive] injection, you see.

I: And did you think yourself of pregnancy?

R: No. Well, people was telling me, like, you know, 'Oh I think you're pregnant' and I said, 'Well how would I be pregnant, like, I'm on the injection? I'm not pregnant anyway.' ... I get one injection and then I go back in three months' time, because its every three months, and then I was getting other injections. But what he should have done was gave me, for the second injection he should have gave me a pregnancy test to make sure that the first one worked. But he never did that, and I was going down and he was telling me that I [had cystitis]; he gave me anti-inflammatory tablets.

I: For the cystitis?

R: Yeah, and when I'd tell him I was feeling bloated he just gave me anti-inflammatory tablets and said that I was swelling up from the injection, like. I was here [indicates distended belly].

I: And you'd had your second injection by this time?

R: Yeah, and then I think I had a third one. Yeah, so I had the third one; yeah, I did have the third one and then I was getting no better so I said to mammy 'I may go somewhere, there must be something wrong with me', because you couldn't get a kidney infection one after the other like that. So mammy said to me, 'Go down to the doctor and see what he says in the morning', so I said 'No I'm not going down there. I'm sick going to him and he's telling me nothing's wrong with me. I'll go down to the hospital and check'. I got the letter then and I went up to the gynae and I said [to a nurse] 'Excuse me could I see a doctor?' and she said 'How far are you gone?' and I said 'Excuse me, but I'm not pregnant.' And she said to me, 'You are heavily pregnant ... could you just lie up on that bed for me?' and then she kept listening to my stomach and she said, 'There's a heartbeat there, but I'm just telling you, you are pregnant, I don't know how far you are.'

R: [My GP] told my mother how many times I was there. 28 times.

I: Up until that point from when you got the injection?

R: Yeah until the time the baby was born.

I couldn't be [pregnant], that was my opinion: that I wasn't because I can't be pregnant and my friend was saying to me, 'You do look pregnant'. I've known her for a long time and she said, 'Whatever way you are standing you look pregnant to me.' ... And I said 'Yeah! I do look it, I look pregnant most of my life'. That's what I said to her, joking about it. Sure, it was only a while after I had [the baby]. But there was no way I knew that I was pregnant, no way.

[Lisa]

While the characterisation of the 'unconscious denial' typology reported in the literature fits with the accounts of three women in this group, when we examine the factors that gave rise to their lack of awareness, the common pattern was failure to detect the pregnancy on the part of their GPs.

In contrast, the literature reviewed tended to explain such a lack of subjective awareness for the majority of the pregnancy as a coping mechanism invoked by women. Bonnet (1993) and Vallone and Hoffman (2003) argued that the idea of pregnancy can be so unimaginable to the woman this then results in denial when pregnancy occurs. In explaining the processes entailed in such 'pervasive denial' (Miller 2003), Finnegan et al. (1982) argued that women went through a process of rationalisation of symptoms; e.g. weight gain being attributed to 'getting fat' or, as Craig (1997) reports, thinking the delivery was a 'bowel movement'. Miller (2003) asserted that the lack of psychological awareness of pregnancy on the part of the woman can often mimic itself in a lack of physical signs of pregnancy.

As noted earlier in the critique of the literature, the implication of characterising this phenomenon as a coping mechanism on the part of the woman attributes the processes entailed in pregnancy denial or concealment to individual women, as opposed to acknowledging the possibility that they also could be attributable to other actors, systems or factors. The evidence generated in this research indicates that in all three cases where women described having no subjective awareness of being pregnant throughout the majority of the pregnancy this was an outcome of failure to detect the pregnancy on the part of physician's women were attending.

This suggests a need to refine the term applied to a pregnancy characterised as:

'having no subjective awareness of being pregnant throughout the majority of the pregnancy or even up to a totally unexpected sudden delivery'

to being an 'undetected pregnancy', as opposed to 'unconscious denial of pregnancy'. This would be in keeping with Spinelli's (2001) argument that to deny something, prior knowledge of the fact must exist.

5.2.2   *Assessing fit of 'conscious denial'*

The second typology of the process entailed in concealed pregnancy identified in the literature – 'conscious denial' – has been characterised as follows:

Where the fact of the pregnancy is recognised but the woman continues to deny it to herself and others, thereby cognitively realising the pregnancy but not displaying emotions associated with pregnancy.

Four women interviewed for this study fit with this typology. An abridged version of one of their accounts, presented below, illustrates how the woman related to the pregnancy. Her account captures the sense of denial to self and the absence of any adaptation to the pregnancy. The accounts of the other three women are presented in a similar format in Appendix 6.

EILEEN

R: I suppose when I missed my periods I just knew straight away. Every pain or cramp I got I said, 'This is my period coming now', and I just couldn't accept that I was pregnant, even though I knew at the back of my mind I was; I couldn't accept it. So I just kept denying it to myself and I'd go into work and I'd just kill myself working. If [anything] needed moving I'd move it. I never ate a thing in the hope that I'd miscarry the baby and I never told anyone. I just kept saying 'I'm not, its not really happening'. I never missed a day at work; I was never sick- nothing. I just kept as normal: going out at the weekends and everything, drinking and smoking and just having a ball. I'd pull everything real tight on me so it would just look like I had a spare tyre coming over my trousers.

I: Missed period was the first thing, but there were other symptoms there as well?

R: Just the gaining of the weight. I never ate, as I said, just trying to do everything in my power to lose the baby and then I had this plan in my head that ... I had my plan then set in my head that when I would start labour I'd go down to the house and I had a babygro and a little, do you know the all-in-one thing, to bring the baby to the hospital. I had the towels got and I said I'd boil the kettle for the towel. I had all that set up and the one thing that was at the back of my mind was how was I going to get the child from [home] to [nearest hospital] after I'd have it. So that was all set in my head – that was the plan. I said I'd get something before the day, I'll get some sort of seat to put the child into. I'd all intentions of just going to [the] hospital and leaving it at the doorstep and that would be the end of it. I'd come home and back to work, nobody would ever know anything.

I: And you had been through a labour before so you knew what that was like and felt you could manage it yourself?

R: Yes. It didn't even enter my head that I'd need anybody or that anything bad would happen to me when I would be in labour.

I: Thinking back, saying you would have always known but at the same time you didn't believe it, how would you describe that? Was it sometimes you'd go 'I know this is going on' and most of the time you'd forget, or what do you think it was?

R: I think two days after my period was due I just couldn't be, there was no unearthly way now I'm worrying and I've myself uptight over the whole lot and that's why my period hasn't come. But behind it all I knew. I knew from the minute I missed my period. My period is never late. I was the same with [my first pregnancy]: I knew the minute I had a miss that time. But I kept telling myself any cramp, pain, anything this was it and I'd poke myself in the belly button to try and bring it on. I just kept ignoring, just kept ignoring the fact that, yeah, I was pregnant.

But even in [the hospital] they gave me a scan and told me to look over it; still didn't click with me that I was pregnant. Blocking. Then I said to the doctor, 'What is it?' and he said, 'Well I can't see a penis so I think it is a girl,' and mammy was mad when I went out and told her it was a girl. Mammy was raging: 'What did you find out for?' and I said, 'What difference does it make? I don't care.' That was the whole attitude I had.

[Eileen]

In all four cases the women had acknowledged the pregnancy and begun attending antenatal care by the time they came to give birth. In two cases, Pauline and Eileen, the women were confronted by family members and forced to acknowledge the pregnancy. Aisling voluntarily disclosed her pregnancy to her brother in month seven. All three of their families then impelled them to attend the family doctor and subsequently the hospital. In all cases their families were supportive and offered help and emotional support. It is interesting to note that all three described how they continued to be in denial of the pregnancy after disclosure, and even while attending for antenatal care. Indeed, Pauline, almost one year after giving birth, still finds it difficult to imagine herself as pregnant.

In Michelle's case, the physical fact of the pregnancy broke through her denial by the start of the third trimester and she herself initiated contact with the health services. She attended hospital for antenatal care from six months' gestation. She did not disclose the pregnancy and instead put arrangements in place through the social work services to deliver the baby in another hospital and place it for adoption. In this way she planned to conceal the pregnancy entirely from her partner, family and social network. She did eventually disclose the pregnancy to her partner before travelling to give birth to the baby, but confined her disclosure to him.

All four expressed a sense of feeling detached from the pregnancy and of having a very different relationship to the pregnancy and the 'bump' than is expected; none of the four described any process of adaptation to the pregnancy. Their accounts indicate that this was a coping mechanism they invoked because the reality of the pregnancy was unimaginable to them and its possibility represented anxiety or pain, as well as a very real threat for them. Thus it seems that the characterisation of 'unconscious denial' as "where the fact of the pregnancy is recognised but the woman continues to deny it to herself and others thereby cognitively realising the pregnancy but not displaying emotions associated with pregnancy" seems to fit with the accounts of these four study participants.

5.2.3   Assessing fit of 'concealment of pregnancy'

The third typology identified in the literature was termed 'concealment of pregnancy' and was characterised as:

  A woman acknowledging the pregnancy to herself but hiding it from others.

It is argued that for concealment to occur, some knowledge of the pregnancy must be present (Wessel et al. 2003, Spinelli 2001, Treacy et al. 2002). Concealment is also considered to be a coping strategy. In the literature concealment was often related to social factors, such as stigma of non-marital pregnancy and lone motherhood, or religious beliefs regarding pre-marital sex. Retaining control over the outcome of the pregnancy has also been associated with concealment of pregnancy.

More of the women we interviewed fitted this characterisation than either of the previous two, and this group comprised of six women. An abridged version of the account of one of the six women is presented below, while the accounts of the remaining five are presented in Appendix 7.

GRAINNE

R: I knew nearly straight away.

I'm going out with the guy for about four and a half years and I couldn't even tell him. Like, I had kind of said in the beginning, I had said I would tell [my partner and family], like. So I said I'd wait till I was about three months and then I'd tell them. But three months made it coincide with my father getting [seriously ill] so I thought, 'Jesus I can't tell them now.' ... I'd to take time off work and help out at home. There was no one else to help at home, the rest of them were all [away] and my mother was working ... so from then on I just put it to the back of my mind and I never rang anyone; I never went to a doctor; I never told anyone. I just went about things as normal and worked harder, like, to put it to the back of my mind and I was just, every night time I'd be thinking, 'What am I going to do about it?' And the longer I'd left it the worse it was. How could you tell someone you are five months pregnant, or six months or...? It was becoming worse.

But that's the way I was. I had nearly myself convinced until the day I was having [the baby], like, even that day I said, 'Jesus what am I going to do?'

I: Then you said right up to the day of the delivery you were worrying about how to tell people. Do you mind talking about that?

R: Oh no. I was working on the Saturday and I came home and it was about half past eight or nine and I stayed up till about half past twelve, one o'clock on Saturday night and I stayed up till about then. Knackered going to bed and woke up about half an hour later – just felt awful sick. So I got up and went to the toilet and my back was, my back does be sore enough anyway but it was unbearable. ... I said if I could just make it to the morning now, it was a Sunday morning when the others would go to mass, I would go to the hospital. I was trying to go in and out to the toilet every five to ten minutes unnoticed.

I: And not be heard?

R: Yes. I went downstairs and had a shower, hopped in the car and...

I: Drove yourself in to hospital?

R: Yeah, it [labour] was all night, but once I got into the car as I was driving I was on auto pilot; I was just, I couldn't even turn on the radio; I couldn't listen to anything, I couldn't. I went to [hospital].

[Grainne]

Characterising concealment as 'a woman acknowledging the pregnancy to herself but hiding it from others' does fit with the account above, as well as those of the other five women in this group. All six women acknowledged the pregnancy to themselves from early on.

Liz, Sarah, Jackie and Grainne were accepting of the pregnancy and displayed a range of ways in which they were pleased about being pregnant. Liz and Sarah concealed the pregnancy from their families, in particular their parents, because they felt by being pregnant they were letting their parents down. Liz disclosed to her mother during the seventh month of pregnancy when she felt she could no longer manage the concealment. During the preceding months she had told friends and embarked on assembling some clothes for the child, as well as planning for her needs by consulting magazines and catalogues. Her mother was supportive and accompanied her to the GP and hospital antenatal care. Sarah herself embarked on attending for antenatal care, prompted by encountering back pain. Her parents were told of her pregnancy by a third party who had seen her at the antenatal clinic; her parents then confronted her about the pregnancy. Again, her parents were supportive and her mother accompanied her on subsequent visits to both the hospital and the GP. She had also been making preparations for motherhood by saving for the financial demands she anticipated in early motherhood. Jackie concealed her pregnancy from her parents to ensure they would not seek to intervene in her decision to continue the pregnancy and parent her child. She considered them to be strongly opposed to her becoming a parent, as they thought she would find it hard to cope. While she lived independently her family were closely involved in her life. She herself acknowledged her pregnancy from early on and began to attend antenatal care, as well as putting in place the practical arrangements she would need to care for the baby and assembling clothes for the child. She did disclose the pregnancy to her partner and some friends as well. She only disclosed the pregnancy to her family after the baby was born. All three – Liz, Sarah and Jackie – were pleased to be pregnant and demonstrated a range of ways in which they were adapting to the pregnancy and the prospect of motherhood during the pregnancy.

Grainne also described feeling positive about the pregnancy when she first detected it and she originally planned to disclose it to her family and partner at three months' gestation. However, her father became seriously ill in the interval between her confirming the pregnancy and the three months stage. She felt that the pregnancy now represented an added stressor for her family on top of her father's illness, and so she felt she could not disclose it. From this point onwards, while she acknowledged the pregnancy and engaged with the foetus, she did not embark on any planning for the birth or motherhood; nor did she attend any health or support services.

In contrast to these four women, the remaining two women in this group described how the pregnancy they concealed, while acknowledged by them from an early stage, represented a crisis pregnancy to them from the outset. Madeline was a migrant worker living in Ireland for over two years. Her family network was all in her home country but she had established a close network of friends from her home country in Ireland who represented her closest support network. Because of the stigma attaching to non-marital pregnancy in her country of origin she concealed the pregnancy from her family at home and her compatriot friends in Ireland throughout the entire pregnancy. She disclosed the pregnancy to her partner, who was also a compatriot, and he agreed with her plan to conceal the pregnancy and place the baby for adoption. She made contact with a crisis pregnancy support service incorporating an adoption agency and planned to place the baby for adoption so as to maintain concealment of the pregnancy from her family. From this point on she attended antenatal care. However, she did not enter into a significant process of adapting to the pregnancy or any process of anticipating motherhood as a coping strategy to prepare for adoption. At seven months pregnant she visited her family at home and kept the pregnancy concealed. She did not proceed with the adoption and only disclosed the pregnancy and baby to her network of friends when the child was returned to her from foster care at three months. Her sister came to visit her when the child was four months of age and she disclosed the birth of her child to her at that point, representing her first disclosure to her family.

Imelda was older than the other five women and had an established independent family unit with her partner and children when she discovered she was pregnant. Her relationship was in difficulties and the pregnancy represented a crisis. She was not sure she wanted to have another child from this relationship. She wanted to conceal the pregnancy from her partner and all others in order to retain control over the outcome of the pregnancy. When she first attended the hospital at 37 weeks pregnant, she was contemplating placement of the baby into foster care. However, she realised that concealing the birth would be too difficult and in the end disclosed the pregnancy to her partner when she found herself in the early stages of labour.

In the literature on concealed pregnancy it is argued that for concealment to occur, some knowledge of the pregnancy must be present (Wessel et al. 2003, Spinelli 2001, Treacy et al. 2002). In all cases the women were certain they were pregnant by the time they had missed a second period at most. In the literature, concealment is considered to be a coping strategy invoked by women and this is related to social concerns such as stigma of non-marital pregnancy and lone motherhood or religious beliefs regarding pre-marital sex. Retaining control over the outcome of the pregnancy has also been associated with concealment of pregnancy. These factors all featured across the six cases discussed above. An additional factor observed in this research was the presence of an external stressor. This arose in two cases. In the case of one woman a parent was diagnosed with a serious illness, which brought distress as well as new responsibilities. Another woman was in a difficult relationship and described how the pregnancy and baby created a new dynamic that generated an impetus to continue the relationship, which the woman had contemplated leaving. Thus the characterisation of concealment as a coping strategy does seem to fit with the accounts of participants of this research.

It is interesting to note how some women in the group entered into a process of adapting to the pregnancy and the prospect of motherhood and others did not, evoking elements observed in the 'conscious denial' group. Grainne, Madeline and Imelda did not enter into any such process of adaptation. Madeline and Imelda contemplated adoption and never projected towards the prospect of becoming mothers. Grainne ignored the progression of the pregnancy as she struggled to cope with the illness of her parent. However, features of their accounts – such as acknowledging the pregnancy from an early stage, engaging with the foetus through 'talking to the bump' or engaging with services to plan the placement of the baby for adoption – indicate a level of continuous acknowledgement of the pregnancy inconsistent with 'conscious denial'.

5.3   Refinement of typologies

Where a woman describes 'having no subjective awareness of being pregnant throughout the majority of the pregnancy or even up to a totally unexpected sudden delivery', this was attributed to the typology of 'unconscious denial' in the literature. This was explained as a coping mechanism invoked by the woman. However, the evidence generated in this research indicates that such a characterisation of women's experience of the pregnancy was an outcome of failure to detect the pregnancy on the part of physicians women were attending. Rather than attributing the processes entailed in being pregnant without having any subjective awareness to individual women, this indicates that such processes may be attributable to other actors, systems or factors. Based on analysis of this study data the typology attributed to having no subjective awareness of being pregnant is an 'undetected pregnancy'.

The second typology, 'conscious denial', has been characterised as 'where the fact of the pregnancy is recognised but the woman continues to deny it to herself and others, thereby cognitively realising the pregnancy but not displaying emotions associated with pregnancy'. This typology and characterisation did fit well with the accounts of four study participants. All expressed a sense of feeling detached from the pregnancy and of having a very different relationship to the pregnancy, their growing 'bump', foetal movements and scan pictures of the foetus than would be expected normally. Their accounts indicate that this was a coping mechanism they invoked because the reality of the pregnancy was unimaginable to them and the possibility of pregnancy represented anxiety or pain, as well as a very real threat for them.

The final typology of concealment, characterised as 'a woman acknowledging the pregnancy to herself but hiding it from others', seemed to fit with the accounts of six of the study participants. All six women acknowledged the pregnancy to themselves from early on. Four of them related an acceptance of the pregnancy and prospect of motherhood to the extent of feeling pleased. Two women acknowledged they were pregnant but the pregnancy continued to represent a crisis throughout. Concealment as a coping strategy invoked by women fitted the accounts of these six participants, and, while the factors related to concealment in the literature were observed in the analysis, two other emerging aspects supplemented them. One was the presence of an external stressor, giving rise to concerns about the context into which the news of the pregnancy and the baby would enter. The second was the way the pregnancy and baby created a new dynamic in a relationship.

5.3.1   Discrete typologies or continuum of typologies?

A final consideration in relation to these typologies is the extent to which they discretely characterise the entire account of the pregnancy or whether women can move between typologies within one pregnancy experience.

Taking the first typology of 'undetected pregnancy' all three women accepted they were pregnant when told, and in two cases at least had displayed an openness to pregnancy before it was confirmed. They went on to display the emotions associated with pregnancy, such as making preparations for motherhood, both psychologically and logistically. All three also went on to disclose the pregnancy to their significant others and attend for antenatal care at the earliest opportunity. Thus, this would seem to operate as a discrete typology.

The women in the 'conscious denial' group challenge the notion underpinning this research that engaging with antenatal care represents a key turning point in acknowledging and disclosing the pregnancy. The first interesting point here is that two of this study group described how they could embark on the expected behaviours associated with pregnancy – that is telling others and attending for antenatal care –

while continuing to suspend emotions associated with pregnancy. Thus, the women described a persistent sense of disbelief that they were/had been pregnant, even while attending antenatal care, going through birth and assuming the role of mother. Secondly, women can move out of the typology of 'conscious denial' by engaging with antenatal care services only to enter into a process of 'concealment'.

Furthermore their practices challenge the notion of 'concealment' or disclosure as discrete events and rather suggest that there are multiple domains relevant to the process of 'concealment'. Michelle attended a crisis pregnancy counselling service, a GP, hospital antenatal services, hospital and health board social workers and hospital maternity services to give birth (the services domain). She concealed the pregnancy from all significant others – her partner and family (the family domain) and friends (the social domain) for part of the time. Eventually she told her partner only, so that she continued to conceal the pregnancy from family and friends until some time after she had given birth. Eileen attended a GP, hospital antenatal services, hospital and health board social workers and hospital maternity services to give birth (the services domain) after disclosing to her mother and two sisters only. She continued to conceal the pregnancy from her father, other siblings and her child (family domain), and, having placed the baby for adoption, she continues to conceal the pregnancy from others (social domain). These two cases demonstrate that by disclosing to the services domain women can move out of 'conscious denial' into a process of 'concealment' from one or more domains. In addition, within each domain disclosure can be full or partial, such that in the latter case some features of concealment persist.

Finally, it is interesting to note how some women in the concealment group never entered into a process of adapting to the pregnancy, thereby evoking elements observed in the 'conscious denial' group. However, features of their accounts, such as acknowledging the pregnancy from an early stage, engaging with the foetus through 'talking to the bump' or engaging with services to plan the placement of the baby for adoption, indicate a level of continuous acknowledgement of the pregnancy inconsistent with 'unconscious denial'.

5.4   Refinement of definition

Referring back to our review and synthesis of the literature on this issue we constructed a stream of definition for pregnancy denial and concealment of pregnancy based on our learning from that literature (see Figure 3.1). Taking this analysis into account the following revised stream of definition for concealed pregnancy is proposed:

Figure 5.1: Stream of definition for concealed pregnancy based on analysis of study data set

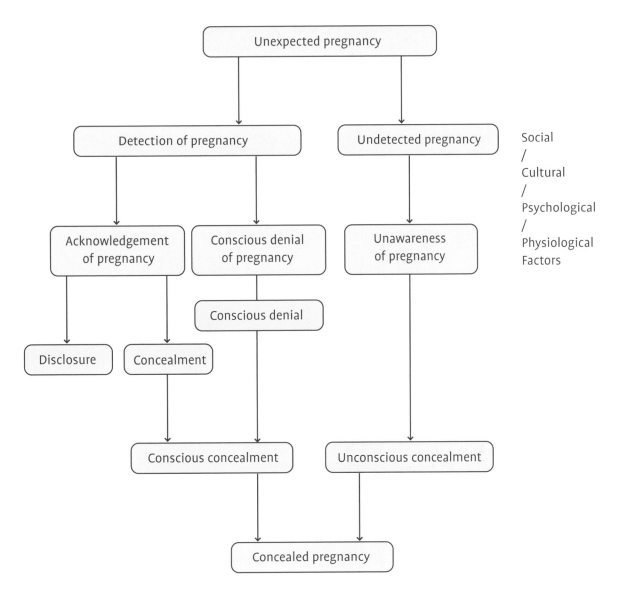

In this diagram a concealed pregnancy is the outcome of either an undetected pregnancy or a detected pregnancy that a woman actively conceals. A woman whose pregnancy is undetected until advanced pregnancy or even labour is concealing the pregnancy without even being aware of it herself. In contrast, women in the conscious denial group recognise the fact of the pregnancy but continue to deny it to themselves and others, thereby cognitively realising the pregnancy but not displaying emotions associated with pregnancy. Concealment of the pregnancy is consciously carried out by women who acknowledge the pregnancy and in some cases welcome it. Women who consciously conceal often engage in a process of adaptation to the pregnancy and the prospect of motherhood, including displaying emotions associated with pregnancy, engaging with the foetus or making preparations to care for the baby after delivery.

Thus, figure 5.1 demonstrates the range of processes entailed in concealment of pregnancy and illustrates the diversity of factors that give rise to a concealed pregnancy.

6.0 Factors and processes involved in undetected, denied and concealed pregnancy

6.1 Introduction

This chapter presents an analysis of the factors that gave rise to concealed pregnancy, together with a description of the processes entailed therein. The factors refer to the reasons women cited as to why their pregnancy went undetected or why they entered into a process of denying or concealing it. This gives us an insight into the social, cultural, psychological and physiological factors contributing to these outcomes. The processes refer to how women account for their pregnancy going undetected or how they succeeded in denying or concealing the pregnancy. In particular, this analysis will focus on the strategies women employed to maintain denial of the pregnancy to themselves and to manage to conceal the pregnancy from others.

6.2 Factors contributing to concealed pregnancy among total study group

The factors recorded in the case notes of the 51 women in the overall study group explaining why they presented late to hospital give a broad overview of the factors contributing to concealed pregnancy. A significant factor recorded was 'fear of upsetting or disappointing parents', which featured for 51 women, while 'fear of parents' reaction' was recorded for thirteen women. A further three women indicated they feared being rejected by their parents. Sixteen women presented to hospital late in pregnancy in order to 'conceal their sexual activity'.

'Avoiding stigma related to pregnancy' – including protecting their family from such stigma – was recorded for 20 women. Nine women presented late in order to prevent others becoming involved in their decision-making about the pregnancy, while another eleven women presented late to hospital to facilitate placing the baby for adoption.

For one woman 'fear of rejection by biological father' was a factor in her late presentation, while five women presented late in pregnancy to hide their relationship with the biological father. Three women thought revealing their pregnancy would threaten their relationship with the biological father.

These are very general categories and do not allow for much exploration. However, the qualitative interviews are analysed in detail below to supplement this general information source.

6.3 Factors contributing to undetected pregnancy

The factors that gave rise to the three cases of undetected pregnancy were quite distinct, while there was more similarity in factors that featured in the accounts of women who denied or concealed their pregnancies. Thus the analysis details the factors entailed in an undetected pregnancy separately first and then goes on to look at those entailed in pregnancy denial or concealment together.

6.3.1 Undetected by physician

In the three cases of undetected pregnancy, the women had been attending their GP while pregnant and their doctors had failed to diagnose the pregnancy. Their accounts of why this evolved are set out below.

In the case of Lisa, her GP had administered the injectable contraceptive to her. Before doing so, a pregnancy test he administered had shown a negative result. Once the contraceptive injection had been administered it seems he never entertained the possibility of pregnancy during her 28 presentations to him up to 39 weeks of pregnancy. During this time he administered two further contraceptive injections to Lisa. She eventually sought a referral to the gynaecological unit of her local general hospital where she was immediately diagnosed as 39 weeks pregnant.

Finola presented to her GP with symptoms similar to those reported by other people in the area due to a virus. When it persisted she herself contemplated the possibility of pregnancy and discussed this with her GP. However, the doctor accepted her accounts of her partner's belief that he was infertile (coupled with Finola having a menstrual-like bleed) as indicative that she was not pregnant. The doctor administered a range of tests and focused her attention on Finola's reported history of irregular menstrual cycles. On her third presentation to the GP at 30 weeks' gestation she believed herself to be pregnant and the doctor confirmed it with a pregnancy test.

> She had never offered pregnancy tests beforehand and maybe that was silly on her part. She said to me, 'Do you think you are pregnant?' and I explained about my partner [believing he was infertile] and that was it: the matter was kind of dropped.

[Finola]

Geraldine was attending her GP for about six months, first presenting during the second month of pregnancy. At the outset the GP had administered a pregnancy test but it showed a negative result. When symptoms of dizziness, heart palpitations and nausea persisted he investigated for a range of causes and noticed irregularities in her hormone levels. The GP then referred her to the general hospital for further tests over concerns that she may have polycystic ovaries or an irregularity in her heart. Scans ordered as part of these investigations revealed the pregnancy, which by that stage was 36 weeks' gestation. The hospital doctors informed Geraldine that abnormalities in her hormone levels made it impossible for her GP to diagnose the pregnancy using regular pregnancy tests.

It is important to note how these women deferred to the expertise of their doctor when they were told that they were not pregnant. They believed their doctors in the face of doubts and questioning by themselves and others. This must be understood in the context of the unexpectedness of the pregnancy: all three were not intending to become pregnant and were happy to have this ruled out by their GP. As Lisa explained:

> R: Well, people was telling me, like, you know, 'Oh I think you're pregnant,' and I said, 'Well how would I be pregnant, like, I'm on the injection? I'm not pregnant anyway.'
>
> ...
>
> I: You never thought of doing a home test?
>
> R: No I didn't.
>
> I: Because you were going to [the GP]?
>
> R: Yeah, and I said if he, you know, like, I didn't put the idea of being pregnant in my head with the injections, you know.

[Lisa]

Thus for these women – Geraldine, Finola and Lisa – the failure on the part of their physician to either contemplate or detect the pregnancy is the central explanatory factor in their pregnancy going undetected for 30, 36 and 40 weeks' gestation respectively.

6.3.2   Inconsistencies with usual symptoms of pregnancy

In a further elaboration of why their pregnancy went undetected by both themselves and their physicians, the women went on to explain how there were significant unusual features in their pregnancies that led to inconsistencies between their pregnancy experience and the usual symptoms in pregnancy. Geraldine explained that during her pregnancy she had a hormonal abnormality, such that usually reliable pregnancy tests did not diagnose the pregnancy:

Because all my hormone levels and everything were all over the place a previous pregnancy test had shown up negative. Because I had been going to the doctor for about six months. This was in June I found out, and I had been at the doctor since the January[8]... The GP was gobsmacked; he literally was gob-smacked, but [the hospital] had phoned me [to say] that it was possible for me to be pregnant and for it not to pick up because of different hormones, the different hormone levels.

[Geraldine]

In the case of Finola it was noticed during her delivery that she had an irregularity in the shape of her womb. The doctor explained that this would have impeded the movement of the foetus in the womb and thus accounted for the low level of movement she had felt during the pregnancy. In turn, this meant that a key indicator of pregnancy was significantly diminished in her case.

So he briefly explained that the reason I had very little movement and the reason I was breech birth is the child turned to give herself as much space as she could possibly have.

[Finola]

Finally Lisa's baby was stillborn due to a congenital anomaly and she explained how this meant that her 'bump' was shaped differently to the shape of a usual pregnancy.

You look at anyone, a normal pregnant woman, and you'd be able to tell, but [my baby had a foetal anomaly] so my bump was kind of a different shape because [of that], which you'd want to think of that, to understand, like, you know.

[Lisa]

In addition to these specific, individual issues, both Finola and Geraldine had irregular menstrual histories coupled with some bleeding during pregnancy. Taken together, this discounted the likelihood of pregnancy for them not only in their own minds but in the minds of their GPs also. Meanwhile, Lisa was using the injectable contraceptive, which also suspends menstrual bleeding. Thus, in all three cases, a principal indicator of pregnancy (a missed regular period) was not in evidence for these women.

---

8 Months here are changed to protect anonymity.

I got a period over Christmas. Because my periods have always been irregular, so to skip two to four is nothing for me: I've always been doing it since I was about seventeen ... The periods being irregular were definitely the key to this. The way it is I don't worry about this. If I was a person who had regular periods I probably would have said, 'Nah, hang on – something is wrong.' But when you are run down, stressed and you miss a period, for me [it's nothing unusual].

[Finola]

Finally, in Geraldine's case another explanation advanced by her GP for her symptoms diverted her attention from pregnancy.

[Weight gain] no, that never registered with me, but, then being told that I probably had a cyst I never noticed that I was getting bigger, but looking back now half my clothes didn't fit me by the end.

[Geraldine]

6.4   Factors contributing to pregnancy denial or concealment

There was significant overlap in the factors cited by women who either denied or concealed their pregnancy as contributing to this behaviour and so they are discussed together here. Where there is any difference in emphasis on a factor between women who denied the pregnancy and women who concealed the pregnancy, this will be highlighted. Additional factors specific to either denial or concealment are then discussed separately.

6.4.1   *Unconventional social circumstances for pregnancy*

For women who denied or concealed their pregnancy the social contexts in which they became pregnant were unconventional, such that it made it difficult for them to accept the pregnancy. A key factor here was the absence of a partner. The profile of the total study group illustrated that many women were not in a relationship when they discovered they were pregnant. In qualitative interviews women who cited this issue described how keenly they felt the absence of a partner and how strongly it was factored in their inability to accept the pregnancy or in their belief that others would not accept it. This factor was most pronounced for those who denied their pregnancy; although it was also cited by one of the women concealing her pregnancy.

Pauline, in the denied pregnancy group, described how her partner rejected her when she told him of her concerns about being pregnant, which triggered her denial of the pregnancy.

I found out that I was pregnant [and] I said it to him and he was really kinda negative: he turned around and he was, like, 'Well it's nothing to do with me, I don't want anything to do with it.' So that's kinda how it started then, that I got such a negative reaction of him that I didn't want to tell anyone else. ... The guy that got me pregnant, I mean he walked away from it, I mean he was getting on with his life, he doesn't care.

[Pauline]

Eileen, who also denied her pregnancy, was already a lone parent. Her child's father was quite involved in her life. She was not in a relationship with the man with whom this pregnancy was conceived and could not contemplate having a child where the father would never be involved, alongside a sibling who had a strong relationship with their father.

> *I already had a child to someone else, the child's father is involved in its life and this was more or less a one-night stand ... I had a hard time with [my child's] dad and now everything was perfect with him and [our child] and me and we all have a great relationship. Here I was, then, going to have another baby and this baby's father would be nowhere to be seen or found, and what kind of life would this child have growing up looking at [a sibling] going off with her dad every weekend and asking me questions and I just felt I wouldn't be able to deal with it. I felt also that it wasn't fair on the child to be looking at [a sibling] going off every weekend and having nothing, nobody only me.*

[Eileen]

Just as with Eileen, though in different circumstances, the complete absence of a father during the pregnancy was also something Aisling and Sarah perceived to be a very difficult problem.

> *That would have been a lot of why I went against the pregnancy and didn't want nothing to do with it, you know? Because at the end of the day I was going to be on my own ... I was carrying that guilt and that shame that you didn't want to tell anybody because there was nobody there. I think that was the biggest problem.*

[Aisling]

For other women, even though they were in a relationship, not being married was a strong factor for them in not being able to accept the pregnancy themselves or in anticipating that others would react negatively towards them being pregnant.

> R: *As happy as I was with the pregnancy, this was not the right time. It was just, 'Oh, like, I'm not married', and you know yourself in a small village.*
>
> I: *What were the things about it that you felt would make it so unacceptable?*
>
> R: *Just not married mostly, more than anything. [My partner] he's still he's at home and his mother is there and she's, I thought, 'God, she'd say that was an awful shame because all the rest of them are married.'*

[Grainne]

6.4.2   Concern about parents' reaction

The issue of being outside of the 'right' social circumstances to become a mother, particularly being unmarried, was a recurrent factor cited by women across both groups. However, it was often the case that women deferred more to what their parents would consider to be the right circumstances than to their own stance on this. Concerns expressed about not being married or being without a partner were sometimes expressed in the context of how this would be greeted by her parents, as opposed to how the woman herself felt she might cope with this.

Michelle described how her mother had reacted very badly when her sister became pregnant while unmarried. She could not contemplate causing the same reaction in her mother and cited this as the sole factor in her denial and subsequent concealment of the pregnancy until two months after the birth of her child.

R: *I decided because my parents would be very religious and very ashamed of it all, kind of, even though I'm [20-25] years of age, very narrow minded. I was thinking, 'No I can't do this: mam is going to kill me.' ... I was afraid she was going to kill me. I was afraid of my life.*

I: *Do you think that was it [Michelle], it was that fear of your family that was the one factor?*

R: *Oh that's all it was. That was it when I look back on it: that was it. A [20-25]-year-old girl afraid to tell her mother she is pregnant – that was it. ... The shame I would have brought on them. Mam was so upset the last time [when my sister got pregnant] and so sick; she made herself run down; she wouldn't go outside the house; she wouldn't eat a thing for you. ... When you are so afraid of something that you think you are going to die if you tell someone, you would rather pretend yourself [you're not pregnant].*

I: *Do you really think is the sole explanation: that strength of fear that you had?*

R: *Yes I was so afraid, that's all I was. I can tell you now that is all, basically.*

[Michelle]

Jackie described how her parents had reacted very badly when she had told them she was pregnant on a previous occasion. She attributed this to their doubts about her ability to parent a child independently, as well as their aspirations for her career. She described how she felt her parents had made the decision for her to terminate her previous pregnancy. She decided to conceal this pregnancy so that she could retain control over its outcome.

Jackie and Michelle had witnessed a very adverse reaction by parents to a previous pregnancy and had a good basis to believe that their pregnancy could cause such trauma and distress again. Michelle could not contemplate causing such a reaction and so went into denial about her pregnancy. Jackie, on the other hand, decided she would challenge her parents' stance by continuing the pregnancy with the intention of keeping her child. She considered concealing the pregnancy would facilitate her in achieving this.

Others who concealed their pregnancy expressed similar concerns that their parents might react badly, but to a lesser degree. Sarah recounted how her mother had warned her to avoid pregnancy and this stuck in her mind when she did discover she was pregnant.

R: *There was one time I remember. You know the way you have mother-and-daughter tiffs and you have a few words then, and she turned around one night and said to me, 'If you ever got pregnant don't come home – I'll disown you,' she said.*

I: *And what age would you have been, do you remember?*

R: *It was only that year, it was only the start of that year, like, around my birthday and she had said that to me and I think that's what put me off.*

[Sarah]

Meanwhile Liz, Madeline and Aisling described sensing that their parents might react negatively, even without the 'hard evidence' cited by Michelle, Jackie and Sarah. These accounts illustrate how impressions given by parents to their daughters of their unwillingness to accept them becoming pregnant until 'the right time' can come to the fore in the mind of a woman when this does happen unexpectedly.

There were other aspects to the concerns women expressed about how their parents might react. For some, disclosure of the pregnancy would also represent the first open disclosure to their parents that they were sexually active.

> *Because, like, I was away at college, and away from home, that they'd be kind of angry at me for, like, doing stuff like that when I'm away from home. And, like, then, you know, they wouldn't trust me .... 'Cos I didn't know what their stance was, like, 'cos we used to, we go to Mass every Sunday, so it's, like, 'my God', like, if they're really strict on that kind of a thing. Do they think it's bad, you know, having sex before marriage? You wouldn't really know. 'Cos they never talk about it .... Would they be really annoyed at me for having sex, would they be, you know, kind of condemning you because of it?*

[Pauline]

Pauline was also concerned her parents would be angry at how the pregnancy jeopardised her life-chances, which they had worked hard to make available to her. She also worried that as the eldest sibling her parents would feel she was setting a bad example:

> *They'd paid for me to go away to college and it felt like I was going to throw it all away or something... 'Cos, like, I'm the oldest as well, so it's, like, you know, having to set an example for everyone else.*

[Pauline]

Pauline denied her pregnancy and the strength of the responsibility she assumed towards her parents and family featured very strongly in this.

6.4.3   *Retain control over outcome*

The discussion of Jackie's case above demonstrates how a woman can decide to conceal a pregnancy so that she retains control over the outcome of that pregnancy. From Jackie's perspective, she could use the time during the pregnancy to put in place the support systems and facilities necessary to enable her to parent her child independently. This would enable her to resist any attempt by her family to intervene on her decision when they learned of her pregnancy and motherhood after the child was born.

Eileen, who initially denied her pregnancy, then planned to deliver the baby alone, bring it to her local hospital and leave it there to be found and cared for by staff. In this way she hoped to keep the fact of ever being pregnant entirely secret from her family and community. In order to carry this out she had to ensure that her pregnancy remained concealed throughout. For Eileen, keeping the pregnancy concealed would allow her to retain control over placing the baby into the care of others so that she could retain her life intact.

I had my plan then set in my head that when I would start labour I'd go down to the house, and I had a babygro and a little all-in-one thing to bring the baby to the hospital ... I'd all intentions of just going to [the general] hospital and leaving it at the doorstep and that would be the end of it. I'd come home and back to work, yeah, and nobody would ever know anything.

[Eileen]

6.4.4   Pregnancy represented a threat

There was a range of ways in which some of those who denied or concealed the pregnancy described how it represented a threat to their life-chances or those of their family. Acknowledging the pregnancy meant facing up to this threat and they found that very difficult.

I couldn't really see what my future would be like, I was there thinking, 'How could I go back to college, how could I?

[Pauline]

How will I cope, you know? Two [children] already. I said two kids is enough, that's all I want, and do you know what I mean, they're grown up now. I said I can't go back to that stage again ... The finances, everything like that, 'How am I going to afford it?' I said to meself. It costs money nowadays- the nappies and food, you know what I mean.

[Imelda]

This theme of the threat the pregnancy posed to the woman's existing family featured strongly in the analysis of the data from the case-notes for women whose pregnancy was the outcome of an extra-marital relationship. While none of these women consented to interview, the threat the pregnancy posed to the maintenance of their marriage and existing families had featured as the principal factor in concealing the pregnancy.

6.4.5   Inconsistent with self-image

In a related theme, another factor cited in pregnancy denial or concealment was the view that pregnancy and motherhood were inconsistent with the image women held of themselves or, indeed, with the image they believed others held of them. Thus the pregnancy operated as a threat to women's self-image or others' established images of them. It is interesting to note how this theme operated differently for both groups: Women who denied their pregnancy tended to see it as inconsistent with their self-image. Women who concealed the pregnancy tended to view it as inconsistent with others' images of them.

Three of the women who denied their pregnancy discussed how they had never envisaged themselves becoming pregnant. The prospect had been anathema to the image they held of themselves and also the life trajectory they had for themselves. Aisling, Michelle and Pauline – all of whom denied their pregnancy – referred to this as a factor in that denial.

R: *I never thought that would be me, I never thought. You see girls my age going round with kids but you're, like, well they're different, they're not me, you know that sort of way? They come from rougher areas of town and you think, 'Yeah that's them,' or whatever, but it wouldn't be me. You know, I thought I'd finish college and I was having a great time in college and I'll be [a professional] and I'll earn lots of money and I'll have a nice car and everything and then, like, all of a sudden you're faced with a child and you're, like, 'Oh my God, what do I do?'*

I: *This just wasn't part of your life plan?*

R: *Yeah, it wasn't part of the plan, I wasn't expecting kids for at least ten or fifteen years.*

[Pauline]

Meanwhile, women from the concealed pregnancy group were more likely to perceive it would be difficult for others to accept that they were pregnant and about to become mothers. It is noticeable in their accounts how less pronounced a concern it is for these women. It is interesting to note, however, that these women themselves accepted their pregnancy quickly and felt happy about the prospect of becoming mothers.

Yes, well, my own family as well. But everyone was shocked – they didn't think it would happen to me; neither did I. Mammy always knew that I was quiet; I wouldn't be one going out getting drunk and coming home drunk, I'd be quiet like that. That's why they were shocked, very shocked. ... Mammy was very shocked: she said, 'I thought it would never happen to you [Liz].'

[Liz]

6.4.6   *Unpronounced symptoms of pregnancy*

Moving from the psychological to the physiological realm, a number of women who either denied or concealed their pregnancy referred to how some of the indicators of pregnancy did not feature very strongly for them. Some referred to not having developed a very large bump or not experiencing morning sickness.

Pauline, Michelle and Aisling, who denied their pregnancy, described how for them the absence or minor nature of the principal symptoms associated with pregnancy operated to minimise the extent to which they were forced to consider the possibility of being pregnant. In Michelle's case missing a period was not an issue as she took the pill continuously – never taking the advised break of a week between packets – in the belief that this would mean greater efficacy. This had the effect of stopping menstrual bleeding. This removed missed periods as a key indicator of pregnancy in her case.

Pauline and Grainne described how other symptoms were hardly noticeable.

I was lucky in a sense that I didn't have morning sickness; my bump wasn't that big.

[Pauline]

This was also the case for women who were concealing their pregnancy. The expected symptoms associated with pregnancy impacted on them in a very limited way.

I wasn't sick one day, one morning for one minute – that's all. It didn't bother me at all.

[Grainne]

6.4.7   Locked into concealment

The notion of becoming 'locked into concealment' was the final factor cited by women in both groups as accounting for why they denied or concealed the pregnancy. Two women who concealed their pregnancy until after delivery described how, as their pregnancy proceeded into an advanced stage, the concealment began to take on a momentum of its own, whereby they passed a point where it would be reasonable for them to tell their families and communities.

Grainne explained:

The longer I'd leave it I said, 'Jesus how can I tell now I'm seven months pregnant?' and then [partner] have to tell his mother and she probably thinking he knew all along.

[Grainne]

Michelle denied her pregnancy until six months' gestation after which she attended services but concealed it from all family and social networks, initially only disclosing to her partner before the birth. After the delivery, she placed the baby in the care of the health board to be adopted. By this time she felt she was locked into a particular path and it was too late to disclose the pregnancy.

R: *I started on that road of, straight away the minute she told me I was pregnant, 'Okay. I'm getting it adopted.' That was it, and that was the start of it. And I never looked forward to twenty years, only when [partner] said to me. I never looked forward, 'I wonder what [the baby will] look like,' and when [they would] go to school, I never looked at a life with [the baby], never. ... I was afraid then that I'd make such a fuss about giving him away they will all think, 'She is such an eejit and now she's keeping him.' It's like embarrassment: what are you doing?*

I: *Did it seem out of control a bit?*

R: *Totally – it was like, 'There's nothing you can do about it now: you've made your decision, there is happy people being asked do they want a new baby and how can you do this now they think they are getting a baby and they are looking for a baby.' It was all over the place.*

[Michelle]

6.5   Factors specific to concealment of pregnancy

The final set of factors – discussed below – was specific to women who concealed their pregnancy.

6.5.1   External stressor

Two women cited factors external to themselves and the pregnancy as crucial to their concealment of the pregnancy. In the cases of both Grainne and Imelda their pregnancy came at a time of other difficulties in their family life. Having regard to these circumstances, both women felt that to reveal the pregnancy now would compound those difficulties. These external stressors were key factors in both women concealing the pregnancy.

In Grainne's case her pregnancy, though unexpected, was acknowledged and accepted by her from an early stage. She planned to tell all of her family and her partner when she was three months pregnant. However, between confirming the pregnancy and telling everyone when she planned, her father became seriously ill.

I had kind of said in the beginning, I had said I would tell them, like. So I said I'd wait till I was about three months and then I'd tell them, but three months made it coincide with my father getting [seriously ill] so I thought, 'Jesus, I can't tell them now' … When that happened I'd to take time off work and help out at home; there was no one else to help at home: the rest of them were all in college and my mother was working. So, it was if he thought that all this work was at home and no one was doing it, it would make him worse. So from then on I just put it to the back of my mind and I never rang anyone; I never went to a doctor; I never told anyone.

[Grainne]

It is interesting to note that in the case-note data analysis illness in the family was cited as a key factor in the concealment of pregnancy by another woman in that study group.

In Imelda's case her relationship with her partner was difficult: she described how communication between them had broken down, her partner's participation in home life was minimal and he was drinking heavily. She also referred to a history of abuse and controlling behaviour by her partner, particularly monitoring where she went when she left the family home. She indicated that she had been planning to exit the relationship now that herself and her two children were at a stage where they could cope independently. The pregnancy meant a newborn baby, which would change the dynamic in the relationship and make her more dependent and vulnerable.

I was dealing with problems with him, he was drinking a lot and, you know what I mean, he was putting more pressure on me … he was getting aggressive and everything and drinking and coming home here drunk. So I said, 'No, I can't have another one now' … [After I told him] he says, 'Why didn't you tell me, why didn't you tell me?' and I said, 'I couldn't, sure, you're never here: the weekends you were gone out, during the week you're gone out, and when you were here', I said, 'you're only sitting looking.' I'd be down in the kitchen, washing and ironing, you know what I mean? … He'd be saying to me, then, 'Are you sure it's mine?' I said, '[N], please, just accept it. Do you not believe me?' You know, this is the craic, as well: 'Are you sure it's my child?' and all this craic.

[Imelda]

6.5.2   'Could not say the words'

One issue that emerged as particular to a small number of the women who concealed their pregnancy was how it was uncharacteristic of their personality to be open – particularly with their parents – about feelings or worries that they had. This learned behaviour was a factor in the difficulty they experienced in disclosing the pregnancy. For these women difficulty actually verbalising they were pregnant played a large part in them not feeling able to disclose the pregnancy to their families.

I: You were saying you never discussed contraception or anything within the house. Would your other sisters with your mother, or would your mother tend to discuss it with you?

R: No, never with me. I think she might have with the two younger ones, I'd say 20 and 21, but a couple of years ago. But even if she brought it up with me, like, I'd nearly run

out of the room. You know it wasn't that either I didn't want to be talking about. ... My
mother was expecting me when they got married, which you think would be able to make
me talk to her, but I just don't like talking to people about things like that.

[Grainne]

6.5.3   Complicity of others

Finally, some of those who concealed their pregnancy described how, after they did
make the disclosure, others indicated to them that they knew were pregnant but hadn't
confronted them. Rather, they waited until the woman disclosed it to them.

Grainne's mother had asked her if she was pregnant when she was seven months
pregnant, but she had strongly denied it and her mother did not persist. Her account of
telling her mother after delivery indicates that her mother believed Grainne to be
pregnant, but it seems she respected her decision not to disclose.

[After giving birth in hospital] I rang them, I rang my mother. She just said, 'What?' I said,
'I'm in hospital' and she goes, 'Jesus are you all right?' and I said, 'Yeah, I'm after having
a baby boy,' and she was absolutely delighted, so she goes, 'Thank God it's over.'

[Grainne]

Imelda described how one of her work colleagues told her she knew she was pregnant
all along.

One of the girls said in work, one the girls said to me after it all, she said, 'I knew you
were pregnant'. She said, 'You were in denial of it.' 'Cos she called here twice to see me
one night and said, 'You were in denial of it,' and I said, 'I know I was; I didn't want to
know I was pregnant.'

[Imelda]

6.6   Summary of factors contributing to concealed pregnancy

Referring back to our review of the literature, we noted that explanations of why women
concealed or denied a pregnancy cited a range of social, cultural, psychological and
physiological factors. The factors identified in the above analysis of women's qualitative
accounts can also be categorised under the headings of physiological, social/cultural
and psychological factors.

6.6.1   Physiological factors

The factors arising under this heading can generally be explained as the symptoms of
pregnancy being inconsistent or under-pronounced for women in this study group. This
set of factors operated to either contribute to the pregnancy going undetected or to
facilitate denial or concealment of pregnancy.

The principal sign of pregnancy is missing a monthly menstrual bleed or period. Four of
this study group described how they had not been having regular monthly bleeding prior
to the pregnancy, so that missing a period was nothing of note. Furthermore, in two of
the four cases the women reported having some bleeding during the pregnancy. The GPs
took any bleed as a strong indicator that the woman was not pregnant and did not
proceed to use any other method of ruling it out; e.g. administering a pregnancy test or
performing an ultra-sound scan.

For a number of women other principal symptoms associated with pregnancy were either absent or only very minor, such that they did not prompt the women to consider the possibility of being pregnant. This included not experiencing morning sickness, no reports of changes in energy levels, no feelings of tiredness, and not developing a very large bump. It is important to bear in mind that women not expecting to become pregnant may not be alert to these indicators of pregnancy. Even those who did notice symptoms, such as tiredness or change in body shape, explained them away with reference to their lifestyles or other conditions, e.g. a GP's suggestion that the woman had an ovarian cyst. Significantly, many of the women were pregnant for the first time and, again, had not been anticipating becoming pregnant; therefore their awareness of and sensitivity to the symptoms of pregnancy beyond a missed period was in many cases minimal.

It is notable that in the three cases of undetected pregnancy the women explained how there were significant unusual features in their pregnancies that led to inconsistencies between their pregnancy experience and the usual symptoms in pregnancy. These took the form of unusual hormonal levels, which rendered pregnancy tests void, abnormal womb shape, which restricted foetal movement, or a foetal anomaly, which led to an irregular pregnancy 'bump'. These women had been attending their GP while pregnant and the doctor had failed to diagnose the pregnancy. It is important to bear in mind how they deferred to the expertise of their doctor in telling them that they were not pregnant and believed it in the face of doubts and questioning by themselves and others. This must be understood in the context of the unexpectedness of the pregnancy: all three were not intending to become pregnant and were happy to have this ruled out by their GP.

6.6.2   Social/cultural factors

For women who denied or concealed their pregnancy the social contexts in which they became pregnant were unconventional, making it difficult for them to accept the pregnancy. A key factor here was the absence of a partner. A number of women became pregnant outside an established relationship and so were single when the pregnancy was detected. They perceived strong social stigma and condemnation attaching to women who became pregnant outside of any relationship. For most of the women the implications of this for their reputations in the eyes of parents, families and their communities was what they were most sensitised to. They felt that they would be viewed as 'not knowing who the father was' and strongly condemned for this. Meanwhile women expressed mixed views on the implications of this for the child. Some found the prospect of the father being uninvolved in the pregnancy and the life of the child very difficult to reconcile. Others accepted this easily and conversely felt that an independent unit comprising them and their child was preferable.

For other women, even though they were in a relationship, not being married was a strong factor for them in not being able to accept the pregnancy themselves or in anticipating that others would react negatively towards them being pregnant. A number of women had strong fears about how their parents would react to discovering they were pregnant at this stage in their lives, and not being married was a key factor in this. For one woman her parents' opposition to her assuming the role of mother featured in her decision to conceal the pregnancy.

There were other aspects to the concern the women expressed about how their parents might react. For some disclosure of the pregnancy would also represent the first open disclosure to their parents that they were sexually active. Other concerns expressed were that parents would be angry at how the pregnancy jeopardised life-chances parents had worked hard to make available to their daughters.

There was a range of ways in which some of those who denied or concealed the pregnancy described how it represented a threat to their own life-chances or those of their families. Acknowledging the pregnancy meant facing up to this threat and they found that very difficult. This theme of the threat the pregnancy posed to the woman's existing family featured strongly in the analysis of the data from the case notes for women whose pregnancy was the outcome of an extra-marital relationship.

Beyond the issues of stigma, disapproval or condemnation women perceived they may encounter from their significant others if they revealed the pregnancy, there were other ways in which significant others featured in women's accounts of the pregnancy going undetected or being denied or concealed by them. Two women demonstrated how they had kept the pregnancy concealed so as to allow them to retain control over the outcome of the pregnancy.

Finally, there were some indications that significant others had been complicit in women concealing the pregnancy. In some cases women did disclose to someone else – usually a partner or friend – who then complied with their wishes to conceal the pregnancy. Other women described how significant others indicated to them after disclosure that they knew they were pregnant but had not confronted the woman. This could be perceived to be either complicity in denial or concealment or else respecting women's right to determine the outcome of the pregnancy in their own way.

6.6.3   *Psychological/social factors*

The decision here to term these factors psychological/social or psychosocial factors reflects how they relate to psychological processes that have social factors as an underlying cause.

The first factor here could generally be described as a belief by the woman that pregnancy was inconsistent with her self-image to the extent that she cast from her mind the possibility that any of the symptoms she noted could be caused by pregnancy. Four of the women discussed how they had never envisaged themselves becoming pregnant, and the prospect had been anathema to the image and life trajectory they held for themselves. This led them to form the belief that 'a pregnancy could not happen to me' and they retained this belief, even in the face of symptoms indicating pregnancy. This created the conditions for denial of pregnancy.

In addition, other women from the concealed pregnancy group who accepted their pregnancy quickly and felt happy about the prospect of becoming mothers themselves, perceived it would be difficult for others to accept that they were pregnant and about to become mothers.

The context under which two women in the qualitative study group concealed their pregnancy demonstrated how conditions external to their pregnancy could act as stressors, which made it very difficult for them to contemplate revealing their pregnancy. In the case of both, the pregnancy came at a time of other difficulties in their family life. Having regard to these circumstances, both felt that to reveal the pregnancy now would compound those difficulties. These external stressors were key factors in both women concealing the pregnancy. Illness in the family featured as one such 'external stressor'. A difficult relationship featuring communication problems, alcohol problems, minimum participation by her partner in the relationship or family and a history of abuse and controlling behaviour represented the second 'external stressor' noted in the study. This was compounded by the fact that the woman had begun to act on plans to exit the relationship which she could not contemplate proceeding with in the event of another baby entering the family.

One issue that emerged as particular to a small number of the women who concealed their pregnancy was how it was uncharacteristic of their personality to be open, even with their parents, about feelings or worries that they had. They found sexuality issues, in particular, difficult to deal with openly. This learned behaviour was a factor in the difficulty they experienced in disclosing the pregnancy. For these women difficulty actually verbalising they were pregnant played a large part in them not feeling able to disclose the pregnancy to their families.

Finally, two women who concealed their pregnancy until after delivery described how as their pregnancy proceeded into an advanced stage the concealment began to take on a momentum of its own whereby they passed a point where it seemed reasonable for them to tell their families and communities.

6.7   Processes entailed in concealed pregnancy

This part of the analysis looks at the 'how' in women's accounts. The focus here is on the processes women described by which their pregnancies proceeded undetected, denied or concealed. These processes meant the pregnancy went undetected by a physician, or they were strategies employed by the women to deny or conceal the pregnancy.

6.8   Processes entailed in an undetected pregnancy

The accounts of the three women whose pregnancies went undetected by their physician until between 30 and 40 weeks' gestation have been well documented in earlier sections (see, for example, section 6.3). Certain aspects of their accounts are pertinent to the issue of the process by which this came about and are presented here in summary. In the cases of both Lisa and Finola their GPs discounted the possibility of pregnancy because they did not present with straightforward symptoms indicating pregnancy. Lisa's GP ruled out pregnancy because she was using the injectable contraceptive; Finola's GP ruled it out because of Finola's reports of her partner's doubts about his fertility and her history of irregular menstrual cycles. Neither GP sought to rule out the possibility of pregnancy.

Geraldine's GP, on the other hand, did consider pregnancy early in the six-month period she was attending him with an undetected pregnancy. However, the hormonal pregnancy test administered did not diagnose pregnancy due to an abnormality in Geraldine's hormonal levels. This prompted the GP to explore other possible causes for her symptoms, finally leading to referral for MRI scans and ultra-sound scans. The ultra-sound scan diagnosed the pregnancy at 36 weeks' gestation. Referral for an ultra-sound scan would have been an alternative means of checking for a pregnancy earlier. The failure to refer her for such a technologically advanced test is understandable, given the high efficacy levels of the hormonal pregnancy test. However, the question remains as to whether a more low-level technological option would be available for use in general practice, such as a hand-held heart-beat detector, which could act as a back-up to the hormonal test.

As well as considering the role of the GPs in not detecting the pregnancy, the stance of the women must also be considered. All three of these women were not anticipating a pregnancy and so were pleased when their GP ruled it out initially. They went on to defer to the expertise of the GP in the face of suggestions by anyone in their family or social network that they might be pregnant. Indeed, they deferred to this in the face of any doubts they had themselves that this might in fact be the case. In all three cases the women were highly relieved to finally receive a diagnosis of pregnancy as the alternatives being investigated or the persistence of unexplained symptoms were becoming a source of worry and distress for all of them.

6.9   Processes entailed in denial of pregnancy

Four of the women in the qualitative study group fit with the characterisation of conscious denial of pregnancy. The process by which they maintained denial can be categorised in two ways. Firstly, they did not take on board the full implications of the pregnancy; secondly, they employed a range of strategies to manage their own thought-processes in line with the belief that they were not pregnant.

6.9.1   *Not taking on the full implications of the pregnancy*

Three of the four women in this group were aware that pregnancy was a possibility for them when they first missed a period. They described a process whereby they never accepted that the pregnancy would either become established or reach its full conclusion. The women described 'hoping the pregnancy would go away', 'hoping I'd miscarry' or 'hoping it just dies'.

Pauline and Eileen reasoned that they would miscarry the pregnancy based on either statistics for miscarriage or as a result of engaging in activities not consistent with sustaining a pregnancy.

I wasn't really thinking, you know, what was going to happen a few months down the line and stuff like that. I was just kind of thinking, 'Oh it'll go away,' 'cos, I don't know, something like one in four or one in five pregnancies end in miscarriage or something, so I was there thinking it could be me.

[Pauline]

In keeping with this mindset that 'it's not happening' or hoping the pregnancy 'would go away', another strategy adopted by women denying the pregnancy was not to project towards the birth of a child. They tended to describe their outlook during this time as taking one day at a time:

You're just getting through it: you don't really sit down and analyse the situation. You're kind of, you know, there's another day over, there's another day over, you know that sort of a way, like? You're not really sitting down and thinking the whole thing through. You're not analysing the whole situation, you're just getting through it one day [at a time].

[Pauline]

Those in denial never thought beyond the pregnancy to anticipate a baby or motherhood. Aisling described being in denial right up to the time she went into labour; she had never anticipated the labour stage at all:

I don't think labour even crossed my mind. I didn't have a clue. … Because I hadn't thought about birth, it was never mentioned or I didn't want to talk about it.

[Aisling]

In all cases the women never contemplated rearing the child themselves and if they did think about it, their attitude was that they would place the baby into the care of others, either through adoption, or, for one woman, by leaving the baby in a local hospital. Thus, as the pregnancy progressed the birth came to represent an end or 'solution' to the situation they were in, rather than the start of motherhood.

I can't ever remember thinking where would [the baby] go. I can't remember thinking what would [the baby] look like. I never let myself. I remember thinking the solution must be giving birth – that was the hardest thing I have to go through because that is painful. Not the actual the emotional pain of having the baby; then I'd be rid of it and you would forget about it.

[Michelle]

I: *Did you ever think about how will I be afterwards? Did you ever think beyond it?*

R: *No, that never entered it – as long as I got the baby to the hospital. No, I never thought how I'd, would I be all right or would I collapse and they'd all know then that I was after having a baby. None of that as long as I got the baby up to the hospital.*

[Eileen]

The families of three of the women became aware of the pregnancy by the time they were giving birth. In all cases this was followed by the woman's mother accompanying her to the GP and from there to a hospital appointment. It is interesting to note how all three said that even in this context they were still not able to take on the reality of the pregnancy and either could not engage with the care being offered to them or found it upsetting:

[The doctor] was kind of just talking and stuff like that. I was still kind of like, you know, 'no I don't want to be pregnant, I don't want this,' and stuff like that. So I was still kind of getting upset, I wasn't really accepting it, like … I kept crying in the hospital. I think nearly every time I went in I was crying … Every time I went in it was a kind of reality check, you know, 'cos they'd be scanning and everything like that.

[Pauline]

During their pregnancy none could contemplate the prospect of motherhood. Where they did have moments of contemplating the possibility of having a child, their tendency was to see the delivery as the end to an entirely unwanted episode in their lives. This entailed placing the baby into the care of others.

Two of the women, Pauline and Aisling, did not proceed with their plans to place the baby for adoption. Both were younger and still dependent on their parents and in both cases their parents knew of the pregnancy by the time they gave birth. Their parents' wishes were instrumental in both of them deciding to keep the baby.

In the case of the other two women, Eileen and Michelle, they had decided to place the baby for adoption by the time they came to give birth. Some of Eileen's family became aware of her pregnancy before she had the baby after confronting her about suspicions they had. This meant she had to give up her plans of unassisted birth followed by leaving the baby. She decided to place the baby for adoption instead and resisted her family's efforts to dissuade her. She concealed the pregnancy and birth of the baby from the remainder of her family, her friends and social network to facilitate adoption.

Michelle acknowledged her pregnancy when she reached six months' gestation. She told her partner after another month but proceeded to conceal it from her family, social network and everybody else. She put arrangements in place to deliver the baby in a distant hospital and place the baby for adoption.

> R: *I needed to get out of [my town] because I didn't want to go into labour walking down the street or in the shop one day. So what I arranged was, a week before I was due I moved down to this place in [City A], which I did. Had all my medical files from [the hospital]. I made them photocopy everything. Went into [City A] hospital a day after arriving, saying, 'I'll be having my baby here, thank you. This is a concealed pregnancy and I won't be keeping him, I'll be leaving him here.' Now, because I'm in Health Board [Area X] they had to organise this with me, my social worker from Health Board [Area X]. I had got in contact with her just before I left. … So I had him in [hospital] on the Tuesday, left hospital Wednesday morning bleeding so badly, in so much pain, I thought I was going to die. I went home to that apartment, sat there.*
>
> I: *Leaving the hospital, was it to get away from the situation?*
>
> R: *The baby – because, so I didn't have to look. I saw [the baby] once, you see, and I had [the baby]. I gave birth and the nurse said 'Do you want to take [the baby]?' [I said], 'No'.*
>
> [Michelle]

The baby went into foster care to be placed for adoption but after six weeks Michelle changed her mind and decided to keep the baby and tell her family.

6.9.2   Managing thought-processes

Throughout this process of not taking on the reality of the pregnancy, women who denied their pregnancy described employing a range of strategies to manage their own thought-processes in line with the belief that they were not pregnant.

It is interesting to note how they referred to processes of 'blocking out', 'denying' and 'trying to keep the thoughts away':

> *I just kind of blocked it out. … Acting normal and concentrating on my studies and going out, kind of blocked it out then. … I concealed it for so long and the fact that, you know – what's the word? – I was denying it, as such … You just try to think of other things, you just, I don't know. You can't really, you know, you're like, 'Oh God this isn't me,' you know, that sort of a way.*
>
> [Pauline]

Strategies women used to block out the pregnancy were typically to keep very busy both physically and mentally. During leisure times getting drunk played a key role in suppressing any thoughts of the pregnancy.

I ignored it, then, by working and going to college and I was grand.

[Aisling]

Cleaning like mad and you are thinking, 'Right: on the Thursday I'll get the prescription' ... Now I'm not a big drinker, but I found out if you drink a bottle of vodka you forget about a lot, there's a happy place there. ... During pregnancy, once or twice I just remember thinking, 'Just drink and forget about it.'

[Michelle]

Any thoughts that they might be pregnant were managed by rationalising away the symptoms of pregnancy and attributing them to other causes. Missed periods were to do with being tired or stressed, and changes in body shape were just getting fat or caused by thyroid problems. When they compared themselves with their peers they did not feel they were really showing any signs of pregnancy.

I missed my period; I kinda thought, 'Oh maybe it was too many late nights, and college and everything,' so I didn't really pass any remarks ... It was strange 'cos even when you have a bump and everything, like, you just go, 'Oh I'm getting fat,' or whatever. And even when it's kicking and everything, I don't know, it's just, it's strange, I don't know how you could explain, like ... 'Cos I couldn't imagine me with a child.

[Pauline]

6.10   Processes entailed in concealment of pregnancy

Six of the women in the qualitative study group fit the typology of concealing their pregnancy whereby they acknowledged the pregnancy to themselves but concealed it from others. In addition, as noted above, those who fit the typology of having consciously denied their pregnancy also engaged in a process of concealing their pregnancy. The strategies all of these women employed to conceal their pregnancy are discussed below to provide an insight into how women managed to conceal their pregnancy totally or partially up to, in some cases, advanced pregnancy or the onset of labour, or until after they had given birth.

6.10.1   Carrying on as normal

As the earlier discussion on the factors in concealment and denial of pregnancy demonstrated, while some of the women were happy themselves to be pregnant, most had difficulties reconciling themselves with the pregnancy and the prospect of motherhood in the current circumstances of their lives. They were, therefore, trying to come to terms with the pregnancy and keep the evidence of it concealed at the same time. A principal strategy of concealment for all of them was to 'carry on as normal' so as not to alert anyone to any changes in them lest they should suspect they were pregnant:

I never missed a day at work; I was never sick – nothing. I just kept as normal: going out at the weekends and everything, drinking and smoking and just having a ball. ... Just acting the normal way [] I was out on the beer with all the rest of them, and me, I'd be sick with heartburn and I could never tell anyone that. They'd know straight away I was pregnant.

[Eileen]

As women were concealing the pregnancy from their family also, they had to be sure to maintain the same pattern of work in the home in case changes to work habits gave any indication of the pregnancy.

He started getting, asking me questions, 'What's wrong with you? You haven't much housework done here today, are you all right?' I said, 'I'm fine, just leave me alone', I said. I thought, 'Is it that obvious, does he know himself now, or what?' ... And he said to me, 'Are you sure you're all right?' he said, 'cos I was going down the garden with a bucket of turf and I dropped it and he'd seen me. I said, 'I'm fine, I'm after pulling a muscle or something, me back is after hurting'.

[Imelda]

Where women were attending the hospital for antenatal care while concealing the pregnancy this often entailed devising ways to fit appointments in with their work schedule so as not to alert anyone. Women were highly sensitised that these changes to their work schedule might alert colleagues to their pregnancy, particularly where they were now regularly taking a weekday as their day off, instead of the usual preference for a day at the weekend.

Eileen maintained this approach even when she went into labour on a morning when she was due to be in work:

R: At 9 o'clock that Saturday morning my waters broke and I nearly died. I said, 'The one day I'm after asking to work so I could have that appointment in [the hospital next week].' I kept working and the pains kept coming and I just kept at it. But I'd rang my sister and said I had to work 'til two so I just kept it up and I was bent over like that now and again with the contractions.

I: And your waters had broken?

R: Yeah. I had tissues everywhere. I worked away anyway, and then my sister rang the actual workplace and I went onto the phone and she said, 'If you don't tell [your boss] shortly that you are sick or something I'm coming down and I'm going to tell her what's going on'. And she's real bossy, real stern, so I was getting afraid and this was half past eleven and I had been in pain since five that morning but real strong pains from nine. So I said to [my boss] that I had awful bad period pains and I had to go home and I went out with the big long white coat on me so nobody would see anything.

[Eileen]

Three of the women even tried to ensure that the birth took place within a very short timeframe so they could return to their lives without it being noticed. Michelle and Imelda both described pleading to have an elective caesarean so as they could contain the delivery and get back to jobs or home without raising suspicions. Eileen delivered within twenty minutes of arrival at the hospital and immediately sought to be discharged.

The day he was due I said, 'I'm going in and that's it', and I cried and pleaded for them to do something because I had arranged, I had taken two weeks' holidays off work. That's where I was gone – a sun holiday, so I had to be back by a certain time because I probably would have lost my job. ... So I had [the baby] on the Tuesday, left hospital Wednesday morning, bleeding so badly, in so much pain, I thought I was going to die.

[Michelle]

6.10.2   Wearing concealing clothes

As well as trying to continue life as usual so as not to prompt suspicions in anyone that anything had changed for them, women described having to conceal any noticeable changes, particularly changes in body shape. A common strategy for all of the women was to wear clothes that would conceal their changing body shape. Clothes were also used to restrict the extent to which these changes were visible. This entailed women wearing heavy, oversized clothes, even in the summer or when they were too warm. It also meant for some wearing restrictive clothing that was highly uncomfortable and then seeking out any private opportunities where they could loosen their clothes.

I was always very stylish, dressed up, went out a lot and then suddenly at seven months, suddenly when I came back from [holidays] I'd wear big jumpers; even though I wasn't huge I'd wear big jumpers in the middle of summer going to work. I used to collapse with the heat.

[Michelle]

I made myself fit into the trousers, and all this craic. Made sure I put on a jumper and made sure I pulled it out a good bit, and put on coats. Anyway, summer came anyway and it was grand. ... The tracksuit bottoms – alright, one of the girls said to me, 'God, you're, they're very tight in the back your tracksuit bottoms'. I said, 'Yeah, they're a smaller size, they're the wrong size'. And I was always a 10; they were a 14. Round the back alright was noticeable, I didn't mind, but, I just passed it off.

[Imelda]

6.10.3   Isolating self from others

Another common strategy women used was to create situations where they isolated themselves from those close to them to avoid the pregnancy becoming detected. They would reduce frequency of visits home to family, avoid going out and even initiate quarrels so as to have an excuse not to have to be in conversation or company with those most likely to notice the changes the pregnancy had generated in them.

I kept a low profile then for a while within the area. Yeah, I didn't, I was so ashamed of myself. I was, I wouldn't even go to the shop. I never went out around [my home town] or nothing, you know, my parish, like. I wouldn't do nothing. Even when it was told then, when everybody knew I still wouldn't bother. ... I wouldn't be going out as much in college. I'd be saying I was sick and that I was tired and I was going to go home and do a bit of study, or none of the other girls in the house were going out and all this, kind of. Or I'd say, 'Jesus I was out last night with the girls in the house' or 'I'm broke'. All kind of excuses. ... I wouldn't go outside the back door; I'd be afraid to go in the car with mom to go shopping in case somebody would come over talking to me when she'd be doing the shopping.

[Aisling]

6.10.4   Keeping busy

Just as described by those in denial of their pregnancy, women concealing the pregnancy purposely kept themselves busy to both minimise the time they spent with family and friends and to distract themselves from the worry of the pregnancy.

I got two part-time jobs and I was constantly going. Like, I worked in a bar and I worked until three o'clock in the morning and back up again at eight o'clock so I had no time to myself. I was just [keeping busy] by getting the jobs and then I didn't go home as much.

[Sarah]

6.10.5   Minimising weight gain through exercise and diet

Some women described how they tried to limit the weight they would gain during the pregnancy by exercising and dieting so as to avoid others noticing.

I used to go for walks even I knew I was pregnant and [thought] 'I hope I don't blow out altogether'.

[Liz]

6.10.6   Considering placing baby for adoption

Of the six women in the concealment group the pregnancy represented a crisis for two, Imelda and Madeline, and both contemplated adoption. Both saw it as a means of keeping the pregnancy concealed entirely. For Madeline this would mean no one in her home country would ever know she had been pregnant. For Imelda placing the baby for adoption would mean that her position in a difficult relationship remained unchanged and she would have more control over the direction it was taking.

6.11   Summary overview of processes entailed in concealed pregnancy

The processes women described by which their pregnancies proceeded while being undetected, denied or concealed are summarised here. These processes entailed the pregnancy going undetected by a physician or strategies women employed to facilitate denial and concealment of the pregnancy.

The process by which pregnancies went undetected by a physician in the case of three women has been well recounted. Other issues relevant to the pregnancy going undetected include having an irregular menstrual cycle (such that missed periods did not feature to indicate pregnancy for this group), encountering unusual symptoms during pregnancy and deferring to the expertise of a GP in the face of suggestions by others that they might be pregnant.

The process of consciously denying pregnancy described by the women entailed firstly believing that the pregnancy would never become established and that they would never have to take on parenting a child as an outcome. Where they acknowledged that a pregnancy could have been conceived, they firstly hoped that it would not proceed, either due to a miscarriage or the death of the child. This meant that they did not engage in any planning for childbirth. During their pregnancy none could contemplate the prospect of motherhood. They tended to see the delivery as the end in itself and planned to place the baby into the care of others. Three women envisaged adoption while one woman had put in place a plan to deliver the child herself and then bring it to a local hospital where she would leave it. They described employing a range of strategies to manage their own thought-processes in line with the belief that they were not pregnant up to advanced pregnancy. This involved blocking out the possibility of pregnancy, despite encountering symptoms indicating the evidence of a pregnancy. To manage this process of 'blocking it out' they typically kept busy – both physically and mentally – with their jobs, college and housework. In some cases or at some times women supplemented this with drinking to forget. Any thoughts that they might be pregnant were managed by rationalising away the symptoms of pregnancy and attributing them to other causes, while comparisons with peers were made to confirm in the woman's mind that all was usual for her.

The four women in our study group who consciously denied their pregnancy did so up until advanced pregnancy. Two of the women were confronted by their families at an advanced stage in the pregnancy, and they described being forced to attend antenatal care and plan for a baby while still not being able to accept they were pregnant. A third woman described telling her family also at advanced pregnancy and again having antenatal care and plans for childbirth arranged for her while not accepting the pregnancy. The fourth woman accepted she was pregnant at around six months' gestation and entered into a process of concealment, attending antenatal care and putting arrangements for adoption in place; she only told her partner. Thus women who were consciously denying the pregnancy were also engaged in a process of concealment and employed strategies similar to the concealed group, as described below.

The strategies women employed to conceal their pregnancy involved a fine balance of taking action so as to hide the pregnancy while at the same time not appearing to look or act any differently in any aspect of their lives to avoid raising any suspicions that they might be pregnant. Actions they took to hide the pregnancy involved wearing concealing clothing, isolating themselves so as to go unnoticed, trying to contain the development of the pregnancy by exercising and dieting, planning to place baby for adoption, and, in the case of three women, even hiding the signs of labour. Meanwhile, they consciously made a point to carry on as usual, especially in relation to work or studies and even in socialising. They tried to manage the worries generated by the pregnancy by keeping busy, not thinking ahead and getting drunk. As these accounts suggest, the process of concealment was complex and there was consensus among the women on the intensity of the time and effort entailed in keeping the pregnancy concealed. The strategies were often simple yet finely detailed. The most striking aspect of the concealment process was the need to be constantly alert to maintaining the concealment, as this final quote from Liz illustrates:

When you were watching telly you had to have a book in front, you know, have your hands in your [hoodie] pocket the whole time, or a book in front of you, doing the crossword, you know – trying to hide it.

[Liz]

7.0 Implications of concealed pregnancy

7.1   Introduction

The previous chapters explored women's accounts of their pregnancy experiences and the factors and processes entailed in undetected, denied or concealed pregnancies. This chapter looks at the implications of concealed pregnancy. In the literature reviewed (see Chapter 3.0) studies principally focused on the stress associated with concealed pregnancy and consequent negative psychological outcomes for the mother, as well as poor outcomes for the baby. Findings from the literature agree that low birth weight is more likely following a concealed pregnancy (Wessel et al. 2003, Treacy et al. 2002, Geary et al. 1997); although Wessel et al. (2003) confine this to where concealment is due to denial of pregnancy. Treacy et al. (2002) and Geary et al. (1997) further argue that delivering pre-term, neonatal death and risk of maternal mortality are more common in pregnancies that have been concealed. However, Wessel et al. (2003), whose study group was larger and the only one focused entirely on the issue of concealment, contest these claims.

Treacy et al. (2002) and Geary et al. (1997) – working in an Irish context – associated these poorer outcomes with the absence of antenatal care. Wessel et al. (2003) challenged this view, arguing that obstetric care is not an independent variable in determining the outcome of a denied or concealed pregnancy. They argued, rather, that the primary reason for worsened foetal outcome is the absence of adaptation to pregnancy by the women simply because they did not know about being pregnant or were not acknowledging the pregnancy (Wessel et al. 2003: 34). They also refer to findings from other research regarding how in retrospect women feel intensely embarrassed by their denial, and guilty for putting their babies at risk and consider this would be a factor.

The discussion of outcomes for women with a concealed pregnancy arising out the review of the literature is brief and indicates that more research is needed, particularly at the psychological and social levels. While a systematic analysis of foetal outcomes for our study group is beyond the scope of this research, women did highlight issues raised by the concealment of their pregnancy that limited their capacity to care for themselves during the pregnancy and engage in usual preparations for birth. The concealment process impeded their participation in the full programme of antenatal care, set down by current practices in the medical management of pregnancy, and placed a heavy emotional toll on them. A further implication they noted arising out of concealment of the pregnancy was on their personal relationships. All of these implications are explored below.

7.2   Implications for medical management of pregnancy

The first set of implications explored below relates to issues raised by women's late presentation to any healthcare professional for the medical management of the pregnancy. Women highlighted concerns this raised for the well being, or, in medical terms, 'outcomes', for the baby. In general, the issues raised relate to how concealment of the pregnancy impeded the application of the standards applicable in current medical management of pregnancy in the cases of the women studied.

7.2.1   *Hard to determine estimated date of delivery (EDD)*

Some of the women in the study were quite certain about when their pregnancy had been conceived and were accurate in their own estimation of their date of delivery. In general, however, presenting for antenatal care past twenty weeks' gestation created difficulties for the determination of the estimated date of delivery. Where women were unclear as to when their pregnancy had been conceived this presented a significant problem. This problem was emphasised in particular by the women whose pregnancies had gone undetected until an advanced stage. Both Lisa and Finola described how difficult it had been to have the pregnancy diagnosed while at the same time being faced with uncertainty about the stage the pregnancy had reached and expected date of delivery.

Lisa described trying to determine her dates when she first presented to the hospital, five days before she actually delivered.

> *The doctor was coming in to tell me; 'I can't get a clear picture,' he kept saying to me. I was too far gone. They said [] that I was too far gone for him to tell me how far I was gone or whether, what way, was it twins, or what. I remember lying on the bed and they were scanning me and a nurse said to me, 'How would you feel about a double surprise?' or something, and I looked and I said, 'Sorry?' And she said, 'I think myself there's two there,' and I kept saying to the doctor, 'Well,' I said, 'do you not even have [an idea]?' and he said 'I think myself that you are pregnant with one child, maybe about six months. If you were pregnant with twins it would be about three.'*

[Lisa]

At delivery her gestation was recorded as 39 weeks and the pregnancy was a single pregnancy.

Finola's pregnancy was detected at 30 weeks' gestation, and when she first presented for antenatal care her doctor also advised her that there was difficulty in determining gestation given how advanced the pregnancy was. She described how this later led to confusion between doctors attending her and criticism being directed at her because the birth weight indicated by scans did not match the gestation determined by the doctor.

7.2.2   No opportunity to detect foetal anomaly or other complications

Because women whose pregnancies are concealed have limited attendance at antenatal care and present at an advanced pregnancy this means that some conditions that would usually be detected during routine antenatal care may go undetected. This arose for two women in our study group.

Tragically, Lisa's baby had a severe foetal anomaly that was incompatible with independent life outside of the womb. Lisa's pregnancy went undetected for thirty-nine weeks. When she presented to the maternity department of a local general hospital the doctors there did detect a problem but wanted to refer her to a specialised maternity hospital to have a diagnosis confirmed. While awaiting an appointment for the referral she went into labour and returned to the local general hospital; from here she was transferred by ambulance to the maternity hospital. Soon after arrival her waters broke while she was being scanned by the consultant on call. Simultaneously, the severe anomaly was confirmed.

Finola had an irregularity in the shape of her womb (a bicornate womb), which would usually mean close monitoring during pregnancy. She presented to the hospital at 30 weeks' gestation and this went undetected in the four assessments – including scans – she had between presentation and delivery.

*I had the [caesarean section] operation, came out into the room and the guy who
operated on me – he was another doctor – and he said to me afterwards, 'The problem is
you have a bicornate womb'. 'What is a bicornate womb?' and he goes, 'Did you not
know?' and I was, like, 'No'. So he briefly explained that the reason I had very little
movement and the reason I was breech birth is the child turned to give herself as much
space as she could possibly have. And a bicornate womb pregnancy usually don't carry to
full term anyway so I should have been on either a list or something or been brought into
hospital early.*

[Finola]

A second issue is that women may be experiencing symptoms that would usually cause
them to be referred for immediate hospital attention during pregnancy but go
undetected or untreated in a concealed pregnancy. This happened in Imelda's case. She
first presented to her GP at 36 weeks' gestation because she was feeling unwell. The GP
immediately diagnosed high blood pressure, which raised her concerns and she wanted
Imelda to attend hospital immediately. However, Imelda was concealing her pregnancy
from her partner and did not manage to get to the hospital until the next day.

7.2.3   *Risk of unassisted birth*

In the overall study group of 51 women, eight women had presented to hospital in
labour, while a further four had presented at 40 weeks' gestation or over. In the
qualitative study group of thirteen women, one woman first presented to the hospital in
labour. A woman whose pregnancy goes undetected or denied, or is concealed until after
the onset of labour is at a real risk of unassisted birth, as Grainne's account
demonstrates.

*When I went to [Hospital A] they sent me to the waiting room and they said we have no
maternity section here and I said, 'Oh God,' and she said, 'Hold on there's a maternity
nurse here. Take a seat.' ... So I had to go in an ambulance into [Town B hospital] ... She
came with me in the ambulance in the end and it could have been about half an hour
after being in [the hospital] when [the baby] was born.*

[Grainne]

Meanwhile, other circumstances reported by women in the qualitative study group
demonstrated how they had come close to an unassisted birth. Eileen had planned to
give birth in secret and unassisted as a means of concealing her pregnancy and only
missed doing so when her mother and two sisters confronted her about being pregnant
just one week before she did give birth.

Like Eileen and Grainne, Imelda continued to conceal her pregnancy even after the onset
of labour, causing her to delay going to hospital until almost 24 hours after the onset of
contractions. These accounts illustrate how close women whose pregnancy is concealed
can come to an unassisted birth.

7.3   Implications for adaptation to pregnancy

The next set of implications discussed relate to the consequences posed for the well-being
of the woman and her developing child during pregnancy, as well as the extent to which
the woman was prepared for both the onset of labour and meeting and caring for her baby.

7.3.1 Doing things 'wrong' during pregnancy

Not knowing about the pregnancy because it was undetected, not acknowledging the pregnancy through conscious denial and the behaviours entailed in the concealment of pregnancy sparked concerns in women that they had compromised the well-being of the baby, as well as their own, during the pregnancy. Concealing the pregnancy often entailed not attending for any antenatal care or adjusting one's lifestyle to accommodate the pregnancy in accordance with widely held practices.

I didn't take folic acid or nothing; no, I'd never been to the doctor about it.

[Aisling]

Women were often conscious that if they did adjust their lifestyle (for example by stopping smoking or drinking, avoiding physical work or activities, or starting a healthy eating regime) this may alert others to the pregnancy.

I never missed a day at work; I was never sick, nothing. I just kept as normal: going out at the weekends and everything – drinking and smoking.

[Eileen]

Some also mentioned drinking as a means of escaping from the emotional distress they were feeling.

I drank an awful lot at the start of my pregnancy, but after I told my parents I would still worry at the back of it, because I was going, 'What if I have done something to this child?' … I didn't say it to anyone but I was worried about it, but yet I was hoping it wasn't [affected].

[Sarah]

Michelle had consciously denied her pregnancy until six months' gestation, during which time she took the contraceptive pill, diet pills and engaged in occasional drinking binges to manage her feelings.

I have thyroid problems so my weight can go up and down, always has, so every time I had weight on [it was that]. I was on diet pills at five months pregnant, and still took the [contraceptive] pill up till I found out I was pregnant [at six months]. … I did everything wrong. … You would be so low that you would drink yourself into stupid. Now I'm not a big drinker but I found out if you drink a bottle of vodka you forget about a lot: there's a happy place there … During pregnancy, once or twice, I just remember thinking, 'Just drink and forget about it.'

[Michelle]

Like Michelle, other women continued to use hormonal contraception during pregnancy, as well as taking other medication that would usually be advised against. Lisa's pregnancy went undetected until 39 weeks, throughout which time she was using the injectable contraceptive. It then emerged that her baby had a severe foetal anomaly and was not capable of living independently. The baby was stillborn. Lisa experienced a lot of stress related to guilt over any possibility that her behaviour during the pregnancy had contributed to the baby's condition.

[Afterwards] I got real stressed and got counselling, then, and I'm grand now since I got the counselling, you know, but I used to blame myself terrible. I used to blame myself that I didn't know I was pregnant and maybe, I said if I was taking, like, something, you know, [folic acid] – if I was taking that maybe it wouldn't have happened, you know? ... You know if you were on that maybe I would have prevented it.

[Lisa]

Both of the other women whose pregnancies were undetected until 30 weeks and 36 weeks respectively shared these concerns and were also worried about how the work they had been doing might have impacted on the baby.

I was still working. I was working [] up until I was about eight months pregnant and I was lifting the whole time. Then when I found out I was like, 'Oh my God – there has to be something wrong with the child now. I'm after straining myself, or whatever.' ... [If I'd known] I wouldn't have drank, because I drank the whole way through it. I wouldn't have worked as hard because my job is very physical: I was lifting and pulling and dragging and things like that. I know now it didn't do [the baby] any harm but if I had known I would have taken it a lot easier.

[Geraldine]

Imelda, who had concealed her pregnancy, described how she had to continue with her usual tasks at work (which in her case included heavy lifting) while knowing this was not advised in pregnancy. She described talking to the baby in her womb explaining why she had to take these risks. When born, the baby had a condition she attributed to the behaviours she engaged in to keep the pregnancy concealed.

You're lifting these parcels, you're trying to throw them down so they won't do damage to you, you know what I mean? This is what you're up against ... And nearly everyone used to lift the boxes and then people would be looking at you, get your strength, in under, underneath it, you know what I mean? I had to do it ... At night time in bed, [I'd talk to the baby] 'You'll be all right now; tomorrow's another day. Keep [the bump] in', you know what I mean? 'Do this for me, 'cos I have the crowd to face, I have the manager to face, I don't want him getting suspicious either,' you know? ... I'd say that's why he was blue: he was stressed out. When he was born he was very blue. I kinda cried when I seen him, you know? I thought, 'What am I after doing now with this child?'

[Imelda]

7.3.2   *Being unprepared for childbirth*

In many cases women discussed how they were not prepared for labour or childbirth because their pregnancies had been undetected, denied or concealed. Some women were still concealing the pregnancy from their families while in labour in the family home or from their employer while in labour at work. Being unprepared included not knowing what to expect, not having chosen a hospital to attend, not having booked with any hospital, having no arrangements made to be transported to the hospital while in labour and having no knowledge of the labour process – including breathing techniques or pain-relief options.

Grainne concealed her pregnancy until after giving birth while living with her family. Despite acknowledging she was pregnant from the second month of pregnancy she had never entered into any preparations for labour. When she went into labour she described the difficulty of deciding on which hospital to go to and driving herself there, while trying to prevent other family members becoming aware of her situation. Because she had not planned in advance where she would deliver the baby, the hospital she arrived at in advanced labour did not actually have a maternity department.

Like Grainne, Eileen and Imelda also concealed their pregnancy until they were in labour. Although Eileen recognised she was in labour she went into work. Even after her waters broke at nine o'clock she intended to continue working until two o'clock so as not to alert her employers to a problem. She had telephoned her sister, who insisted she make an excuse to leave and allow her to bring her to the hospital. She arrived at the hospital at two o'clock and her baby was born twenty minutes later. Imelda was concealing her pregnancy and went into labour at home. She tried to maintain concealment of the pregnancy and labour from her partner but eventually told him. This situation meant she delayed going to the hospital from noticing contractions on Tuesday evening until the following afternoon.

Other women who had disclosed the pregnancy still had not prepared for labour or motherhood. Aisling was in conscious denial about her pregnancy, and while she did tell her family she was pregnant at seven months' gestation, she still found it difficult to accept she was having a baby. When she went into labour she did not recognise the signs of labour or accept that she was in labour. She described having no knowledge about the process of labour, including pain-relief options.

> I was sitting there and the sweat was out through me and my back, I thought I was going to fall apart ... I don't think labour even crossed my mind: I didn't have a clue. So she [her mother] told me to go into bed and lie down and that. But as soon as I jumped into the bed I jumped out the other side: I couldn't. So she said, 'Do you want to go to [hospital]?' and I said, 'Yes.' So we went up to [hospital] and we were in there and I was on the bed and I said to one of the midwives that I'll have the epidural and she just started laughing at me and said, 'You are far too gone for that – you will have to have natural labour.'

[Aisling]

Another aspect of being unprepared for labour was not having any arrangements made to be absent from work. As discussed earlier, Eileen concealed the pregnancy and planned to conceal the birth and place the baby into the care of the hospital after birth. She wanted to keep the pregnancy concealed from her employer and colleagues at work. She went into work while in labour so as not to give any indication of something being amiss with her. Michelle planned to deliver her baby during her two weeks' annual leave from work when she was supposed to be on a sun holiday. In doing so she put enormous time pressure on herself and then returned to work still feeling very sore and in emotional turmoil so soon after the birth. Finola, whose pregnancy was undetected until 30 weeks, described how this did not allow enough time to organise a replacement for herself in her retail business when she suddenly found herself in labour at 38 weeks.

I had another two weeks in my head to get everything organised. When you are driving in full-on labour trying to organise staff that morning like I was; doing the ordering, driving down in the car, ordering stuff for the next few weeks – which probably isn't the most normal thing to do.

[Finola]

Finally, being unprepared for labour further extended to being unprepared for first contact with the baby, as Aisling, who had consciously denied the pregnancy, described. Her lack of engagement with the pregnancy left her entirely unprepared for 'meeting' the baby and it took some time for the reality that she had a baby and was now a mother to sink in.

I wasn't even prepared for a child; I didn't even know what was happening to me. When I had the child I was sitting in the hospital and I was like, 'Ok, right, it's a baby'. And then she was down in intensive care and she wasn't with me then so I was sitting in the hospital 'What am I doing here?' and then in another while I'd be like, 'Oh my God: I have a baby.'

[Aisling]

7.3.3   Seeking early discharge from hospital

A number of women sought early discharge from the hospital after giving birth or else tried to arrange to have a caesarean section followed by early discharge to facilitate concealment of the pregnancy. Meanwhile, it was their plan to return to their daily routine of jobs, working in the home, socialising, and so on, so that nobody would notice any changes in them. In thinking about or carrying out these plans, women paid no regard to their own well-being.

Michelle had arranged to stay in residential supported accommodation in another city away from home and give birth in a hospital there. She described discharging herself within hours of the birth and soon afterwards embarking on a long bus journey back home.

I had [the baby] in [hospital] on the Tuesday, left hospital Wednesday morning, bleeding so badly, in so much pain I thought I was going to die … [The baby] was only a couple of hours old, so then I got a taxi home to that apartment and I cleaned the apartment from top to bottom. I remember every time I went to the toilet I was really sore, even though I had no stitching I had tears. There was no bath, there was only a shower and I couldn't sit in the bath. So I used to get a jug of water and tried to wash myself out and it was killing me, and I said, 'What's this? I'm going back up to [my home] – I need to have a bath somewhere.' The pain was unreal. So on the Thursday I went into the woman in the residential centre and said, 'I'm leaving.' So I paid up and I didn't see [the baby] again. I didn't go into the hospital. So I got on the bus on the Thursday and the pain on the bus – I thought I was going to die.

[Michelle]

7.4   Emotional toll on woman

We saw above how Wessel et al. (2003) attributed worsened foetal outcomes to absence of expected adaptation to pregnancy by the woman, as well as feelings of intense embarrassment of their denial and guilt for putting their babies at risk. The qualitative accounts of women in this study illustrate the intensity of the emotional toll a concealed pregnancy imposed on them. While Wessel et al. (2003) refer to these only in the context of worsened foetal outcome, women's accounts suggest that the implications of such a toll are borne by the woman herself as well as by her baby.

7.4.1   Emotionally difficult

Women described the emotional turmoil they went through during the pregnancy, including intense distress and upset, even to the point of experiencing suicidal-like feelings.

So many times I was thinking, 'Wouldn't I love to be hit by a bus? Wouldn't it be great, like, if something happened me?' and every time I'd see someone that got killed on television or something happened them, they got knocked down, 'Why doesn't that ever happen me?' And that's an awful way to think. But you would be so low ... Or go to bed and cry so much that it will just go away or go into the bathroom and cry. I remember sitting in the bathroom floor bawling for hours and hours.

[Michelle]

While many women had disclosed the pregnancy, were resigned to it themselves and were receiving support in the option they were considering by the time they gave birth, some were still concealing the pregnancy and/or were still not resigned to the fact that they were pregnant and about to become mothers. This meant that the birth was accompanied by a lot of emotions.

I spent from when I had him bawling the whole night and the nurse used to come in and say 'Are you still crying, are you still crying?'

[Michelle]

I don't know what came over me but I just went into the bathroom and I cried and I cried and I never slept the whole night from crying. I asked myself what I'd done and telling them to take the baby, that I didn't want to see the baby or anything.

[Eileen]

7.4.2   Missed any enjoyment of the pregnancy

A strong recurring theme among the women was how the situation they were in meant that their experience of pregnancy differed greatly from the stereotypical image of pregnancy as portrayed in contemporary popular culture. While popular culture presents pregnancy as something to be proud of, embraced and celebrated, with the pregnant woman taking on a revered status, this is the antithesis of how the women interviewed experienced their pregnancy.

When I see a pregnant woman and they've lovely maternity clothes on them and the bump is all [showing] I get awful jealous. Something I had myself that just, always pulling belts, hiding under everything else. But I always say to my sister I can't wait until I get pregnant again just to let it all hang out.

[Eileen]

It's supposed to be the most beautiful time in your life and the most exciting time, and the whole lot, but yet for nearly six months of it I was terrified of it. I was absolutely terrified.

[Sarah]

Michelle described how her experience of childbirth was silenced because of the circumstances in which she gave birth. She also expressed regret that her baby was in foster care during the first six weeks of life.

No-one had asked me [about the birth]. I hadn't got a card; I hadn't got flowers like mothers usually do; I hadn't got, 'Oh you're gorgeous,' [about my baby] ... [My mother] still doesn't ask me how I had [the baby], how was the birth, where I had it, who was there, it's just now, like, [my child] was always there ... I regret that I was actually denying it. I regret I didn't have [my baby] for six weeks as a real baby. I'll never have it back.

[Michelle]

7.4.3   Sense of isolation

Throughout the pregnancy and birth women often described an intense feeling of isolation. Michelle concealed her pregnancy from everyone except her partner. She then gave birth in a distant hospital and insisted to her partner that she did not want him there. She found the birth an intensely lonely experience.

When I had [the baby] that day and the loneliness being inside with the midwife and knowing that next door there's a woman, and her husband is rushing in and out getting water and ice, and it was that there was no-one in this world that knows what you are doing right now. Your mother is at home making the dinner and she doesn't know that her daughter is having a baby. [My partner] didn't even know, so no-one knew. And thinking that if I died now no-one will actually know because people didn't know. If I died who'd be there? No-one ... I hate that, I hate that I did that, that I put myself through that. It wasn't fair on me what I did to myself – wasn't fair. I shouldn't have had to do that all by myself.

[Michelle]

7.4.4   Feeling judged for concealing

Women described how the disclosure of the pregnancy or the pregnancy coming to an end did not mean all of the issues raised by it were resolved. A number described a sense of feeling judged for concealing the pregnancy at all.

Sure, anyone else looking in would say, 'That is cracked. Isn't she a sly one – she didn't tell?' It was never anything like that.

[Grainne]

I look back now and I just feel so stupid for what I did.

[Eileen]

Somebody said, 'You know, you're selfish in ways. You should have told people.'

[Imelda]

For both Madeline and Michelle, who had placed their baby in foster care while considering adoption, the feeling of being judged was strong enough to become an impediment to giving consideration to not going ahead with the adoption and taking the baby home. Both felt guilty that those who were hoping to adopt her baby would be disappointed and both anticipated negative judgements against her among the community should she disclose the birth at this time.

I was afraid then that I'd made such a fuss about giving [the baby] away they will all think, 'She is such an eejit and now she's keeping him'. It's like embarrassment, what are you doing? It was like, 'There's nothing you can do about it now – you've made your decision. There is happy people being asked do they want a new baby and how can you do this now they think they are getting a baby and they are looking for a baby?' It was all over the place.

[Michelle]

In addition, the one woman whose pregnancy continued to be concealed by the time she was interviewed – facilitated by the option of adoption – described how she was subjected to scrutiny and rumour in her hometown as people speculated as to whether she had been pregnant or not and what the outcome of the pregnancy had been.

[A good friend] was saying to me how the girls were all talking about me in the house one night that I had this baby and dumped it. This is what annoys me, that I dumped it. Yeah, that was my initial plan, but I didn't. I've given the child a good life and nobody can see that ... I broke down again and I told her everything and she came over and she gave me a big hug and she said, 'Do you realise what a strong person you are to do it? Don't be worried about all them talking about it. You've done a good thing and let them talk away.'

[Eileen]

Finally, women also described encountering guilt for not having confided in people who expressed disappointment to them that they had not represented a potential source of help and support.

[My friend] felt bad 'cos she didn't know and because she didn't pick up on anything when I was in college. She was like, 'But you were being so normal' and 'I should have known, I should have picked up on something.' She felt bad then, but I was kind of just, 'Look, I didn't tell you,' and I felt bad then for not telling her and this whole thing.

[Pauline]

It came to the stage where I knew I was lying to [my parents]. I didn't like that because we were very close to begin with.

[Sarah]

7.5   Impact on personal relationships

A third theme in the implications women identified as arising out of concealing their pregnancy was becoming isolated from their significant others. In the discussion in Chapter 6.0 on the process of concealment we saw how women isolated themselves from significant others so as to facilitate concealing the pregnancy. Meanwhile, women were aware that the decisions they had taken during the pregnancy had implications for others, particularly their families, partners and partners' families. In this sense the pregnancy, even if never disclosed, had implications for women's personal relationships.

7.5.1   Persistent sense of stigma

Women sensed stigma attaching to them during the pregnancy, and this sense of stigma persisted after the baby was born and continued to impact negatively on their confidence in public spaces.

> *Even now [a year later] if I was going out now I'd wouldn't like to go out and I'd be like, 'Oh my God, I can't go in there, now, to such a place.'*

[Aisling]

> *After I did have [the baby] I was living closer to the town and I was living near that girl [who gossiped] as well and then I moved away. I used to finish work; I used to go into work and I'd finish work; I'd do my grocery shopping in a petrol station; never wanted to see anyone. I'd come up here and lock the back door and lock the front door and go upstairs and cry. I never wanted to go out or see anyone, constantly worried about being haunted every time I seen her, so in that aspect that I've moved away. I'd never leave [my home town] but I have some regrets I had to move away [from my area].*

[Eileen]

7.5.2   Reproaches from family or partners

Some women described how they had to deal with reproaches from their family for not telling about the pregnancy. Imelda described how she encountered recriminations from her partner that were hard for her to deal with.

> *'You were selfish' and all this kind of stuff – 'self-centred' [my partner] was going. As I said to him, he was first to be told, he was never here, and why tell other people and he hears down town.*

[Imelda]

Eileen and Madeline described how both their mother and sister respectively were deeply disappointed they had not confided in them. They handled this differently from Imelda's partner, however, conveying the disappointment indirectly through feelings of hurt rather than blame.

> *I don't know why I couldn't have went to mammy. She was awful hurt for months after that I didn't go to her and say it to her. She kills herself now even because she [feels she] should have brought the baby home ... She knew, mammy knew that she couldn't bring the baby home and I was trying to explain to mammy that I wouldn't have let her take the baby home because it would have been too hard on me ... So mammy is, to this day it still affects mammy awful bad and mammy never says it to me.*

[Eileen]

Meanwhile it is important to note that most women found their families were hugely supportive and did not, in fact, advance any of the criticism or admonishments they had anticipated when they were concealing the pregnancy.

I: *Were there any recriminations for not telling?*

R: *Never. I was every day expecting some but no-one, nothing, ever. They were all brilliant.*

[Grainne]

I: *Was there ever anything enjoyable about the pregnancy?*

R: *Not really. Probably the fact that me and my mum, we're a lot closer.*

[Pauline]

[My mother] turned around and she goes, 'Look, we know' and I goes, 'I'm sorry you had to find out like that,' and she turned around and she goes, 'Look, we've always been here beforehand for you, we are not going to stop now. You are my daughter and now you are having my grandchild. I'm not going to fall out with you over that,' which was brilliant: it was a weight taken off my shoulders.

[Sarah]

Finally, while most women were not in a relationship, some of those who were and concealed the pregnancy from their partner felt guilty about the impact the pregnancy coming to light at a very late stage or after the birth of the baby had on them.

I kind of felt sorry for him. People said, 'How the hell did he not notice anything?' I did feel really bad for him that way, like.

[Grainne]

Michelle also had regrets about how her concealment of the pregnancy impacted on her partner, who was supportive. As well as worrying about how it impacted on him directly, she also felt that had she pursued her intentions to place the baby for adoption she would have been taking a grandchild from her partner's parents.

7.6   Overview of implications of concealed pregnancy

This chapter explored the implications women recounted of concealing their pregnancy. It looked at the implications of concealed pregnancy for the well-being of the woman and the baby, and explored other emotional and social issues the women had to face.

In the literature reviewed studies focused on the stress associated with denying or concealing a pregnancy and the associated negative psychological outcomes for the mother, as well as poor outcomes for the baby. Findings from the literature agreed that low birth weight is more likely following concealment of pregnancy (Wessel et al. 2003, Treacy et al. 2002, Geary et al. 1997), though Wessel et al. (2003) confine this to where concealment is due to denial of pregnancy. Treacy et al. (2002) and Geary et al. (1997) further argue that delivering pre-term, neonatal death and risk of maternal mortality are more common in pregnancies that have been concealed. However Wessel et al. (2003), whose study group was larger and focused entirely on the issue of concealment, would contest these claims.

While Treacy et al. (2002) and Geary et al. (1997), working in an Irish context, associated these poorer outcomes with the absence of antenatal care, Wessel et al. (2003)

challenged this view. They argued that obstetric care is not an independent variable in determining the outcome of a denied or concealed pregnancy. They argued, rather, that the primary reason for worsened foetal outcome is the absence of usual adaptation to pregnancy by the women simply because they did not know about being pregnant (Wessel et al. 2003: 34). They also refer to findings from other research regarding how in retrospect women feel intensely embarrassed by their denial and guilty for putting their babies at risk and consider this would be a factor.

The discussion of outcomes for women with a concealed pregnancy arising out of the review of the literature is brief and indicates that more research is needed, particularly at the psychological and social levels. While a systematic analysis of foetal outcomes for our study group is beyond the scope of this research, women did highlight how the concealment of their pregnancy resulted in the following range of physiological, social and emotional implications.

The first set of implications related to how a concealed pregnancy impeded women's participation in the full range of antenatal care set down by current practices in the medical management of pregnancy. They highlighted concerns this raised for the well-being or, in medical terms, 'outcomes' for the baby. Presenting for antenatal care at past twenty weeks' gestation created difficulties for the determination of the expected date of delivery. This made it difficult to determine when women could expect to go into labour and some were given conflicting dates. In addition, confusion about dates and related expectations of the growth of the child in the womb resulted in women encountering criticism for not taking due care during their pregnancy to ensure the well-being of the foetus.

Another implication cited in relation to medical care was how conditions that would usually be detected during routine antenatal care could go undetected in concealed pregnancies. There was no opportunity to detect foetal anomalies, and for one woman this left her entirely unprepared for the delivery of a stillborn baby. Other conditions that would usually be monitored very closely, require intervention or be a determining factor in deciding on the type of delivery advised for a woman also went undetected. A woman whose pregnancy goes undetected, denied or concealed until after the onset of labour is also at a real risk of unassisted birth.

Women described a set of consequences arising from not having adapted to the pregnancy. They were concerned that they had put their own well-being and that of the child at risk during pregnancy. Many described how they did not attend for any antenatal care or adjust their lifestyle to accommodate the pregnancy in accordance with widely held practices, such as stopping smoking or drinking, avoiding physical work or activities or starting a healthy eating regime. This was part of the process of concealment: engaging in any of these behaviours may have alerted others to the pregnancy. Women also described continuing to take medication, including hormonal contraceptives, dieting pills and prescribed medicines.

Women also described a range of implications relating to being unprepared for labour. This included not knowing what to expect, not having chosen a hospital to attend, not having booked with any hospital, having no arrangements made to be transported to the hospital while in labour and having no knowledge of the labour process, including breathing technique or pain-relief options.

Women who concealed their pregnancy up to labour also delayed getting to the hospital so they would not raise families' or employers' suspicions. In some cases women had no arrangements made to be absent from work and attempted to fit childbirth in with their usual working conditions. Being unprepared for labour further extended to being unprepared for first contact with the baby. This meant that it took some time for the woman to allow the reality that she was a mother to sink in, while at the same time being expected to fulfil the role.

A number of women also sought early discharge from the hospital after giving birth, or else they tried to arrange to have a caesarean section followed by early discharge to facilitate concealment of the pregnancy. Meanwhile, it was their plan to return to their daily routine of jobs, working in the home, socialising, and so on, so that nobody would notice any changes in them. In thinking about or carrying out these plans, women paid no regard to their own well-being.

Women's accounts demonstrated how concealment of pregnancy placed a heavy emotional toll on them. Wessel et al. (2003) refer to this only in the context of worsened foetal outcome, while in this study women's accounts illustrated that the implications of such a toll are borne by the woman herself as well as by her baby. Women described the emotional turmoil they went through during the pregnancy, including intense distress and upset, even to the point of experiencing suicidal-like feelings.

A strong recurring theme among the women was how the situation they were in meant that their experience of pregnancy differed greatly from the stereotypical image of pregnancy as portrayed in contemporary popular culture. Normally pregnancy is portrayed as something to be proud of, embraced and celebrated, with the pregnant woman taking on a revered status; yet this is the antithesis of how women interviewed experienced their pregnancy.

Women often described an intense feeling of isolation throughout the pregnancy and birth, which was particularly acute for women who were not accompanied during birth. The birth itself was intensely emotional for those still concealing and those who were not resigned to the fact that they were pregnant when they gave birth. Where pregnancy was concealed beyond delivery the experience of childbirth itself can be silenced, leaving women concerned about how they might cope with this in the future, particularly if the child ever asks about their birthing experience.

The aftermath of concealment included women feeling judged for concealing the pregnancy at all. Those who had placed their baby in foster care while considering adoption described how the embarrassment and guilt they felt became an impediment to them giving consideration to not going ahead with the adoption and taking the baby home. Meanwhile they expressed feelings of guilt and loss for missing out on those early weeks of their child's life. In addition, the one woman whose pregnancy continued to be concealed by the time she was interviewed – facilitated by the option of adoption – described how she was subjected to scrutiny and rumour in her hometown. People speculated as to whether she had been pregnant or not and what the outcome of the pregnancy had been.

The final set of implications women noted arising out of concealment of the pregnancy was on their personal relationships. Becoming isolated from others was a feature of the process women engage in so as to deny or conceal a pregnancy. The sense of stigma women felt while pregnant persisted after the baby was born and continued to impact negatively on their confidence in public spaces. Some women described how they had to deal with reproaches from their family for not telling about the pregnancy. These took the form of either direct recriminations or more indirect means of conveying disappointment. However, many women found that their families did not express any of the criticism or admonishments they had anticipated.

Women were also aware that the decisions they made in relation to their pregnancy had implications for their families, partners and their partner's families. While most women were not in a relationship, some of those who were, and who concealed the pregnancy from their partner, felt guilty about the impact the pregnancy, coming to light at a very late stage or after the birth of the baby, had on them. In these ways the pregnancy, even if never disclosed, impacts on women's personal relationships.

8.0 Women's accounts of contact with medical and support services

8.1   Introduction

In this chapter we document the extent to which women concealing their pregnancy had contact with medical, social, counselling and support services during their pregnancy. This relates to contacts directly dealing with the concealed pregnancy and contacts during the time when the woman was pregnant but the pregnancy was undisclosed or undetected. A range of services are discussed, including general practitioners, crisis pregnancy counselling and support services, social work services, hospital antenatal clinics, hospital maternity units and other hospital departments to which women presented.

8.2   General practitioners

8.2.1   Attendance with general practitioners

Our analysis of the case-note data of 50 women found that two-thirds (33 women) were referred to antenatal care by their GP. In the qualitative study-group of thirteen women, eleven had attended a GP during pregnancy while two had not. These findings indicate a high tendency among women to present to GPs during a concealed pregnancy.

8.2.2   Factors in not presenting to a GP

Both women in the qualitative group who did not attend a GP at all during their pregnancy were in the concealed group. Madeline was a migrant worker in Ireland who had limited contact with the health services and was unclear how the system of antenatal care worked. She attended a counselling service and was referred to a maternity hospital for antenatal care. She continued to attend the hospital exclusively for all her care henceforth. Grainne concealed her pregnancy until delivery, without attending any antenatal care or pregnancy services, including a GP. In discussing this, she referred to her general reticence about discussing contraceptive or sexual health issues with her GP:

> I was never on the pill or anything. I'd always been too very afraid to say anything like that to a doctor … I was always that way anyway when I was younger: I'd never talk. Well, not about contraception or anything really like that. But with the doctor! Jesus, I'd be mortified.

> [Grainne]

In addition she described never feeling unwell enough during the pregnancy to seek a consultation with a GP.

8.2.3   Pathways to attending a GP

The most common pathway to a GP for women interviewed was to experience symptoms that concerned them, which was cited by six of the eleven. Three women – Lisa, Geraldine and Finola – presented to a GP early in pregnancy with symptoms that caused them to suspect pregnancy. As discussed in detail in previous chapters, their pregnancies went undetected until 39 weeks, 36 weeks and 30 weeks respectively. Jackie attended her regular GP early in the pregnancy for antenatal care while continuing to conceal it from her family. The other two women who presented with symptoms presented later in pregnancy, were certain they were pregnant and were concealing it. This represented the first disclosure of the pregnancy for both women. Neither had told their families at that point.

> *Everything was going great and then I got awful back pains. I didn't know what was going on at the time. Mam would say something to me at home and I'd start crying and she could not make it out at all. So it just came to the stage where I had to do something, so I went to the doctor.*

[Sarah]

Both purposely chose not to attend their usual family GP and selected another GP in their area instead. They remarked that they would likely have waited much longer to present had their only option been their usual GP.

The second principal pathway for women to present to a GP during a concealed pregnancy was to disclose the pregnancy to a family member, who then was instrumental in organising for her to attend antenatal care, in all cases beginning with the family doctor. Four women, one in the concealed pregnancy group and three in the conscious denial group attended their GP through this route.

> R: *I was just gone seven months when I did tell her ... Mammy was very shocked: she said, 'I thought it would never happen to you, [Liz], and don't worry about it. We'll go to the doctor tomorrow.' She said, 'I'll ring him first thing – 9 o'clock he's open – and I'll ring the doctor and we'll go down.'*
>
> I: *Would you have thought about going to the doctor on your own before telling your mother. Did that ever cross your mind?*
>
> R: *Not really, no ... Well, I wanted the family at home to be told first and I knew once they knew it would be from there on that we would be visiting the doctors.*

[Liz]

All agreed with Liz's view that they wanted to tell their family first before attending a GP. Three of the women, all in the 18-20 age group and on their first pregnancy, also stated how being unfamiliar with the system of antenatal care was a factor in not attending a GP themselves. Finally, the other principal factor for all of them was not having any symptoms that would have prompted them to attend a GP.

Michelle attended a GP after being referred to one by the counselling service she attended at six months' gestation.

8.2.4   *Views on GPs' response to women concealing a pregnancy* [9]

There were mixed views among women in this study group of how well GPs responded to their needs. Two of the three women whose pregnancy went undetected were critical that their doctor had not administered a pregnancy test, in Lisa's case during 28 visits between approximately 4 and 39 weeks' gestation and in Finola's case until her third visit between approximately 10 and 30 weeks' gestation. Lisa's GP ruled out pregnancy because he had administered the injectable contraceptive to her after a negative pregnancy test. Lisa argued that he should have repeated a pregnancy test before each

---

9 For a discussion on GPs' responses to women presenting with a crisis pregnancy see Conlon 2005.

administration of the injectable contraceptive, particularly in light of his explanation that pregnancy can occur during the first number of days after administration. Finola's GP discounted the possibility of pregnancy on the basis of her accounts of her partner's belief that he was infertile coupled with a menstrual-like bleed during a three month period. Finola felt that her GP was too preoccupied with concerns about her fertility indicated by her irregular menstrual history to the point where the possibility of pregnancy was overlooked.

Where women attended GPs and had their pregnancy confirmed some were pleased with the response they met. Aisling appreciated how her GP did not make an issue of her pregnancy when she attended with her mother.

> He took me weight and blood pressure and said, 'You wouldn't think you were pregnant at all. I'll send away this form and I'll see you back in a couple of weeks.' That was it ... He just acted normal, there was no tone as if he was thick or looking down on me, or there was no tone as if he was one bit excited ... It is a big help when you have to go to him first that they are ok; that you are not getting a feeling from [doctor], that would put you off going in.

[Aisling]

Three other women were also pleased with their GP's response, referring to them being understanding. In Imelda's case this included her GP acknowledging the emotional toll concealing the pregnancy must have taken on her and offering to help her through the coming months with referral for counselling or prescriptions of anti-depressants, if she needed them. Sarah described how the GP she attended gave her time and understanding enough to allow her disclose the pregnancy.

> She asked me what I was doing there and I was just sitting there. She said, 'You know, you can talk: I'm not going to judge you on anything.' So she knew, but she wanted me to say it. I couldn't get it out and she goes, 'Is it what I think it is?' I said, 'Well, as far as I know it is,' and she goes, 'Leave it with me. I'll sort it out from here.' She was very, very good and then, like, she wanted to know about my family and I think it was great. She said, 'I'm not prying, but if you want we can have a conversation,' which was lovely; I thought it was brilliant. I think someone you can actually have a conversation with instead of, 'Who's next?'

[Sarah]

Two women, however, felt their GP had not been adept at handling the distress they expressed when first presenting with the pregnancy. Michelle described how her doctor relayed the experience of another woman who became pregnant at a similar age and had managed fine. On its own this response was inadequate in her mind. Pauline attended with her mother and described how her doctor appeared at a loss when she got upset.

> I was kind of crying then, and stuff, so I think he might have got a bit awkward, and he got, like, a nurse to come in. She was lovely and that, so. So I didn't, you know, when I was sitting there crying, he was kind of feeling a bit awkward. Maybe he hasn't had to deal with it as much, as a nurse would have, or something.

[Pauline]

8.2.5   Referral on for other antenatal care

Of the eleven women who had attended a GP during pregnancy, nine were referred by
the GP for antenatal care, while two were referred to other hospital departments for
other investigations. Four of the nine women referred by their GP highlighted some
difficulties in the process through which women who conceal their pregnancy can be
referred on to hospital for antenatal care and booking for delivery.

In two cases the GP sent a letter of referral directly to the hospital on the woman's
behalf. However, both women grew concerned at the delay in hearing back from the
hospital and either returned to the doctor or telephoned the hospital to highlight their
advanced stage of pregnancy and need for the earliest possible appointment.

> *[The doctor] sent the letter, then, but I never heard back from [the hospital] so I rang and
> then they – over the phone – fixed a date ... It was my mam who [phoned the hospital].
> She told them how far I was gone and I'd been to the GP and how the GP had sent in the
> letter about three weeks ago and they had never got the letter and then they fixed an
> appointment and that was Tuesday and the following Tuesday I was there.*

> [Aisling]

Another potential for delay in referral is where the GP gives the letter of referral to the
woman to give to the hospital and organise her own appointments there. This arose in
both Michelle and Imelda's case, and both women described how they delayed attending
the hospital for longer than their doctor advised.

In contrast, Eileen described how her GP made an appointment for her by telephone
during her consultation. It was scheduled for the next clinic and she attended.

> *I went to the doctor the Thursday. They made an appointment on the Monday for me and
> we went to [the hospital] on the Monday.*

> [Eileen]

These accounts illustrate how it is imperative that GPs follow a system of referral for
women who present late in pregnancy that maximises the opportunities left to them to
access health and support services.

8.3   Crisis pregnancy counselling and support services

8.3.1   Factors shaping attendance with counselling services

In one of the hospitals where the study was conducted a Crisis Pregnancy Agency funded
Crisis Pregnancy Counselling And Support Service was provided on-site, and this
supplemented the role of the medical social worker. All women in the study group
attending this hospital were referred to this on-site crisis pregnancy counselling service.
In the other hospital only medical social workers were available to provide counselling.
Only where women were considering adoption were they referred to a counselling
service that included the option of adoption.

Two of the thirteen women interviewed – Michelle and Madeline – attended a crisis
pregnancy counselling service independently from referrals through hospitals they
attended. In both cases this was to access information and services related to adoption.

8.3.2   Factors shaping non-attendance at counselling services

Some women did not attend a counselling service because they did not feel they needed to. Three women concealing their pregnancy did not perceive it to be a crisis for them and so did not feel the need to attend a crisis pregnancy counselling service. They associated such services with advice on options to resolve a crisis pregnancy and did not envisage they would have a broader role in helping them disclose the pregnancy.

Other women across the three groups identified a range of barriers to attending counselling services. When her pregnancy went undetected until advanced pregnancy the shock of discovering such an advanced stage of pregnancy made Lisa consider contacting a service, even though she was accepting of the pregnancy. However, as her pregnancy was detected at 39 weeks' gestation, this did not leave any opportunity to access a service. Finola, whose pregnancy was undetected until 30 weeks' gestation, felt that her GP, who finally diagnosed the pregnancy, should have been proactive in referring her to a counselling service.

> *For me being so late in the pregnancy just being told, 'Listen you've got to go and talk to this person', not in a nasty way, but kind of being made like a bold school child; just made go talk to this person. It might have been good for me, and, like, if I didn't have the support of my family and the way the doctors, the way there was no support network. It was a case of 'you are on your own now; you are pregnant. Go to [the hospital] and you get checked out and that's it.'*

[Finola]

Three women in the conscious denial group said the reason they did not make contact with a counselling service was because they could not actually verbalise that they were pregnant.

> *I was thinking that I knew I was [pregnant], I just didn't want to admit it. But I didn't want to actually go and ring a crisis [service] because, to have an abortion or whatever, because then I was admitting it and I didn't want to admit I was [pregnant].*

[Aisling]

It is interesting to note that four out of the thirteen women interviewed did utilise the Crisis Pregnancy Agency sponsored 'Positive Options' service without proceeding to counselling. Two women in the conscious denial group sent an SMS to the 'Positive Options' service. When they received back a list of telephone numbers, both described how they were unable to engage any further with services that required them to have telephone or face-to-face sessions where they would have to verbalise the fact of their pregnancy.

> *I saw the things on the bus shelter – the 'Positive Options' thing you text, and I texted that and just got back lists of numbers, so then, like, I wasn't going to go ring them up, that sort of thing, 'cos if I rang them it was, 'Yeah, I'm pregnant', that was kind of like admitting to it and I couldn't really admit to it.*

[Pauline]

Eileen felt that the service should have included some SMS-based counselling, which may have helped her engage better with the services.

I checked out 'Positive Options' and they gave me a list of numbers and I said, 'Feck that. I'm not ringing anyone.' I thought they'd, I don't know why someone couldn't text me back: 'How are you doing?' or 'What's wrong?' or something. You know, 'Was all ok with you?' but I wasn't [going to telephone].

[Eileen]

Sarah, who was concealing her pregnancy, also sent an SMS to the 'Positive Options' number. She went on to telephone one of the services in the return information but was disappointed that they did not offer telephone counselling.

I rang [a number from the 'Positive Options' reply list] and the woman that answered she kind of said, pretty much, go to your GP and he will or they will help you from there ... I kind of expected someone, like, do you know, the Childline that, you know, there's someone there to listen to you even if they never say nothing at all.

[Sarah]

For those concealing their pregnancy who would have liked the support of a service, arranging to attend a face-to-face consultation could be difficult without arousing suspicions about the pregnancy. This deterred Imelda from keeping an appointment she made with a service listed in the 'Positive Options' leaflet she had picked up in a GP surgery.

There was one in [a town forty minutes' away], but, there again, it's real hard to get away. If you [go] now it's 'Where are you going?' 'What you going there for?' [from my partner] ... 'Cos I had made an appointment, remember I was telling you I had? I couldn't go because I had, first of all, no one to mind the kids and then secondly I can't get away because I don't want to be bringing the kids with me either, yet again, [my oldest] is at that age now, she'd be copping on. I had to cancel it.

[Imelda]

The lack of availability of widespread counselling services impeded Imelda's access; she felt she would have attended a service if there had been one available in her local town.

If you had one, say, you could have a, say, little office in every town, I mean, you wouldn't have to travel away then ... If you had somewhere in [every town] where you could take the [children] with you, you know what I mean, I'd be back in half an hour. You could cover yourself then.

[Imelda]

These accounts highlight the real challenge posed to pregnancy support services in reaching out to women concealing a pregnancy, particularly as an outcome of conscious denial. Not feeling able to verbalise the fact of being pregnant is a particular challenge. However, two of the three women who cited this barrier did go on to use the SMS route to contact services. Furthermore women in the group used SMS for other purposes, including disclosing the pregnancy or as a sole means of communicating with a partner or family member after disclosure to establish how they were feeling. They seemed to find this form of communication more acceptable, indicating a need for services to consider how it's application could be extended.

8.3.3   Views of counselling

As noted above, two women attended a service independently, while ten of the women interviewed had attended a hospital with an on-site counselling service to which they had been referred. Women discussed a number of benefits of attending counselling. Women found counselling helpful firstly for providing an outlet to talk after a long period of keeping the pregnancy concealed.

They said they'd send me up to the social worker then and so she came up then and we talked and she wrote down a few things about me and I said in me own mind, I said, 'Oh a big relief, a big relief' ... I felt, when I came out of [the hospital] after talking to [the counsellor], 'Okay, yeah, the bubble has burst.'

[Imelda]

Others referred to how in counselling they talked through aspects of the pregnancy that they felt they would otherwise have kept silent about.

I mean, it was good and it was a help 'cos they'd kind of get me to talk. I probably wouldn't have spoken otherwise. I would have kept it to myself.

[Pauline]

Geraldine found that talking through the options available to her with the counsellor, who was informed on supports available, enabled her to get perspective on her situation and make an informed decision she was happy with.

She told me all the different options – the pros and the cons – and then she told me if I kept the baby about all the different benefits and things like that and then I told her I was planning on going back to college and she was telling me about crèche facilities and different things like that. She was really helpful. She put everything into perspective ... she made it seem that it was possible to keep the child and to go on and do my studies, because before that I just thought, 'This is the end of it now: I'm stuck with [a baby] until about four years old when [the child is] at school. Everything has to stop.'

[Geraldine]

Like Geraldine, other women found the practical support offered through the counsellor useful and helpful. This included:

- information on grants for mothers in education
- equipment grants
- local young mothers' support groups
- the procedure regarding naming the father on the child's birth certification
- the option of placing the baby in foster care while considering adoption
- thoughtful gestures, such as getting women who arrived unprepared for labour some clothes for the baby.

We went through the options for me, to give up the child for adoption or fostering so then she said she was going to contact the Midland Health Board for fostering, you know, a couple would foster the child. [I was worried] was I selfish, then, that I was giving up the child, and I said I didn't know what to do. So I was crying and crying about it and [the counsellor] was saying, 'Well, it could go into a fostering home for a while and you could make up your mind then, if you want to go for adoption, okay, if not, you can gauge after a few weeks then, on your feeling then and on your fears', which I thought was a great idea … [After I gave birth the counsellor] came into me and she says to me, 'Come down to the room,' she said, so I went with her. She gave me a babygro for [the baby], to start me off, and a vest.

[Imelda]

Another important practical help was referral on to other services, for example, the local young mothers' group. Michelle was referred on to a residential support service where she could go and stay while having the baby in a hospital in another region.

The on-site counselling service offered continuity of care, which women appreciated. This was especially the case for Imelda, whose baby was kept in the special care baby unit of the hospital for a number of days after she went home. During this time the counsellor telephoned her to give her updates on the baby's progress. Geraldine also appreciated how the counsellor had supported her when she was admitted to hospital in the early stages of labour.

[The counsellor] came down to me and she was brilliant because mam had gone home so she was coming down and checking on me and walking around with me and giving me pep talks, and that was brilliant.

[Geraldine]

Meanwhile Finola remarked that even though she did not take up the option of any follow-up, knowing it was available helped.

[The counsellor] gave me her mobile number and I didn't use it but it was nice to know that it was there.

[Finola]

However, women in this study group also criticised some aspects of counselling services. The first aspect relates to the referral system for an on-site counselling service. A woman who began her contact with the hospital through the private system and then changed to become a public patient found that she was not referred to the on-site counselling service until an upsetting incident arose during a consultation a number of visits later. After attending counselling she felt it would have been much better had she been referred earlier:

From the beginning maybe it should [be available]. The doctor should have said when I was first down there, 'This person's coming down make sure you see her.' At the time, at the very first visit, maybe that's when I should have been speaking to somebody not literally, ironically, five days before I have [the baby] when I was probably a lot calmer.

[Finola]

While the system of referring women who present late to an on-site counselling service seems to work well in public antenatal clinics, this does not appear to be the case where women attend private clinics.

Some of those who attended counselling were uncomfortable in the counselling setting as they found it to be a much more formal process or forum for articulating feelings and issues than conversations with someone they had an established relationship with.

They were nice; they were lovely people, back and forth, but they weren't personal. They didn't know me well enough to be personal, but yet that's what you need, I think.

[Sarah]

Where a woman felt this way, the system whereby regular scheduled sessions were arranged as part of her package of care in the hospital meant that at times she found herself attending a counselling session that she would not have initiated otherwise.

She was lovely to talk to but at times it was, kind of like, it was arranged, you know, it was very kind of formal ... It had some sort of an air to it, a formality. I mean, it wasn't her fault – it wasn't anything like that. It was, it kind of felt like to me it wasn't a chat, it was like a counselling session ... I mean, she wasn't forcing me, but from my point of view it was kind of like, 'Oh I've to go, I'm going to hospital today and I'll probably have to see the counsellor, I'll have to talk,' you know what sort of a way.

[Pauline]

Michelle attended a two-option counselling service independently before presenting to hospital. She described feeling let down by how the agency responded to her. She contacted the service hoping they would be able to offer a form of support that would alleviate her anxieties but she did not feel that this had been achieved by the end of the session.

I was upset at the time, so upset, crying, 'I can't do this' and 'Oh my God.' They were very, 'Do you want biscuits and tea?' kind of, 'It's all right; you will have adoption. It's great – there are so many people that want children'. ... I thought when I rang [the counselling service], 'Oh the solution will be here tonight, I'll know what to do,' that they would solve everything for me. I would go home that night and a weight would be lifted off my shoulder and everything was going to be grand. No – I went home going, 'Well that was a waste of time.'

[Michelle]

She also commented how the presentation of the service was clandestine, which she found off-putting, and she felt it reinforced of the stigma associated with crisis pregnancy.

It was like, even the house that it's in, it's like a bad place to go; it's in a back alley, you know. It's really weird. It just looks like an ordinary house and you knock on the door. You ring beforehand and then you ring the doorbell, but you ring them on the phone beforehand to let them know you are coming and they will be ready to open the door to let you in so no-one can see you. I think [they], I know they mean well and everything, but still, in year 2005!

[Michelle]

It is interesting to note how a number of women refer to others being present during their meetings with a counselling service – usually their companion at the clinic. In some cases this caused difficulties for the woman where issues were raised that they did not wish to discuss in their companion's presence.

They showed me and [the counsellor] into this room with my mother and I would have preferred that my mother wasn't in the room. I thought that was very wrong because being that there was some tension between myself and my mother and she didn't realise it and she was trying to talk to me and I was like [in my head saying], 'I'm not talking to you with my mother here.' Like, I love my mum to bits but there was tension there.

[Finola]

Similarly, Michelle described that when she had her consultation with the GP, arising out of a referral from the counselling service she attended independent from the hospital, the counsellor was present.

I: *Were you on your own [with the GP] or was the [counsellor] with you?*

R: *She was sitting there. She goes, 'I'll come in with you' and then I was like, 'Okay'.*

[Michelle]

This does not appear to follow best practice and suggests that counsellors and service providers should be more rigorous about always ensuring that consultations with women occur on a one-to-one basis unless the woman actively seeks the presence of a companion.

One specific criticism highlighted by a number of women who were not in a relationship during their pregnancy was the emphasis placed on partners by counsellors. From the earlier discussion on factors in concealment it was clear that this was a source of stigma for a number of women. When a counsellor was perceived to labour the issue women felt this stigma reinforced and resisted the discussion.

There was an awful lot of emphasis, as well, on the father of the child [by the counsellor]. They nearly doubted my, what I was saying, like, and I was looking at them and going, 'Why should you doubt something you don't know?' They pressed that an awful lot, now, I must say, and even the doctors – it was nearly in every conversation at all they would have brought up, and I didn't like that at all because it was putting pressure on, somewhere I just didn't, I couldn't do anything about ... They said, 'You know, you can go behind his back; go to a GP, make sure nothing's wrong, you know, there's nothing wrong with your child's family, heart problems and things like that.' They thought if they pushed it ... and I'm going, 'If I could I would.' You know what I mean? I wouldn't want my [child] picking up something; I would never want her to be sick or anything like that just because, you know, we're after falling out, if that was the case. And I'm going, 'No.' They just didn't want to listen.

[Sarah]

8.4   Social work services

Women in the study group came in contact with social work services through three routes. Firstly, all were referred to medical social work services in the hospital where they attended for antenatal care and/or the birth of their baby. Secondly, women contemplating placing their baby for adoption were put in contact with either Health Service Executive social workers or adoption agency social workers. Finally, one woman contacted a counselling service incorporated into an adoption support service and was referred to one of the agency's social-work staff.

8.4.1   Medical social workers in hospital

All women participating in the study were referred to the medical social-work service of the hospital they attended by staff who were concerned about their late presentation. In the hospital with an on-site crisis pregnancy counselling service it was usual for women to be referred on to that service by the social worker, and so their accounts emphasised the role of the counsellor much more so than that of the social worker. In this situation the woman may have retained contact with the social worker in respect of issues such as placement for adoption or procedures for applying for social welfare entitlements.

In the other hospital the social worker provided counselling, practical support and referral on to other services where appropriate. This included referral on to an adoption service and liaison with support services. Continuity of care also featured, with social workers visiting women who had consulted with them during antenatal care when they came to the hospital as in-patients. Follow-up contact was also offered. Madeline described how she kept in touch with her hospital-based social worker while her child was in foster care and she was making up her mind as to whether to proceed with adoption. When she made up her mind to keep the baby she felt impelled to visit the hospital to tell the social worker and thank her for her support through this time. Jackie described how her hospital social worker had helped her liaise with other social services she was in contact with and telephoned her after her discharge from hospital to inquire how she was getting on, which she appreciated. Finally, Lisa, whose baby was stillborn, appreciated the efforts of the social-work staff to ensure that she had time with her baby and that she got to take away some keepsakes of the child's life.

8.4.2   Health Service Executive social workers

Women considering placing their baby for adoption were put in contact with either an adoption agency's social worker or a Health Service Executive social worker. Two women had contact with HSE social workers, while one had contact with a social worker attached to an adoption agency. Referrals to these social workers all came through the social worker or counsellor women had attended through the hospital where they were attending for antenatal care or, in one case, after giving birth.

The women gave high praise to the social workers for the level of preparation for adoption they received as well as constant reassurance that the decision remained open until the final order was in place[10] and reassurance that they were doing 'a good thing'.

---

10 The Adoption Act 1974 empowers prospective adoptive parents to apply to the High Court to dispense with the final consent of the natural mother if the Court is satisfied that it is in the best interests of the child to do so.

[The social worker] said to me the first time, 'You do realise now he can be adopted into the midlands. You can be walking down the road some day and [your baby] could be walking up against you,' and she said, 'You have to realise all this, you know, [the child] will be adopted into [your area] and you could have the chance of meeting.' That's well, she really went into the whole adoption thing: 'Are you sure? Are you sure?' And I had it right up to, I didn't take [the baby] back until six weeks old. [The baby] was in foster care … You need different views. You don't just need the supportive view: 'Oh, it will be all right. We will do whatever you want to do – it's your choice.' You need people coming along and say, 'If you did this you could also go back to college, you can have crèche.' There are so many other choices, there's no-one kind of, [the] social worker … she did give me alternatives. She was the only one that said, 'These are the alternatives.'

[Michelle]

She's real easy going and laid back; just put me at ease and said to me, 'I'll look after everything – you've nothing to worry about. You are not doing anything wrong.' … [The social worker organised that] I meet [the baby's] foster parents for the first time and she was lovely, just wonderful.

[Eileen]

As well as appreciating reassurance that they were 'not doing anything wrong', women appreciated other aspects of the approach taken by the social workers, including recounting stories of other women who had placed their babies and reassurance that the woman is caring for her child through the act of placing them for adoption.

[My social worker] always says to me, like, 'You're great, you always answer your phone and you're always able to be contacted.' She just makes me feel good … [She] says to me when she lifts out my file, 'You see this, [your child] is going to get that and going to know that you wanted the best for them because you've never missed an appointment and you've never missed a phone call or any of that.'

[Eileen]

All three women also valued social workers accompanying them to see their baby after placement in the home of their foster parents.

[My social worker] was there all the way – she used to collect me and we used to go out and see [the baby] in the foster care. She was there all the time.

[Michelle]

Finally, the follow-on care women found they got from their social workers was strongly appreciated. They described having many on-going contacts by telephone and face-to-face. The social workers would call to see them at home or meet them for coffee and provide an outlet for them to keep talking about their decision. In addition, this on-going contact allowed women feel that they were building a strong, trustworthy, personal connection with their social workers and were able to relate to them on a basis beyond the adoption process.

8.5   Antenatal outpatient departments

Of the thirteen women interviewed, three did not attend for any antenatal care. Lisa's pregnancy went undetected until 39 weeks' gestation, leaving no opportunity to attend an antenatal clinic. Grainne concealed her pregnancy until she went into labour at home, while Imelda concealed until 36 weeks' gestation, at which point she attended a GP with concerns over pain she was experiencing. When referred to the hospital she avoided the outpatient department and went straight to the maternity ward. While an appointment was made for her to attend the antenatal clinic one week later she went into labour in the meantime and so did not attend the antenatal clinic at all. Of the ten women who did attend for antenatal care, two had just one antenatal visit before giving birth while the remaining eight women had more than one visit to an antenatal outpatient department.

8.5.1   Factors shaping attendance at antenatal clinic

Some women attended antenatal care before disclosing the pregnancy to members of their family or social domains. Jackie presented at twelve weeks' gestation but only ever disclosed her pregnancy to health and social service personnel, her partner and friends. The pregnancy was concealed from her family throughout in order that she could retain control over the outcome of the pregnancy. Michelle and Sarah both attended past twenty weeks' gestation without having disclosed to their family or social domain. Sarah's family were alerted to her pregnancy by someone who saw her at her first visit to the clinic and so she disclosed to them at this point. Michelle went on to tell her partner after two visits to the clinic at seven months' gestation but continued to conceal the pregnancy from all others in her family and social domains. Both of these women consulted a GP, who referred them to the antenatal clinic. During the pregnancy Madeline only disclosed it to her partner and employer. She attended antenatal care past twenty weeks' gestation after attending a counselling service that made a referral for her. As a recent migrant to Ireland, Madeline described how she had no understanding of the process of antenatal care before making contact with the support agency.

Other women did not contemplate attending an antenatal clinic until they had disclosed the pregnancy to members of their family and/or partner. Geraldine and Finola's pregnancies went undetected until advanced pregnancy. Once pregnancy was confirmed they immediately arranged antenatal care and also disclosed to their families. Other women in the conscious denial or concealment group described a process of being confronted by members of their family (Pauline and Eileen) or eventually disclosing to them (Aisling and Liz). Pauline, Aisling and Liz were younger women (aged between eighteen and twenty) and they described how they themselves were entirely unfamiliar with what antenatal care entailed. Only after disclosure – when in all cases their mothers took charge of organising antenatal care – did this seem possible for them.

8.5.2   Perceptions of antenatal services

In general women liked to find that they were not singled out for special attention or treatment when they presented to antenatal hospital departments, which many had anticipated. When nurses, midwives and doctors treated them in the same routine way as other women were treated, the consensus was that this made women feel more at ease. Most found this was the case when they presented for antenatal care. They felt that by not probing into their situations staff were respecting their privacy and demonstrating an understanding of their need to be treated with discretion.

However, two women remarked on how surprised they were that staff did not query their situation because they were at such an advanced stage when they presented to the clinic. Both felt that staff could have picked up on their need to be linked in with support services earlier.

R: *They didn't know it was concealed as such, they just thought I was another woman going in. I found it strange: the nurses never asked at the start, 'Why are you coming in six months pregnant for your first scan?' They didn't, but then I think I asked for a social worker because I had to tell them I wasn't keeping the baby eventually. They found it strange that, because I wasn't going back to [the hospital] to have [the baby] … Basically it was, 'This is the weight', it was, 'This is the size. That's it. Goodbye now.' It was never, maybe they thought because I was concealing I didn't want to talk about it. I don't know.*

I: *But you did want to talk?*

R: *I did, yes, definitely. You need something or you will blow up. I went for two months before I sorted everything.*

[Michelle]

Finola had one visit as a private patient before transferring to attend the public outpatient department. She felt that it should have been the responsibility of the doctor she was attending privately to either refer her for support or inform the public clinic that she had presented late and may need referral.

While most women found that they were not singled out for any special attention, one woman did remark on how her circumstances gave rise to particular attention being directed at her, and she was uncomfortable with this. Geraldine's pregnancy was not detected until 36 weeks' gestation and she found that when she presented for antenatal care this resulted in her receiving more attention than she would have liked.

The staff were fine but, like, when they heard the circumstances of it and how I was so far gone and I was only finding out they were shocked, like. There seemed to be staff coming from everywhere to hear my story. It was so strange and I was like, 'Oh God! Don't be making such a big thing out of me,' because I just wanted to be in and out and I didn't want notice taken of me. It was everyone else just seemed to be looking at me. The women out in the waiting room were looking at me because I didn't look pregnant and then all the staff were looking at me because I was eight months gone and I didn't know. It was so strange. I was the centre of attention and it was the one thing I didn't want to be.

[Geraldine]

In addition, three of the women interview cited incidents they felt demonstrated a lack of understanding for their situation on the part of some members of staff. Eileen explained her reasons for attending late to the doctor who examined her; however, she felt that staff went on to be very indiscreet with her details and also misunderstood and were insensitive to her situation.

R: *This is one thing about when you do go into a hospital and you are in that late stage. I went in and the doctor asked me was I happy about it and I said no I wasn't, and I had explained to him that I already had a child to someone else. I said the child's father is involved in its life and I said this is more or less a one-night stand and he said, 'Right, so.' And the next thing he sent me back out to the waiting room and a nurse just came out and announced it to the waiting room*

I: *Your name?*

R: *She said, 'Oh this girl, she has to see a social worker – she isn't happy because she had a one-night stand and it isn't her partner's child.' The whole thing was misunderstood. She said it out to another nurse. Now, if I heard it in the waiting room everyone did. That was, I think, if for girls in future, if they are going in that they should be took away privately because I could have just got up and walked out that day and said, 'Feck the lot of you! I'll stick to my own plan [of unassisted birth].' I was just so mad with that nurse: she just made me feel, like, as if I was a slut that was after arriving in pregnant after a one-night stand. She had misunderstood everything. That's one aspect of what I didn't like.*

[Eileen]

There were two other women who felt, like Eileen, that staff in the clinic demonstrated a lack of understanding of their situation. The primary issue for Sarah was a lack of understanding by staff when she could not estimate the date of her last period or when the pregnancy was conceived.

I had put it off [thinking about the pregnancy] so much that I didn't know when I actually missed my first period. It was funny, like, because when I got to the hospital and they were looking at you kind of going 'Why wouldn't you know?' And I'm going, 'Put yourself in my shoes and see can you remember?'

[Sarah]

Finola's felt that the doctor she attended judged her because she presented late with an unexpected pregnancy and she was no longer in a relationship:

I went in, sat down across the table from [the doctor] and he said, 'You are very late.' He more or less gave out to me and then said, 'Right. We'll have a look at you,' and said, 'Get up on the table.' That was grand and I looked at him and said, 'Can I have a picture [of the scan]?' because my friend who has a small baby said to make sure you get the first picture. And he was, 'It's too big' and then I went, 'Sorry? What?' and he went, 'All you'll get is a head' and I said, 'That's fine. I just want it.' 'No.' and I went, 'Ok.' So at that stage, when I'm in a situation where somebody keeps barking at me, I tend to just sit back and say nothing and listen, so he goes, 'Right now. Sit down and we'll talk' and he says, 'Right. Partner. Where is he today?' and I said, 'He's at work,' and I suppose in his own way he was trying to be very concerned. He was, he said, like, you know, ' I can see him at any time he wants, if he wants to come.' I said, 'Well, we are not really together that much anymore. This wasn't planned.' And the moment I said, 'This wasn't planned,' he kind of just changed attitude altogether to, 'Right. Father of the child is not here, unplanned, you are a single mum,' and he went from talking to me to talking down. I very much felt that. And he said, 'You are not 25 weeks pregnant; you are 30 weeks pregnant.' He was very much barking at me rather than talking to me.

[Finola]

Regardless of how staff responded to women, many described feeling very self-conscious while in the public space of the clinic. Women were anxious about people who knew them seeing them there and realising they were pregnant; they felt the absence of a partner when observing couples together; they noticed how other women looked pleased and confident about their pregnancies, in contrast to their anxieties and desire to hide the pregnancy. All of these anxieties and fears were exacerbated by a system that required long periods of sitting in a public communal waiting area and women's names being called out when it came their turn for treatment. Attending the clinic under these circumstances meant that women did not get to benefit fully from the consultation, as they would forget questions they had or be so distracted and anxious to leave that they would not be able to take in the information being offered.

It's very hard to go into your antenatal appointment and all these mothers there with their husbands and their partner and I wouldn't let [my partner] come with me. And you are sitting there and you are afraid someone will see you, even … I used to cower in the corner where no one will see me and hate when my name was called out. You know, they call out and I was afraid of my life there was someone else there going, 'What in God's name is she doing here?' … To have to sit watching a girl with her boyfriend and he's rubbing her back, or watching a mother with three kids already and her husband's just ringing her on the phone, or [] being called out in public and everyone is going, 'Oh, she has no-one with her. We saw her last week, there was no-one with her then either.'

[Michelle]

Women were appreciative of referrals made for them by the antenatal clinic to counsellors, social workers and antenatal educators. In particular they appreciated the sensitivity of staff to pick up on occasions where they were upset and arrange for a session with the counsellor or social worker.

Antenatal education was welcomed by many women for helping them to prepare for childbirth. In particular women valued one-to-one consultations offered with the educator. Some were happy to attend antenatal classes, while other women only wanted to see the antenatal educator on a one-to-one basis, or they presented at a stage in pregnancy where there was only opportunity for a one-to-one session.

The midwife bringing me down for the day- that was brilliant for me because I had no idea what to expect and she literally took the whole day out to just bring me around the wards, talk me through the labour and any questions or queries I had or worries about anything. Like that she was brilliant.

[Geraldine]

R: The whole thing about what my options were birthing-wise, and it was great, like, to have someone there. You'd have people saying to you in passing and she advised me of the epidural – the whole lot, like. If you listen to everyone walking along the street one person would say it's terrible; the next person would say it won't work, the next person. But she said because I was so young and everything, like, she put everything into perspective for me and I thought it was great. But I think something like that would be a lot better every time.

I: To see her every time?

R: *Yeah. Now maybe not every time but a little more often than before, but just more regularly. She was very helpful.*

I: *Yeah, and did you do antenatal classes as well?*

R: *I did. There was two different women on it as well. I thought I felt things were very specific. You'd never know yourself, or even like my mum, like, my mum had four kids and she still wouldn't know half of it.*

[Sarah]

Finally, Michelle described how staff in the antenatal clinic made copies of all her notes so that she could bring them with her to the hospital where she had arranged to give birth as part of her process of concealing the pregnancy. It was important to her that this facility was made available.

8.6   Hospital maternity department

Twelve of the thirteen women interviewed gave birth in one of the two hospitals where the study was conducted. One of the women transferred to a hospital in another region to give birth to facilitate concealment of the pregnancy.

8.6.1   *General assessment of maternity services*

Overall there was strong praise for the midwifery and nursing staff of the maternity departments they attended from all of the women. Just as in the antenatal clinic, women tended to appreciate when they were not singled out for any special treatment.

I didn't want [special attention] and I found that none of them ever bothered, like. The nurses would be coming around, 'How are you today?' and they'd be messing about, something on the radio or all that, or they could be laughing, one of them passing a joke. They would take your blood pressure and they'd be on about, 'How are you?' and they might say, 'How is the baby?' and all very good. There was no such thing as, 'How did you manage?' or, you know? They were, there was no notice taken. That's what I liked.

[Aisling]

In keeping with this, women tended to prefer being accommodated in a public ward with other women to having special accommodation arrangements made for them. Even though some were sensitive to being much younger than others they still preferred the camaraderie of a group ward, rather than opting for a private ward, which they considered would be isolating.

All the nurses and the staff and everything were lovely down there. I mean, they were such a help, but it was kind of strange for me because, I don't know, I was the youngest one, but at the same time it was kind of good because we were all in the same boat: we were all having kids; we're all women, you know?

[Pauline]

Another issue relating to not wanting any special treatment was how staff handled any emotional upset or trauma women experienced after delivery resulting from the process of concealing their pregnancy. This did not arise for every woman, as most were resigned to the pregnancy by the time they came to deliver. However, Grainne, who presented to hospital in labour, described how one member of the midwifery staff took her own initiative in broaching how Grainne was feeling. Grainne found this helpful.

Similarly, Michelle and Eileen referred to how individual midwives had taken the initiative themselves to sit down with them and discuss how they were feeling. In both cases the midwives had relayed to them aspects of their own experiences or experiences of other women. The compassion shown by these midwives was greatly appreciated by all three women at a time when they were feeling very lonely, isolated and confused.

Most women spoke very highly of the facilities offered to them in the hospitals where they gave birth, and, indeed, aspects such as music in the delivery suite were specifically praised One issue was mentioned, however, in relation to the physical facilities of the hospital and that was the distance between the special-care baby unit and the post-natal wards. Aisling's baby was place in the unit initially after birth. Aisling was very anxious about being identified when she was travelling along corridors and stairs to reach the unit, which was on another floor from the post-natal ward.

> R: *What I found very uncomfortable was I was on the second floor and where the babies are, the care unit, was downstairs and I didn't like having to go all the way out and into the elevator and down and in.*

> I: *What was it that made it uncomfortable?*

> R: *I don't know. Maybe walking by and you would meet anyone; that they'd be looking at you and thinking you were so young and then going in to the care unit.*

> [Aisling]

While the general consensus among participants was that maternity staff deserved high praise for the care they provided, a couple of issues arose in women's accounts that indicated some lack of appreciation on the part of staff for the situation women concealing a pregnancy find themselves in. The first issue arose from Aisling's account of being introduced to her baby after delivery and later being brought to the special-care baby unit to see the baby again. It is interesting to note her sense of being unprepared for meeting the baby, arising from issues discussed in Section 7.3.2 This dealt with how Aisling, who had consciously denied her pregnancy, had not adapted to the pregnancy or begun to prepare for a baby and motherhood by the time she delivered. It took some time for the reality that she had a baby and was now a mother to sink in. However, maternity staff in the hospital had no awareness of the possibility that she may feel this way.

> *I was given [the baby]. Sure, I didn't know what I was looking at and then they brought [baby] off and they put [baby] into the incubator and about an hour after they brought me down in the wheelchair to see [baby] and I was looking in and I could see this baby move about and I was like, 'Ok, sorry now. Oh my God.'*

> [Aisling]

A second issue arose out of Imelda's account of her experience of childbirth and time in the maternity unit. Imelda had concealed her pregnancy from her partner and two children until she went into labour. She initially concealed labour and then eventually decided she had no option but to disclose to her partner. All of these events went on over at least a 24-hour period during which time she delayed going to the hospital. She did not eat or sleep during the time and was highly anxious and stressed. When she arrived at the hospital she was exhausted and still highly anxious as her partner, who accompanied her, had been drinking. She went on to have what she described as a difficult labour and birth, during which time she was administered a variety of pain-relieving drugs. Afterwards, when she went to walk around she was very unsteady and later when she was holding her baby she was clumsy and unsteady. Staff then questioned her as to whether she also had consumed alcohol and told her they had concerns that she was handling the baby roughly. She found this deeply upsetting, particularly in light of what she had endured in the previous hours, days and weeks.

Got up anyway after an hour, [got] off the labour bed and I staggered, and really what hurted me was – I never took a drink for the last seven years, I'd say – they thought I was drunk. Because of [my partner] they thought I had drink in me as well, because of [him]. The midwife said it to me. I thought, 'I'll put on me jammies', 'cos the T-shirt I had on was wringing, and I staggered all right. I remember staggering. But I was so sore and so high from the gas. Anyway, the midwife says to me in the bed, 'Had you drink in you?' I said no. 'I don't drink,' I said. I didn't drink for the last seven years and even at that all I'd drink was nothing. And she said, 'Oh no,' she said, 'you're after staggering.' And I said, 'I'm new to the gas and the pethidine and the hardship.' That took me, put me in bad humour then, hurt me more ... I went down to the ward anyway, and just, one nurse gave me the baby and she thought by me, the way I was holding it, I was rough with it, you know, like, and I said I was fierce nervous holding the baby now. I said, 'All back to me, new again,' and she said to me, 'You look tired,' and I said, 'I am tired.' I said, 'I think I'll go back to the bed and sleep for another hour.' So that was the next thing. She said to me the next morning, then, [the paediatrician] said to me, 'They thought you were a bit rough with the baby.' I said I was tired as well, I had the pethidine, I had the gas, I said I'd an awful lot of gas, I said, and I went down for a cigarette and a cup of tea after it as well. She said, 'Yeah,' and she said, 'but the nurses and myself are keeping an eye on you,' she said, and there she said it again: had I any drink on me? Even the nurse in the special care baby unit thought I had drink on me, as well. Me eyes looked tired, you know what I mean? And I said to her, I said what I went through. I said, 'I'm wondering at meself I didn't take a drink, the pressure and everything, the stress and everything I went through,' I said, 'between work, being pregnant, trying to look after two kids and the situation I'm living in.' You know what I mean?

[Imelda]

Finally, one further issue arose for Imelda, who had been an in-patient of the hospital when giving birth to her previous two children as well as on the occasion of this baby's birth. Imelda had attended a different GP during this pregnancy than her previous pregnancies as part of her process of concealment. When she was being admitted to the hospital she was asked to verify if she was still attending the GP specified on her old charts and she admits that in the midst of so much information she stated she was. Subsequently communication relating to her was sent to this GP, which caused her some further anxiety.

8.6.2   *Managing care of women considering adoption*

Madeline, Eileen and Michelle were all still concealing their pregnancy when they gave birth and intending to maintain concealment after delivery by placing their baby for adoption.

Eileen delivered in her local hospital, where she attended for one antenatal appointment the week before delivery. She was pleased to be accommodated in a private room.

They put me down into a private room ... like, they didn't have to do that. I think if girls are going in – and they do go in – it's a big step to take to actually go in to [a hospital] that they should be took away in private.

[Eileen]

While Eileen had not indicated a definite intention to place the baby for adoption before being admitted to hospital, after the birth of the baby staff facilitated her wish not to have to take care of the baby. The baby was cared for by staff and only brought to Eileen when she requested it.

Michelle attended a different hospital for the birth of the baby than she attended for antenatal care as part of her arrangements to conceal the pregnancy. Her social worker had helped her put these arrangements in place (through liaison with a social worker for the area attached to the hospital). They also arranged to handle the placement of the baby into foster care from that hospital.

I gave birth and the nurse said, 'Do you want to take [the baby]?' 'No,' I said and they didn't put me in [with the child] ... [It] was a brilliant hospital. That's the one thing I'll say, it was a fantastic hospital. Apart from disguising who you were [] they didn't put me into the ward where mothers had all had their babies. They put me into a ward, just a different ward, and I could have had my own room if I wanted to – but I wasn't private or anything – but I could have. And they kept the baby in the nursery so they kept me away from anyone that I didn't want to see and people going, 'Where's your baby?' you know, if you were inside in that ward? ... It was kind of a silent thing that they knew that girl wasn't keeping it.

[Michelle]

Both Eileen and Michelle placed their baby into foster care directly from the hospital. Madeline, the third woman who placed her baby into foster care, described how she had given birth a number of weeks earlier than her expected date and the foster parents identified for her child were unavailable for three days after Madeline was due to be discharged. She had cared for the baby herself while in hospital. When she was offered a choice of either taking the baby home for three days while awaiting placement or placing the baby into the care of the hospital she was happy to take the baby home. The consensus from the three women planning to place their babies for adoption was that every individual has different feelings about whether or not they want to have contact with the baby after birth or with other patients in the hospital. Being offered the option of 'rooming in' with the baby or having the baby cared for in the hospital nursery was important. Women also valued being offered a choice of accommodation – in a private room, a ward other than the post-natal ward or the post-natal ward. These choices are important, as women may decide on any combination of arrangements depending on how they are feeling.

Michelle and Eileen both described how individual staff members took the initiative themselves to talk with them when they heard the circumstances of their pregnancy or when they noticed they were upset. Both appreciated these gestures.

8.6.3   Managing delivery of a stillborn child

Lisa only had her pregnancy detected four days before giving birth. It then emerged that her baby had a foetal anomaly and, tragically, it was stillborn. In this context Lisa was offered – and was grateful for – the provision of a private room where herself and her partner could spend time with their baby and prepare for the burial.

8.7   Other hospital departments

Two women in the study presented at other hospital departments during their pregnancy before being referred to the hospitals where the study took place. Geraldine was undergoing tests in the medical department of a local general hospital when her pregnancy of 36 weeks' gestation was detected. She was critical of the manner in which this information was relayed to her.

> R: *I went in. I was on my own and there was two nurses there and they did the ultrasound and straight away they said, 'You are 36 weeks pregnant.' Like, I thought they could have broke it to me more gently because they knew that I wasn't expecting it at all. They were kind of blunt about it, in a way.*
>
> I: *Did they tell you they were doing a scan of your womb at that stage?*
>
> R: *No. All I'd been told was I was getting an ultrasound and that was it.*
>
> I: *But you're not familiar with that term?*
>
> R: *No, definitely not. Because after hearing that I was supposed to be getting MRIs and all this. I was like, 'Right. An ultrasound. Grand.' and then it was only when they turned around and told me I was like [panicked] ... The nurses that did the ultrasound were kind of, they were blunt. I don't know if that's the best word to describe it but they could have told me in a better way because they knew I was going down with absolutely no idea.*
>
> [Geraldine]

Lisa also attended a general hospital to have symptoms investigated, only to have a pregnancy detected. She attended a gynaecological department and was told she was at an advanced stage of pregnancy but the exact stage could not be determined. Like Geraldine, she felt that the manner in which she was told of the pregnancy was insensitive to the shock she felt.

8.8   Overview of contact with services

Of the qualitative study group of thirteen women, all but one had some contact with health services during their pregnancy. There was a high tendency among women to present to GPs during a concealed pregnancy. Women's attendance with crisis pregnancy counselling and support services was quite low. Two of the thirteen women interviewed, Michelle and Madeline, attended a crisis pregnancy counselling service independently to explore their interest in adoption. One hospital had an on-site crisis pregnancy counselling service and all women in the study group attending this hospital were referred there. In the other hospital only women considering adoption were referred to a counselling service that included the option of adoption. All women in the study group were referred to medical social work services in the hospital where they attended for antenatal care and/or the birth of their baby. Of the thirteen women interviewed, ten attended a hospital outpatients department for antenatal care at some point during their pregnancy, while three did not attend for any antenatal care. All of the women in the study gave birth in hospital. One woman gave birth in a different hospital to the one she had attended for antenatal care; this was part of her strategy of concealing the pregnancy.

The most common pathway to a GP for women was to experience symptoms that concerned them. The second principal pathway was to disclose the pregnancy to family members, usually mothers, who then were instrumental in organising an appointment with the GP. Other routes cited by women were referral by a counselling service and self-referral to organise antenatal care while concealing from family. Reasons for not attending a GP included reticence about discussing contraceptive or sexual health issues with GPs generally, never feeling unwell enough during the pregnancy to seek a consultation or being unfamiliar with the system of antenatal care (in the case of one woman who was living in Ireland less than two years). There were mixed views among women of how well GPs responded to their needs. Two of the three women whose pregnancy went undetected were critical that their doctor had not administered a pregnancy test. Where women attended GPs and had their pregnancy confirmed some were pleased with the support and understanding they received, including acknowledgement of the emotional toll of concealing a pregnancy. Others appreciated the way their doctor did not make any judgmental comments about their pregnancy or stage of gestation. Some felt their GP had not been adept at handling the distress they expressed when presenting first witeh the pregnancy. Finally, some difficulties in the process through which women who concealed their pregnancy were referred on for antenatal care were highlighted, indicating a need for GPs to take particular care in ensuring women access such care as quickly as possible.

Crisis pregnancy counselling and support services were attended by two women independently, while all women attending the hospital with an on-site service were referred there. Some women's did not attend a service because they did not perceive their pregnancy to be a crisis; other women encountered specific barriers to accessing a service. These included:

- a pregnancy being detected too late to allow any opportunity to access a service
- women not feeling able to actually verbalise they were pregnant
- difficulty arranging to attend a face-to-face consultation without arousing suspicions about the pregnancy
- lack of availability of widespread counselling services.

Some of the benefits of counselling and support services described by women that attended them were that they:

- provided an outlet to talk after a long period of keeping the pregnancy concealed
- allowed women to address aspects of the pregnancy that would otherwise have been kept silent
- helped women make an informed decision
- offered information and advice on practical supports and services.

One of the criticisms made of counselling services related to the referral system in the hospital with an on-site service, which seemed to effectively link women presenting late at the public clinic with the service but not those presenting to private clinics. Other criticisms related to women's perception of the counselling they received. Criticisms included:

- the emphasis placed on partners by counsellors where women were not in a relationship
- feeling counselling was a much more formal forum for articulating feelings and issues than conversations with a person they were close to
- feeling let down when an agency did not offer a form of support that would alleviate the anxieties a woman was feeling.

A number of women's accounts of their meetings with the counsellor in the hospital setting included references to others being present and how this inhibited the interaction.

Women in the study group came in contact with social work services through two routes. Firstly all were referred to medical social work services in the hospital where they attended for antenatal care and/or the birth of their baby. Women cited some specific social work undertaken on their behalf, such as liaison with other social services and visits and support from social workers during or after the birth. Secondly women contemplating placing their baby for adoption were put in contact with either HSE social workers or adoption agency social workers. Women appreciated the emotional and practical support they were given in preparing for adoption and the follow-on care they received when their babies were being placed in foster care.

Ten of the thirteen women interviewed attended antenatal care in an outpatient hospital setting. Some women attended antenatal care before disclosing the pregnancy to members of their family or social domains. Other women did not contemplate attending an antenatal clinic until they had disclosed the pregnancy to members of their family and/or partner. In general women liked to find that they were not singled out for special attention or treatment when they presented to antenatal hospital departments. However, two women who were not referred to support services despite presenting late felt that this should have been done as a matter of course. Some incidents were cited that demonstrated a lack of understanding for the situation of women concealing a pregnancy on the part of some members of staff, particularly women's need to remain anonymous and /or to receive a sympathetic response from staff. Regardless of how staff responded to women, many described feeling very self-conscious while in the public space of the clinic.

Women were appreciative of referrals made for them from the antenatal clinic to counsellors, social workers and antenatal educators. Many women welcomed antenatal education as it helped them to prepare for childbirth. In particular women valued one-to-one consultations offered with the educator. One woman who had arranged to give birth in another hospital as part of her process of concealing the pregnancy appreciated staff providing copies of all her notes so that she could bring them with her.

Across all of the study group women gave strong praise to the midwifery and nursing staff of the maternity departments they attended. Just as in the antenatal clinic women tended to appreciate when they were not singled out for any special treatment. Most preferred being accommodated in a public ward with other women than having special accommodation arrangements made for them. A number of women cited instances of individual midwives taking the initiative to talk with and comfort women when they experienced emotional upset or trauma after delivery. None of the women interviewed highlighted any shortcomings in the facilities offered to them in the hospitals where they gave birth and were more likely to praise facilities such as music in the delivery suites. The only issue cited by one woman was the location of the special care baby unit on a floor separate to post-natal wards, making her feel at risk of being identified while making the journey. A couple of incidents were cited by women indicating some lack of appreciation on the part of staff for the situation women concealing a pregnancy find themselves in. One issue was lack of awareness among maternity staff to the possibility that a woman may feel unprepared for contact with her baby, such that no particular steps were taken to manage this process. Secondly a woman who arrived to give birth exhausted and highly anxious was deeply upset when staff suggested she was under the influence of alcohol. She argued that this showed no understanding for what she had endured in the previous hours, days and weeks.

The consensus from the three women planning to place their babies for adoption was that every individual has different feelings about whether or not they want to have contact with the baby after birth and with other patients in the hospital. Being offered the option of 'rooming in' with the baby or having the baby cared for in the hospital nursery was important. Women also valued being offered a choice of accommodation – in a private room, a ward other than the post-natal ward or the post-natal ward. These choices are important, as women may decide on any combination of arrangements depending on how they are feeling.

Two women in the study presented at other hospital departments during their pregnancy before being referred to the hospitals where the study took place. Both were critical of the insensitive manner in which they were told of the pregnancy, which did not take into account the shock they felt when a very advanced pregnancy was detected.

9.0 Health professionals' perspectives on challenges and practices entailed in responding to undetected, denied or concealed pregnancy

9.1   Introduction

Interviews with health professionals provided an insight into the challenges of managing a concealed pregnancy in their daily routine as well as documenting the examples of good practice they have adopted in responding to the issue.

The following health professionals were targeted for participation in the study:

- Midwives
- Nursing staff in antenatal/maternity settings
- Administrative staff in antenatal/maternity settings
- Antenatal educators
- Staff of accident and emergency departments
- Medical social workers
- Consultant obstetricians
- Health board/HSE social workers
- Crisis pregnancy counsellors
- Adoption agency social workers
- General practitioners.

(See Chapter 2.0 for a detailed account of the methodology.)

General practitioners were the only group who could not be recruited for the study. Initially members of the advisory group identified a list of GPs known to them through professional contacts in relation to crisis pregnancy. While five were contacted for participation only one practice agreed to take part. A second strategy was to ask the Irish College of General Practitioners to facilitate us by alerting its members to the research and by asking those who had encountered concealed pregnancy in practice if they would be willing to participate. However, difficulties in implementing such a strategy together with a very limited timeframe imposed by the study schedule meant this was not possible. In the event it was not possible to include the perspective of general practitioners in the research.

The following questions were addressed to these health professionals in both of the geographical areas surrounding the hospital sites chosen for participation in the study [See Appendix 8 for Topic Guide]:

- The challenges they experience when a woman presents at an advanced stage in pregnancy up to the point of delivery without having disclosed the pregnancy to her social network.
- The specific steps taken in responding to a woman presenting with a concealed pregnancy that go beyond the usual practices in their care setting. In particular, a description of procedures which have developed 'organically' over the years in their care settings, as well as examples of specific innovative steps they have taken in particular cases.
- The recommendations they wished to see included in a national framework for the management of concealed pregnancy to apply across the range of services, from antenatal care to other support services.

The structure of the chapter follows this framework in presenting our analysis of focus-group and interview discussions with these groups. The challenges faced by professionals across these areas when a woman presents late in her pregnancy are discussed first. This is followed by a discussion of the practices initiated by healthcare workers across these disciplines in response to the particular needs of women presenting late in pregnancy. Finally the recommendations drawn from the perspectives of practitioners across these professional disciplines will be incorporated into the recommendations chapter presented at the end of the report.

9.2   Challenges for medical management of pregnancy

When a woman presents late in pregnancy for antenatal care this raises challenges for the medical management of pregnancy in accordance with usual protocols or standards of care, as well as challenges in meeting counselling, emotional and support needs associated with concealment of pregnancy. This first section addresses the challenges for medical management of the pregnancy.

9.2.1   Knowledge of medical history

The purpose of booking early is that a woman's medical care can be planned, risk factors can be identified and appropriate screening programmes put into place, if they need to be. There is no opportunity to do this if a woman presents late in pregnancy. Not knowing a woman's medical history is one of the main challenges faced by doctors caring for her. She may have had high risk factors in her medical history that would usually be closely monitored during pregnancy, such as an underlying cardiac disease or a positive family history of diabetes. There is also less time to investigate whether the mother has a medical condition that would usually involve administration of treatment during pregnancy; for example, where a woman who is HIV positive presents, drugs are administered to reduce the risk of transmission of the virus. A woman may present with an established condition representing a risk to her and her pregnancy such as pre-eclampsia. It is impossible to establish how long the condition has been present or the severity of its impact.

9.2.2   Time pressures and extra workload

For staff in busy hospital departments, trying to remain open, friendly and approachable while under time constraints and pressures is one of the main challenges, as a woman will only open up and disclose to somebody who she feels she can trust. Medical staff were conscious of trying to remain approachable during their busy schedules.

A woman's first visit to the antenatal clinic is particularly time-intensive when a woman is presenting late. As well as having to 'catch-up' on missed care, antenatal staff are conscious that they need to prioritise that woman's care, as the woman may not present again during her pregnancy. Where women present unbooked to maternity departments this also creates a greater workload for staff because they have no medical or social history for the woman. In turn, this has implications for the overall workload of the clinic or ward and the care of other women in attendance.

Women who present late without partner/family support may need to stay in the hospital for a longer period than usual so that alternative accommodation arrangements can be made for them. Medical staff have to continue to provide them with post-natal care and support. This has implications for the workload of maternity care staff.

9.2.3   Management of labour and delivery

The care of a woman and her baby can be compromised if there is insufficient time to plan for the delivery and to take reparative action before the birth. If a woman presents in labour she will not have had her bloods taken; therefore there will been no checks for HIV, Hepatitis B, Hepatitis C, blood counting, and blood group. As there has been no planning for the delivery taking account of the position of the baby an assessment needs to be done quickly. There could be problems in terms of a foetal abnormality or growth, which have implications for delivery. A vaginal delivery is always anticipated but there are situations where it may not be appropriate. Staff might have to do an emergency caesarean section because of unexpected findings.

When a woman presents in advanced pregnancy – particularly into the third trimester – it is difficult to determine accurately her stage of pregnancy; there is no information about the maturity of the baby. If the baby was very premature the special care baby unit would need to be placed on stand-by.

If a woman presents in labour, staff need to respond immediately to helping her give birth. Her social and medical history will not be sought until after the birth, before she leaves the hospital. The woman may be very distressed, traumatised and/or in a state of shock and may not know or be fully aware of what is happening to her. A woman who is not prepared for labour and the birth, and has not had any antenatal care or education, may not be able to identify the onset of labour or may not have any preparations in place for how to get from home to hospital. Members of staff are presented with a challenge in trying to extract information from her (such as whether or not it is her first pregnancy) when she is in this condition.

9.2.4   Presentation 'out of hours'

When a woman presents late, a comprehensive and intensive medical and social response is necessary. A challenge arises when a woman presents out of antenatal clinic hours or to another clinic in the hospital; for example she may present to the surgical clinic with abdominal pains or the gynaecological clinic with irregular bleeding. The woman will be seen by the doctors and nurses on duty at that time. This team may not have specific obstetric or midwifery expertise. There is also a possibility that they would discharge the woman, advising her to return for an antenatal visit the following week, without being able to make a complete assessment.

9.2.5   Postnatal care

Concerns were expressed about a woman's medical aftercare where she delivers and seeks to leave the hospital in a very short space of time, with the risk of haemorrhaging cited particularly. On a more long-term basis, where a woman decides to place her baby for fostering or adoption directly from the hospital, the public health nurse in her catchment area will not be referred to attend the woman who has recently given birth. This has implications for the woman's care following the birth.

Where a woman delivers at home unassisted there is a possible risk of infection to her. Crisis pregnancy counselling services described challenges arising for them where a woman makes contact in this situation wishing to bring the baby to their centre to leave anonymously in their care. They find that it is difficult to gain that woman's trust and to encourage her to think of her own medical needs and overcome her anxiety about attending the hospital.

9.3   Challenges for meeting women's support needs

9.3.1   Reaching women

A principal challenge lies in how to reach women who conceal their pregnancy until advanced pregnancy and even up to the point of or beyond the birth of the baby. Counselling and support services discussed how women are seeing their information and 'Lo-call' numbers, but they are not ready to avail of the service at that time or they are in denial. It was felt that issues of privacy and trust are huge for women who present late and so women may have fears about writing the number down in case it is seen. It was recognised that it takes courage to make the phone call. Meanwhile, it is difficult to get the message out there that it's okay for a woman to come forward at any stage of the pregnancy and that there are services that are safe, secure and private, which can help her in a non-judgemental way.

When women concealing a pregnancy do make contact with support services this will often be by telephone or text messaging. Building up trust with a woman on the phone is difficult. Women sometimes prefer to use SMS to contact a counsellor/service, and the counsellor must work with what the woman is comfortable with, even though it can leave the counsellor with anxious feelings in relation to the woman's safety. The counsellor must wait to receive a text message about arrangements to meet.

Finally, professionals perceived there to be very negative attitudes towards women who conceal a pregnancy. For example, messages such as, 'How could you be so stupid?' and 'Why couldn't you have just gone to the hospital?' produce feelings of embarrassment and shame, locking a woman into concealment.

9.3.2   Referrals

As the first point of contact in an outpatient department, administrative staff expressed concerns about their capacity to respond appropriately to a woman who is concealing her pregnancy. Women normally present through a GP referral-letter. Staff had concerns about handling sensitively a situation where a woman self-refers, while adhering to hospital procedure.

9.3.3   Development of rapport/building trust

Developing rapport with a woman and building her trust is crucial – but not always easy – in this context. There is less time to develop a relationship and rapport with the woman. A relationship that would normally develop over a seven-month period now has to develop in a much shorter time. This challenge can be compounded by a woman's particular circumstances, which may give rise to stress, isolation and lack of support.

A woman may be trying to identify someone in the clinic in whom she can confide. Being very busy may mean that a staff member can 'miss out on the signs' given by a woman indicating her wish to disclose or confide in them.

Engaging women and building a relationship of trust sufficient to sustain on-going contact with the services is difficult. Women tend to have put an enormous amount of energy into keeping the pregnancy and birth a secret and so they have little energy left for opening up to a health professional in a counselling relationship. Building up this relationship can also be also hampered by a woman's social isolation, which may have been necessary to keep the pregnancy a secret.

Counsellors are conscious of the medical risks in disclosing the pregnancy late and they encourage women to come into a centre so that they can start a process of care for her. The first step of this process of care is to make contact with the social worker attached to the hospital, then medical appointments can be arranged. There is a further challenge in trying to remain calm, steady and assess a situation quickly in an emergency, for example when a woman makes contact when she is in labour and in a distressed state.

9.3.4   *Time pressures and intensive nature of response required*

A woman may be trying to identify someone in the clinic in whom they can confide. Being very busy may mean that a staff member can 'miss out on the signs' given by a woman indicating her wish to disclose or confide in them. The intensity of the work involved when a woman presents late and the time pressures mean this may not be a relaxed consultation as medical staff may be inpatient or annoyed with her for presenting late. When the disclosure of concealment is made the response a woman needs is wide-ranging, covering the medical, social, psychological, and emotional aspects of pregnancy, as well as the consequences of presenting late.

For counselling and social work staff, building sufficient trust to sustain on-going contact with the services is difficult as women tend to have put an enormous amount of energy into keeping the pregnancy and birth a secret such that they have little energy left for opening up to a health professional in a counselling relationship. The level of support required means that a woman's care is prioritised. The intensified response needed places additional demands on staff time and can take them away from other cases.

Medical staff expressed the view that it was becoming more and more difficult to give time to a woman who presents late because of their increasing workloads. This is problematic, as continuity of care would be their preferred response.

9.3.5   *Managing the contact between mother and baby*

In the case where a woman does not want any contact with the baby, staff will have an increased workload in that the baby, who would otherwise be 'rooming-in' with their mother, needs to be provided with alternative accommodation and care. The extra resources this demands are particularly an issue at weekends.

9.3.6   *Managing contact between a woman and family members*

Managing the contact between the woman and family members after the baby is born can be difficult. Social workers and counsellors working with young women have found that the disclosure of pregnancy to family members, or the birth itself, can trigger unresolved family issues or unexpected feelings. The challenge for social workers or counsellors in this context is knowing when to limit their own involvement and when it's time to refer family members on to other services.

Staff referred to specific challenges raised when the woman is young, particularly under eighteen years old. Where a young woman presents at a youth service, the youth workers let the young woman know that they can work with her for a short timeframe (a couple of weeks) but after that they are required to involved statutory services if she doesn't disclose to her parents or a relative. There is a lack of support for workers working with sexually active minors and there are no national guidelines in this area. Within the hospital setting, it can be very challenging when a woman presents with a family member but makes it clear she wants to keep the pregnancy and birth a secret. Where parents do become aware of the pregnancy some may not want their daughter to attend the hospital for antenatal care. From a social worker's perspective there is a further challenge in dealing with the tension and conflict that can arise with the woman's partner and his family.

9.3.7   Presentation 'out of hours'

Social workers do not have an out-of-hours on-call rota. As women often present 'out of hours' – at the weekend, during the night or during bank-holiday weekends – they could miss the social work service entirely. A woman could be returning home with a new baby and not have had any adjustment or preparation for the role of motherhood. Social workers have to find ways to address these issues very quickly.

Without the back-up support of the social work service during these times medical staff may be unable to provide an answer to a woman if they are not aware of the available services and facilities. This leaves the woman and the midwives in a 'limbo' state, not knowing the outcome for her and her baby.

9.3.8   Lack of facilities

When women are in-patients there are some situations where it would be most appropriate to accommodate them in a self-contained private room. However, lack of facilities makes this difficult. The availability of a private rooms with en-suites is limited, with the result that a woman often has to go out onto the corridor and risk being seen by members of the public. Alternatively, a woman may have to have the screen permanently pulled around her bed in the ward.

9.3.9   Confidentiality procedures

Maintaining a high level of secrecy around the pregnancy and the birth is critical for all women with concealed pregnancies, with some women requiring higher levels of secrecy than others. This level of secrecy may mean that a social worker is not aware of the woman's background, the circumstances surrounding the conception and the pregnancy and the exposure to risk the woman has experienced. It can also be very difficult for a social worker to fully explore with a woman her options in the available timeframe, particularly if adoption is being considered.

Women attending for outpatient appointments are often anxious to leave the hospital as soon as possible because they are uncomfortable in that setting or afraid of being recognised in the public space. Women may also want to avoid attending a public clinic or hospital in their own region due to the risk of identification. A tension thus arises for social workers between providing for a woman's safety and facilitating her wish to conceal the pregnancy.

While medical records containing all a woman's details would be marked confidential, staff are aware that a named woman's file could be seen by a member of the public as files are 'in transit' around the hospital. Meanwhile a woman may have fears that her files could be accessed under the Freedom of Information Act.

9.3.10   Adoption

Various tensions exist in providing support to a woman contemplating adoption. A social worker has to comply with a woman's wishes to maintain secrecy throughout the adoption process, which can be quite lengthy – anything from six weeks to a year. The social worker is continuously looking for feedback from a woman on her understanding of the process to ensure she is making informed decisions (in the context of protecting her need for confidentiality). Challenges connected with safeguarding a woman's need for concealment include a social worker not being able to visit her in her home and trying to encourage her continued engagement in the process. Meanwhile women contemplating adoption may neglect their own wellbeing by not acknowledging the emotional and psychological stress associated with the process.

Where a woman does not wish to disclose to the father a tension arises for the adoption agency, as they are legally obliged to consult with the birth father where possible. There are conditions, however, where the Adoption Board will accept an affidavit from the mother on her wish for non-contact with, and non-disclosure to, the birth father.

Women may not be fully aware of what the process of adoption involves. Counselling services described the difficulties they face when a woman contacts them wanting to bring her baby into the centre and leave the child in their care anonymously without wanting to engage in the adoption process. The services, meanwhile, are aware of how the woman's involvement is central to the adoption process.

9.3.11   Responding to migrant women

Members of minority ethnic communities also present specific challenges. The language barrier makes it more difficult for a social worker to respond effectively to her needs. Staff have to put in place the intensified comprehensive service for a woman who is presenting late with the added problem of the language barrier. The vulnerable situation a migrant woman is in was raised by counsellors and social workers, as the woman's legal situation can feed into concealment. The range of support a woman needs in this situation is greater. Reasons for this include:

- her unfamiliarity with the Irish health system
- her vulnerable position vis-à-vis her employer
- uncertainty around her maternity leave entitlement
- isolation
- accommodation needs
- financial pressures
- cultural differences, e.g. stigmatisation of lone motherhood in other cultures, rejection by family.

Liaising with medical staff so that a woman can stay longer in hospital, checking out a woman's legal situation, exploring alternative accommodation possibilities and negotiating with outside agencies are examples of some of the practical supports staff will be involved in.

9.4   Initiatives taken by professionals in response to concealed pregnancy

Health professionals interviewed were asked to describe any specific steps taken by them in responding to the needs of a woman who presents late in pregnancy without having disclosed it to her wider support network, particularly steps that go beyond the usual practices in their care setting. Their accounts illustrate practices adopted to meet the challenges outlined above. They provide an insight into systems for responding to women who present late in pregnancy; these could be implemented across the entire medical and support service settings represented in the interviews.

9.4.1   Individual nature of response

The fact that every woman's situation is different means that a different response is needed, depending on the particular context of a woman's social, emotional, psychological and medical needs and circumstances. Factors such as age, ethnicity, disability, sexuality and socio-economic background will also influence the response needed.

There usually is an intense level of involvement with a woman who presents late. Counsellors in crisis pregnancy support services described adopting a number of roles in supporting a woman presenting at an advanced stage of pregnancy incorporating both counselling and practical supports. Their involvement can include:

- providing on-going telephone contact and counselling in a calm, sensitive and open way so that she might agree to meet with the counsellor
- arranging meetings in alternative venues than the services premises to facilitate concealment
- being available during the night should a woman go into labour and accompanying a woman to hospital as she wishes.

Other steps that facilitate concealment but encourage contact with the statutory services may be taken, such as contacting a hospital beforehand and making an arrangement to enter through the back door rather than through the main entrance of the hospital. The support of a counsellor is crucial to a woman who presents at the onset of, or during, labour.

Medical staff try to explore with a woman the level of support she has available to her. If she is not inclined to open up to staff, they would look for other signs that might indicate her emotional and support needs, such as body language. Staff anticipate that a woman may be upset at discovering she is pregnant and try to convey to the woman that they are available and supportive by being open, warm and friendly. The view was expressed that a midwife needs to be confident and experienced to be able to sensitively care for a woman who has presented late.

A woman would be referred to pastoral care if an abnormality was detected on her scan or if the pregnancy was not on-going. Pastoral care tends to be used more by family members and relatives.

9.4.2   Integrated response to late/unbooked presentation

In the usual outpatient clinic routine a 'booking' or first visit would not normally be prioritised. However, when a woman presents late in pregnancy the team prioritise her visit. Members of staff work co-operatively and as part of a team to carry the extra workload in order to prioritise her needs. Staff are careful not to bombard the woman with too much information or too many people in the first visit. An antenatal education programme tailored to the needs and wishes of the woman is offered. This includes the option of an intensive, once off, one-to-one session, and this is offered even to those planning to give birth in another hospital. In the antenatal outpatient department, where administrative staff at the front desk have concerns about a woman's situation they will inform medical staff; for example where a woman checks in at the clinic but disappears afterwards.

Where a woman presents to the accident and emergency department with symptoms that are subsequently diagnosed as a pregnancy two priorities are attended to. Firstly, staff arrange for a midwife to take over the woman's care and to transfer her to the maternity unit as soon as possible. Secondly, staff would facilitate a woman's wishes regarding disclosure or non-disclosure to family members who have accompanied her to the hospital. Staff liaising with family members try to deter them from seeing the woman, especially if she has been transferred to the maternity ward.

Normally medical and nursing staff would not have much time to spend with a woman to explore her social, emotional and counselling needs. All women who present late, without an appointment, or whose demeanour gives rise to concerns for medical staff are referred to a social worker. They explain the role of the medical social worker to her, and assure her that she can speak to her in confidence. A woman may or may not agree to meet with the social worker on her first visit. If medical staff are very concerned about a woman's well-being they ring the social worker immediately and arrange a direct appointment with her. Women who do not attend the social worker on first referral are given contact details for the social worker and the social worker will receive a referral card informing her of the woman's presentation. The woman may present at a later stage. If this happens the social worker will be familiar with her situation. If a woman says that she has her own social worker, antenatal care staff would nevertheless inform her of the role of the medical social worker and encourage her to meet with her.

In the case where a woman arrives at a hospital in labour, usually presenting to the accident and emergency department, if time allows she will be transferred. If the woman is in advanced labour, especially where there is no maternity unit on site, efforts are made to source somebody on site with training in the area to assist in the delivery. Accident and emergency staff can organise her scan and analysis of bloods and make contact with the obstetric teams and social worker from their department. Maternity staff explain to a woman who presents in labour the essential elements of antenatal education, including what will happen to her during the process of delivering the baby, pain relief, anaesthesia/analgesia and feeding the baby. Maternity care staff provide a woman with education on breast-feeding at the first opportunity, so that she can make an informed choice about feeding her baby. Most women who are placing their baby for fostering or adoption do not wish to breast-feed, and staff facilitate their wishes in this regard.

A woman who presents to hospital unaccompanied is considered to have high support needs. The maternity care staff do not normally leave a woman on her own in a room and try to be with her throughout the labour. Every effort is made to ensure she has the one-to-one support of a midwife during birth. Medical and nursing staff all recognised the importance of not dwelling on the reasons why a woman has presented late without having attended for antenatal care.

9.4.3   Scheduling of appointments
A woman is encouraged to attend the antenatal clinic regularly after her first visit. More regular visits are scheduled where necessary to ensure a woman attends for the

recommended number of consultations during pregnancy. It is common for women to miss subsequent appointments. If a woman does not present for follow-up appointments, a second one is made for her and if she fails to attend that one, the consultant normally notifies her GP by post. However, this procedure is dependent on having contact details for the woman and her GP. Where women request no correspondence from the hospital the social worker is notified of failure to attend appointments and she follows this up.

9.4.4   In-patient confidentiality procedures

The issue of disclosure during antenatal care and after delivery is discussed with the woman as early as possible. Confidentiality procedures are organised by a social worker, who informs maternity care staff of the arrangements; procedures include:

- no correspondence is sent to a woman's family address
- her details are not available on her chart
- her details are not available at the hospital's reception, as in the usual practice
- no information is given to any member of the public about her hospital visit and stay
- a woman would sign a confidentiality form in which the hospital would deny all knowledge that she is attending there for care
- a woman's name does not appear on the ward notice board; 'occupied' appears instead.

In a general hospital women may be accommodated in another department both before and after the delivery. In this way a woman can conceal the pregnancy and birth by pretending to be attending the hospital for other treatment.

A woman's wishes will be accommodated as far as possible in terms of providing her with a private room. A single room is always requested for a woman contemplating adoption whether she's concealing the pregnancy or not.

When handing over shifts, medical staff inform the nurse coming on duty of a particular woman's need for confidentiality. As far as practicable, one member of staff looks after a woman who has presented late.

In a situation where a woman has had a concealed pregnancy in the past, and placed her baby in foster care or for adoption, medical staff will facilitate her need for secrecy and will, for example, keep her chart in the office. On her chart it is written that it is her first pregnancy and she is being treated accordingly.

9.4.5   Special arrangements

Women can be referred to services providing funded residential accommodation prior to and after delivery if they express an interest in this option. In general the accommodation is available for six months for a woman and baby but it may be longer depending on a particular woman's needs. Women can go at any stage prior to the birth.

Arrangements can be made for the birth to take place in another hospital. Copies of the woman's antenatal care notes can be given to her to bring to that hospital. Social workers from her Health Service Executive area liaise with the hospital and conduct follow-up care on the woman's behalf.

Social workers can make arrangements with a woman to meet her outside of clinic hours and outside of the hospital at a suitable location, as it is not always possible for her to come to the hospital during clinic hours. This is particularly important for women concealing their pregnancy from family members or from an employer.

9.4.6   Postnatal care

Where a woman presents in labour, the question of confidentiality and disclosure is discussed after the birth, along with her options regarding parenting or adoption. Social work staff often organise essential practical items for the woman during her hospital stay, such as clothing for herself and the baby.

Both parenting and adoption are discussed with the woman and parenting is considered in the context of lone parenting, joint parenting or parenting with the support of her community, family or friends.

Medical and social work staff establish women's wishes concerning contact with the baby after delivery in a non-judgemental way. However, there is a consensus that it is better to err on the side of encouraging contact, in the belief that this will help her make a more informed decision on her options. If she has discussed her options with a social worker prior to delivery, maternity staff may be aware of her wish for contact with the baby or not. There is no problem if a woman changes her mind about having contact with her baby after the birth.

Where a woman does not wish to have contact with her baby, maternity care staff make arrangements for the baby to be taken care of in the nursery or the special-care baby unit. A woman can still go and see her baby in the special-care baby unit any time she wishes.

A woman may wish to discharge herself as early as possible after delivery. In this case, social workers always work intensively with the woman, providing her with information on the follow-up supports available to her. In circumstances where the baby is being placed for adoption and not going home with the woman social workers will work to arrange completion of preliminary paperwork. Where there is a possibility that a woman may self-discharge 'out of hours' the social worker will ask her to sign a form granting permission for the baby to be placed in the care of the Health Service Executive, from where s/he can be placed in foster care. Her signature also allows for any medical treatment for the baby or transfer to another hospital.

Where a woman goes to stay in residential accommodation after the baby is born, her social worker will meet her for a follow-up visit. A social worker can arrange the woman's postnatal care by making an appointment with the public health nurse – with the woman's permission. In a situation where a woman does not wish to attend her GP or public health nurse for her aftercare, a social worker can make a specific arrangement for a return visit to the hospital.

Counsellors from counselling and support services can continue their involvement with a woman for as long as she needs it. In terms of follow up, they give a woman their phone number and she is then able to contact them at any stage in the future. A woman may need information related to custody issues, her entitlements, or she may have another crisis pregnancy.

9.4.7   Fostering and adoption

Where a woman decides to place her baby for fostering or adoption, the notification of birth is sent to her local health authority, where the foster parents will also reside. In the case of concealment two separate files are created – one on the mother and one on the baby – so that the baby is not linked to the original information of the mother's. Once a woman has decided to place her baby for adoption the social worker meets with her once a week to discuss the decision in-depth and whether she wishes to see the baby while it is in foster care. Adoption agency staff always let a woman know that she can meet with them at any stage during the process or afterwards.

Before the woman leaves the baby with the hospital a social worker offers to take a photograph of the mother and baby together and – if the woman wishes – a photograph of the baby alone. If a woman places her baby in pre-adoption foster care, the public health nurse for her area will not be contacted to inform her of the birth, a practice intended to protect the woman's confidentiality.

9.4.8   Presentation of young women

If a woman is under eighteen years of age and presents late during normal working hours, medical staff will contact the social worker immediately, and perhaps pastoral care. When a woman presents 'out of hours' members of staff will talk to the parents and try to establish their level of knowledge about their daughter's situation. In the majority of cases family members have no idea that the woman is pregnant.

9.5   Overview of caregivers' response to women concealing pregnancy

There was evidence that caregivers do assume responsibility, through providing a tailored response on the ground to the individual needs and circumstances of women who present with a concealed pregnancy. However, the issue of concealed pregnancy has not been addressed in any structured, systematic or integrated way to date in healthcare settings. Responses are usually implemented on an ad-hoc basis, and in some instances they are dependent on the level of experience, goodwill and sensitivity of individuals.

The accounts of the health professionals who participated in the study demonstrated that there was agreement on the specific challenges they experience when a woman presents in an advanced stage of pregnancy. Their response to these challenges, however, differs according to their professional background and training, be that from within a medical, social work, or counselling approach.

Health professionals' accounts revealed evidence of good practices that have developed organically in response to women who present late. These good practices can be drawn on in the development of a national framework for the management of concealed pregnancy. Caregivers have adapted their approach, processes, and systems to facilitate aspects of concealment; for example, using a pseudonym when a woman attends at the antenatal clinic to facilitate her need for confidentiality.

10.0   Conclusions

10.1   Conclusions

A review of international and national literature indicates that concealed pregnancy is not a thing of the past but rather remains present throughout contemporary western societies. This study of concealed pregnancy focused on researching the accounts of women who give birth in hospital after concealing their pregnancy for a substantial part or all of the pregnancy. It is important to bear in mind that this represents one group of women who conceal their pregnancy. Women who conceal a pregnancy either present late to hospital and deliver the baby there or never present to hospital and usually have an unassisted birth resulting in either a live birth or death of the baby before, during or after birth. Death of the baby following birth can either take the form of death by passivity, due to a lack of care and sustenance or due to infanticide. Women may leave live babies in a public place in the hope they will be found and cared for. Each year reports emerge of bodies of newborn infants found or newborn infants anonymously abandoned. In Ireland for the ten-year period between 1996 and 2005 there were 24 such reports; eighteen referred to bodies of babies found and six referred to live babies. For the six months from January to June 2005, bodies of two infants were found in the West and Midlands. These reports indicate the presence of a group of women not covered by this study who conceal their pregnancies and give birth without ever making contact with health or social services. The deep sensitivity surrounding this issue means that these women's accounts could not be included in the study. However, in considering the issue from the perspective of service responses it is important to bring these women back into the frame.

The question remains as to how complete is our understanding of the prevalence of concealed pregnancy. At the international level a number of initiatives indicate the persistence of this issue as an area of concern. However, international studies highlight difficulties in estimating prevalence. Nationally and internationally data on the incidence of concealed pregnancy is inadequate. In the Irish context the information-recording and reporting systems of maternity hospitals do not allow for any reliable conclusions to be drawn on the number of deliveries in hospital following a concealed pregnancy.

Notwithstanding these limitations, the present research does represent a significant contribution to our understanding of concealed pregnancy. The research draws on a range of data sources. It involved a study group of 51 women in secondary data analysis, thirteen women in qualitative interviews and focus groups with health professionals. In the current study the focus of inquiry was extended beyond the usual concern with medical outcomes to include the social factors and processes entailed in concealed pregnancy. A synthesis of literature reviewed demonstrated that three typologies of concealed pregnancy have been advanced: unconscious denial, conscious denial and concealment. These are discussed in detail in Chapter 5. The qualitative interviews generated for this research were analysed to assess the 'fit' of these typologies to the phenomenon of concealed pregnancy as observed in contemporary Irish context and seek to refine them.

In the literature 'having no subjective awareness of being pregnant throughout the majority of the pregnancy or even up to a totally unexpected sudden delivery', was attributed to the typology of 'unconscious denial' and explained as a coping mechanism invoked by the woman. However the evidence generated in this research indicates that those whose experiences of pregnancy could be characterised in this way were an outcome of failure to detect the pregnancy on the part of the physicians' women were attending. Thus rather than attributing the processes entailed in being pregnant without having any subjective awareness to individual women, this indicates that such processes may be attributable to other actors, systems or factors. Thus, based on analysis of this study data the typology attributed to having no subjective awareness of being pregnant is an 'undetected pregnancy'. The second typology 'conscious denial' has been characterised as 'where the fact of the pregnancy is recognised but the woman continues to deny it to herself and others, thereby cognitively realising the pregnancy but not displaying emotions associated with pregnancy'. This typology and characterisation did fit well with the analysis of some women's accounts, which indicated that this was a coping mechanism women invoked because the reality of the pregnancy was unimaginable to them and the possibility of pregnancy represented anxiety or pain as well as a very real threat for them. The final typology of 'concealment', characterised as 'a woman acknowledging the pregnancy to herself but hiding it from others', also seemed to fit with the accounts of the larger group of study participants. The notion of concealment as a coping strategy invoked by women also fitted, and while the factors related to concealment in the literature were observed in the analysis, two other emerging aspects supplemented them.

A final consideration in relation to these typologies is the extent to which they discretely characterise the entire account of the pregnancy or whether women can move between typologies within one pregnancy experience. The first typology of 'undetected pregnancy' seemed to operate as a discrete typology. However, this was not the case for either typologies of 'conscious denial' or 'concealment'. Considering the second typology of 'conscious denial', our analysis demonstrated that women could embark on the expected behaviours associated with pregnancy, such as telling others and attending for antenatal care, while continuing to suspend emotions associated with pregnancy. Secondly women moved out of the typology of 'conscious denial' only to enter into a process of 'concealment'. In relation to concealment, women's practices challenge the notion of 'concealment' or disclosure as discrete events and rather suggest that there are multiple domains relevant to the process of 'concealment' spanning the services domain, the family domain and the social domain. Women demonstrated a capacity to move out of one typology, 'conscious denial', by disclosing to the services domain while continuing the process of 'concealment' within the family and/or social domain. In addition, within each domain disclosure can be full or partial such that in the latter case some features of concealment persist.

The three typologies outlined above demonstrate how a diversity of factors give rise to a concealed pregnancy and a range of processes are entailed in that concealment. Analysis of women's accounts illustrated that a range of physiological, social, cultural and psychological factors converge in the concealment of pregnancy. Analysis of the processes or strategies women employed to conceal the pregnancy illustrated how they were related to the typologies outlined above. Women were involved in a fine balance of taking action so as to hide the pregnancy while at the same time not appearing to look or act any differently in any aspect of their lives to avoid raising any suspicions that they might be pregnant. The process of concealment was complex and there was consensus among the women on the intensity of the time, effort and stress entailed in keeping the pregnancy concealed.

The implications of concealed pregnancy discussed in the literature emphasised poorer outcomes for the baby in terms of birth weight in particular. This was attributed to the dual absence of antenatal care and adaptation to pregnancy. While a systematic analysis of fetal outcomes for our study group is beyond the scope of this research, the analysis broadened our understanding of how the concealment of their pregnancy results in a range of biological, social and emotional implications, as well as impacting on women's personal relationships.

These insights into the factors, processes and implications arising from concealed pregnancy provided an important backdrop for our analysis of women's accounts of contacts with services. Difficulty in engaging with services at all, acute feelings of stigma and sensitivity, and the intensity of stress and anxiety women felt all shaped their needs and expectations when they eventually made contact with services - in some cases only at the point of delivery.

11.0 Recommendations on responding to needs of women concealing a pregnancy across relevant care settings

A primary objective of this study was to generate recommendations to guide and inform the planning and development of a national framework of services responding to concealed pregnancy in medical, social, counselling and support services settings throughout the health services on a national basis. The findings of this research highlight how the situation for every woman concealing her pregnancy is unique and requires a tailored response depending on her particular social, emotional, psychological and physiological circumstances. The recommendations below strive to ensure such a tailored approach is forthcoming. They seek to address the range of social, cultural, psychological and physiological factors that give rise to concealment of pregnancy as well as setting out best practice principles for responding to women concealing a pregnancy across all relevant care settings.

11.1 Recommendations to the Crisis Pregnancy Agency

11.1.1 Cultural context

Until the cultural stigma of non-marital pregnancy is addressed, women will continue to feel a need to conceal their pregnancies. In its 2004-2006 Strategy to Address the Issue of Crisis Pregnancy the CPA has committed to actions in relation to influencing cultural change. These incorporate an advocacy and cultural changes project, public information campaigns and specific work with the media. The factors contributing to concealment of pregnancy should be centrally addressed in these actions. The persistence of stigma towards non-marital pregnancy and, in particular, the strong stigma attaching to a pregnancy outside of the context of an established relationship described by women in this research should be addressed. The latter issue relates both to social attitudes towards lone mothers and the role of men in assuming responsibility when a pregnancy occurs. The range of social and emotional implications of concealing a pregnancy identified through this research should also be taken into account in designing initiatives in this area.

Media treatment of concealed pregnancy should be closely monitored by the Agency and representations made to newspaper editors highlighting examples of insensitive reporting. Contact information for relevant support services should also be made available to editors for inclusion in stories relating to this topic.

11.1.2 Include concealed pregnancy in education initiatives

The Agency's strategy document for 2004-2006 identifies the Department of Education as a partner organisation in its work relating to preventative actions, particularly through the delivery of relationship and sexuality education. The strategy also cites plans to develop national information-, knowledge- and skills-based programmes, including specific initiatives aimed at third-level students. These programmes should incorporate two components relevant to the issue of concealment of pregnancy. Firstly, as a preventative measure, programmes should teach participants to recognise the symptoms of pregnancy and raise awareness of the benefits of early pregnancy testing and antenatal care attendance. They should also inform of the range of professional support services available for women who do not wish to disclose a pregnancy to their family or social network. Secondly, the factors, processes and support needs associated with concealed pregnancy should be incorporated, so as to build the capacity of young people to recognise and provide support should members of their peer group conceal a pregnancy.

11.1.3   *Address concealment of pregnancy as specific theme within 'Positive Options' campaign*

Drawing on the insights generated by this research, particularly regarding the factors and processes entailed in concealed pregnancy, a public information campaign should be devised as part of the 'Positive Options' campaign. This should aim to connect with women who may be concealing a pregnancy and inform them of the range of professional support services available, as well as highlighting the benefits of early pregnancy testing and antenatal care attendance. These messages should be targeted both at women who suspect they may be pregnant but find it difficult to acknowledge this possibility and those who suspect someone close may be pregnant but are unsure how to broach the subject. The latter could take the format of public information campaigns highlighting signals a person may convey when concealing a pregnancy, similar to campaigns highlighting the issues of depression or suicide.

11.1.4   *Address perceptions of adoption*

An information campaign on the contemporary process for adoption should be developed, emphasising new 'open' forms of adoption and informing women of what modern-day adoption entails. This should include information on services, including residential support services to support women during their pregnancy who plan to place a baby for adoption.

11.1.5   *Develop and deliver skills training programme for frontline staff on responding to women concealing a pregnancy*

A core part of a strategy to respond to women concealing a pregnancy is raising awareness of this issue among 'frontline' caregivers. The Agency should develop a 'sensitisation training' programme aimed at:

- Raising awareness of concealed pregnancy. This should address aspects such as prevalence, contributory factors, processes of concealment, implications of concealment, related support needs and a comprehensive list of support services.
- Providing basic counselling-skills training to develop caregivers' capacity to be understanding and provide reassurance to women who disclose a pregnancy either in advanced pregnancy or at point of delivery. This could include informing women of others who have had similar experiences.
- Informing caregivers of the range of support services available to women concealing their pregnancy and providing resource materials enabling them to pass this information on to women.
- Providing training on appropriate ways of informing a woman about the detection of a pregnancy at advanced pregnancy, emphasising that no assumptions should be made that the woman will be prepared for or accepting of such information.
- Addressing different cultural understandings and responses to pregnancy and the consequences of these; for example, in some cultures pregnancy is

connected more with a community focus whereas in other cultures pregnancy is situated in the individual and family context.

The target group for receiving this training should at least reflect all of those professional caregivers who were targeted for this research, including:

- midwives
- nursing staff in antenatal/maternity settings
- administrative staff in antenatal/maternity settings
- antenatal educators
- staff of accident and emergency departments
- medical social workers
- consultant obstetricians
- HSE social workers
- crisis pregnancy counsellors
- adoption agency social workers
- general practitioners.

A range of partnerships will need to be developed by the Agency to deliver the training across the range of professional groups and settings necessary to ensure that all the appropriate caregivers are targeted. Many of these partnerships have already been forged by the Agency, so that this initiative could form an extension of existing work. Models of delivering training on domestic violence across diverse health settings and caregivers could be referred to for guidance in designing the delivery of the training.

Some suggestions on approaches to delivery are:

- Training should be delivered on site in all maternity hospitals and hospitals with maternity departments. It should target consultants in obstetrics, registrars in obstetrics, midwives, nurses, antenatal educators, medical social workers, administration staff involved in booking patients and accident and emergency staff.
- Through partnership with the Irish College of General Practitioners (ICGP). Training could be delivered to GPs though the ICGP's regional colleges or through the co-operative structure recently established at county level. Opportunities to incorporate this issue onto the curriculum of professional training for General Practice should also be explored.
- The Institute of Obstetricians and Gynaecologists should be consulted on a strategy for delivering training to consultants in this area.
- Training should be delivered to counsellors through their affiliate agencies. Opportunities to incorporate this issue onto the curriculum of professional training in counselling should also be explored.
- Opportunities to incorporate this issue onto the curriculum of professional training for general practice, social work, midwifery and/or nursing and obstetrics should be explored.

11.1.6   Host regular forum for continued sharing of information on concealed pregnancy

As demonstrated throughout this report, each woman's concealed pregnancy is individual. Caregivers can generate significant learning and insights by reflecting on the situation of and challenges arising for each individual woman presenting with a concealed pregnancy. To facilitate on-going learning in this area, it is recommended that the Crisis Pregnancy Agency host a regular symposium, bringing together staff from all antenatal/maternity hospitals and departments to share accounts of cases of concealed pregnancy presenting in the interim period. The focus would be for caregivers to draw out common learning in relation to understanding concealed pregnancy, identifying challenges arising and highlighting good practice in responding to concealed pregnancy. Medical social workers in each hospital/department represent the most appropriate professionals to liaise with the Agency in this initiative and to lead their workplaces' input into the seminar. Given issues of confidentiality this should be a closed symposium. Regularity of the forum should be no more than every year but no less than every three years.

11.1.7   *Include concealed pregnancy in 'Key Contacts' project*

Resources developed to build competency among groups identified as 'Key Contacts' (including public health nurses, youth workers and teachers) should be extended to include a section on concealed pregnancy. The aim should be to raise awareness of the factors, processes and support needs associated with concealed pregnancy, to develop competency among key contacts to take an assertive, non-judgemental approach to checking out suspicions of pregnancy and to resource them to provide information and assistance to women concealing a pregnancy on accessing support services.

The principles cited in the 'Key Contacts Resource' developed by the Crisis Pregnancy Agency and the Southern Health Board for responding to a teenage client should be reiterated when dealing with concealed pregnancy. In particular, while acknowledging that parents should be involved from the earliest stage where possible, women should be reassured that they can consent to medical treatment and examination without parental consent if they are over the age of sixteen years.

The Agency should also target other therapeutic environments where women at risk of concealed pregnancy may present (such as treatment centres for substance use or rape and sexual abuse) with resources to build competency in dealing with a concealed pregnancy. In these settings the aim should be to provide a comprehensive, non-judgemental response that integrates obstetric care with the other appropriate therapeutic treatments.

11.1.8   *Include concealed pregnancy in resources developed for parents*

Resources developed to build competency among parents on sexual health, relationships and crisis pregnancy should be extended to include a section on concealed pregnancy. As with Key Contacts, the aim should be to develop competency among parents to take an assertive, non-judgemental approach to checking out suspicions of pregnancy. The resource should also help parents to provide information and assistance to women on accessing support services. More generally, parents should be advised and assisted on how to combine messages encouraging sexual responsibility with encouragement to disclose a pregnancy should this occur.

11.1.9   *Include concealed pregnancy in resources developed for primary care*

A comprehensive guide to antenatal care should be developed for distribution by primary caregivers. The guide should outline:

- providers of care and their roles
- current guidelines for antenatal care
- advice on additional recommended care e.g. antenatal classes
- universal medical schemes applicable to antenatal care
- maternity and postnatal care (i.e. Combined Antenatal Care system)
- semi-private and private systems
- pregnancy counselling and support services
- social work services
- basic information on what women should expect during the different stages of pregnancy and at the on-set of labour.

The particular need among members of migrant communities for this information should be taken into account. Multi-lingual versions are necessary, and these should begin with a simple, basic guide to the structure of the health services in Ireland.

11.1.10   Enhance linkages between crisis pregnancy counselling services and antenatal/maternity care settings

The experience from the two hospital settings where this research was conducted demonstrated that women concealing their pregnancy are more likely to attend counselling when the service is directly linked with the antenatal or maternity departments of a hospital. The Agency should explore how linkages can be further enhanced between crisis pregnancy counselling services and all antenatal and maternity care settings.

11.2   Recommendations to Crisis Pregnancy Counselling and Support Services and Agencies funded by the CPA

Crisis Pregnancy Counselling and Support Services attached to each HSE area should initiate contact with Medical Social Workers in every antenatal and maternity department within their region to devise a shared protocol ensuring that each woman presenting with a concealed pregnancy will be referred to a CPCSS counsellor.

Services and agencies should ensure that all staff participate in sensitisation training on concealed pregnancy when this has been developed by the Crisis Pregnancy Agency.

Counselling services and agencies should develop a protocol referring women who present with a concealed pregnancy without having attended for antenatal care for same. Following the combined care system, the referral should be to a GP acceptable to the woman. It should further be explained to the woman that the GP will refer her on to a maternity hospital. Resources developed by the Crisis Pregnancy Agency outlining antenatal care (as part of the 'Key Contacts' initiative) should be distributed to women continuing a pregnancy.

Where staff accompany a woman to a GP surgery, they should take great care to respect a woman's right to a confidential consultation with her GP and only accompany her into consultation where the woman makes a clear, informed decision that she would like the counsellor to be present.

The recommendation made in Conlon's (2005) report on crisis pregnancy counselling services regarding enhancing access to services by developing alternative formats for delivery is reiterated here. Alternative formats include out-reach, drop-in and out-of-hours options and exploring the potential of a counsellor-staffed telephone help-line to reach women. In particular, telephone counselling and out-reach services would have gone some way to addressing barriers cited by women in this study.

11.3   Recommendations to General Practitioners

GPs should routinely but sensitively question young women in their client group about sexual activity, and the benefits of responding early to suspicions of pregnancy should be discussed.

GPs should be more proactive in the administration of pregnancy tests and adopt a principle of testing to screen for pregnancy rather than testing to confirm a pregnancy. Taking this approach, reporting one indicator of pregnancy would be sufficient to prompt the administration of a test. GPs should not take the absence or contra-indication of another symptom as disconfirming a pregnancy (such as continuation of bleeding or reports of episodes of unprotected sex without a pregnancy in the past by either partner). Recommendations are made below to the Health Service Executive regarding the funding of pregnancy testing to resource GPs for such an approach.

In particular, GPs should administer a pregnancy test before administration of each round of injectable contraceptives, in light of the possibility of pregnancy during the first number of days after administration or in the event of any gap in cover due to delays in repeat administration. At an absolute minimum, pregnancy tests should be administered before the second round of injectable contraception.

Where a woman presents with persistent symptoms indicating pregnancy following a negative result from a test to detect the presence of hormones in the urine or blood, other methods to rule out a pregnancy should be considered. This would include the use of a handheld ultrasound device, which can generally pick up and transmit the sounds of the baby's heart rate after twelve weeks. Referral to hospital for an ultrasound scan should also be considered.

When a woman presents to a GP in advanced pregnancy it is imperative that this – often first – engagement with health services regarding this pregnancy is fully optimised as regards retaining women's engagement with the care system. The GP should take an active role in ensuring that the woman makes further appointments to continue her antenatal care. The GP should always take responsibility for organising booking appointments with hospitals where a woman is concealing a pregnancy. Before the woman leaves their surgery the GP should:

- fully advise her of her entitlements under the Combined Antenatal Care scheme
- telephone the hospital to make an appointment at the earliest possible time, explaining that the woman is presenting late
- send a follow-up letter of referral directly to the hospital confirming the woman's details and, again, highlighting that the woman is presenting late in pregnancy
- make an appointment for her return visit to the surgery.

11.4   Recommendations to antenatal and maternity hospitals/departments

11.4.1   Addressed to hospital managers

A holistic, integrated approach to providing for the care needs of a woman who is presenting late is important, where doctors, midwives, nurses, social workers, counsellors, antenatal educators and administrative staff work together. This should be led by the on-site social worker or crisis pregnancy counsellor. To facilitate its early implementation, a protocol should be established throughout all hospital departments that social workers/counsellors are notified of all women who are more than twenty weeks pregnant at their first presentation.

Medical social workers play a key role in responding to the needs of women who conceal their pregnancy. It is imperative, therefore, that every antenatal/maternity hospital/department have at least one on-site social worker. Consideration should also be given to making this service available on an on-call basis during out-of-hours periods. Throughout this research we saw how it is highly likely that women concealing a pregnancy will present out of hours. Moreover, turnover of patients in maternity departments can mean that women presenting in labour may be admitted, delivered and discharged within the out-of-hours period. An on-call social work service would ensure all women presenting with a concealed pregnancy would get the opportunity to meet with a social worker.

This research highlighted how women felt very self-conscious while in the public space of antenatal clinics. Anxieties and fears were exacerbated by a system that required long periods of sitting in a public communal waiting area and women's names being called out when it came their turn for treatment. Having to discuss personal details with staff in public areas or hearing staff discuss patients' personal details in public areas also caused alarm. This system should be reviewed to consider:

- how women's confidentiality can be better safeguarded
- how long waiting times may be eliminated, e.g. by replacing block booking with staggered appointments or by offering women the option of attending smaller outreach clinics, where available
- how facilities can be organised so that appropriate private spaces are available for all medical and social assessments.

This study highlighted significant discrepancies in the extent to which women attending antenatal care as private patients were linked in with support services, as compared with women attending public clinics. Managers should review procedures for referring women who present late in pregnancy with consultants operating private clinics. The protocol recommended above, that social workers/counsellors should be notified of all women who first present when they are more than twenty weeks pregnant, should be implemented in private as well as public clinics.

11.4.2   Addressed to Nurse Managers of antenatal outpatient departments

Once a woman discloses a pregnancy either in advanced pregnancy or at the point of delivery, caregivers should prioritise being empathetic and reassuring. Staff should be encouraged to give one-to-one attention to the woman and share their experience and knowledge of women in similar situations. Caregivers should not focus on negative aspects when a woman presents late, but should focus on developing a relationship with her and encouraging her to come back and attend appointments. Issues like difficulty estimating estimated date of delivery should be handled sensitively and the reasons for such difficulty fully explained to women in a non-judgemental way.

As stated above, a holistic, integrated approach to providing for the care needs of a woman who is presenting late is important, where doctors, midwives, nurses, social workers, counsellors, antenatal educators and administrative staff work together. This should be led by the medical social worker. To facilitate its early implementation, a protocol should be established that medical social workers are notified of all women who are more than twenty weeks pregnant at their first presentation. The medical social worker is in turn responsible for liaising with colleagues in the antenatal department to brief them appropriately on specific issues that will enhance their capacity to be empathetic and reassuring to the woman throughout her care there. Notwithstanding the recommendation above calling for an on-site Medical Social Work service in each hospital with antenatal and/or maternity departments, where this is not yet in place referral should be made to the community social work service.

Any probing to establish reasons why a woman is presenting late should only be undertaken by the medical social worker who has the highest level of counselling skills training.

Continuity of care is important, especially for women with concealed pregnancies. A woman concealing a pregnancy should ideally meet the same midwife, nurse, doctor or social worker each time she visits.

Close attention should be paid to handling women's information sensitively, and confidentiality should always be prioritised. All medical and social assessments should be conducted in appropriate private spaces. Patient details should never be discussed among staff members within audible range of other patients or members of the public.

Where a woman has arranged to give birth in another hospital, she should be provided with a full copy of her antenatal chart by the antenatal clinic to pass on to the maternity department of that hospital.

11.4.3   *Addressed to Medical Social Work Managers*

In this research on-site medical social workers emerged as key supports for women presenting late to antenatal or maternity departments. The following recommendations reflect our conclusion that as such medical social workers should play a lead role in caring for women who present to antenatal or maternity departments in advanced pregnancy or labour.

The first set of recommendations below relates to the care social workers should provide directly to a woman who presents late in pregnancy. Social workers should:

- Promote the implementation of a protocol that social workers are notified of all women first presenting when they are more than twenty weeks pregnant.
- Ensure that all women presenting late are offered a consultation with the social worker at this first presentation.
- Be proactive in ensuring the woman is clear that her consultation is intended to be on a one-to-one basis, and pursue this unless the woman explicitly requests the presence of a companion.

- Prioritise being empathetic and reassuring to women in all consultations. In particular, sensitivity should be shown in addressing the issue of partners, given the findings in this study regarding the stigma women felt about partners being absent. To reassure them of the reasons why partners feature in consultations women should have relevant legal and policy issues clearly explained; for example, legal requirements regarding the role of partners when a baby is being placed for adoption and the duty to pursue partners for maintenance support where a woman submits a claim for social welfare supports.

- Be alert to possible suicidal feelings in women concealing a pregnancy and screen for it, given that some women in this study encountered such feelings during their pregnancy.

- Undertake careful planning with the woman to agree on measures the hospital can put in place to safeguard her confidentiality in future communications with the hospital. Women should be advised on what information can be withheld from her chart should it become the subject of a request under the Freedom of Information Act.

- Refer all women concealing a pregnancy to the Crisis Pregnancy Counselling and Support Service attached to the region where the hospital is based.

- Make appropriate referral to health-board social workers, or adoption-agency social workers where the woman is contemplating adoption. Women contemplating adoption should have on-going contact and counselling with a social worker from the birth of the baby up to a period after signing the final consent forms.

- Inform women of other locally available counselling and support services for further help in coping with the emotional and social impact of the pregnancy, and make appropriate referrals. In particular, community-based services to support mothers such as young mothers' groups or community mothers' schemes should be highlighted.

- Act on the interest women in the study expressed in a peer-counselling approach to supporting women concealing their pregnancy. This would involve social workers asking women who concealed their pregnancy if they would be willing to be contacted to provide peer counselling to others who present in the future with a concealed pregnancy at the point of discharge from the service. All those agreeing could be placed on a register of peer counselling volunteers. Women subsequently presenting to the social worker with a concealed pregnancy could be offered the option of being introduced to a peer counsellor.

- Assess women's needs for emotional, social and practical support on an on-going basis at the point of discharge from the maternity ward. Women should be offered post-natal counselling to address issues including grief associated with placement of the baby or feelings of guilt about concealment of the pregnancy.

- Offer women who concealed a pregnancy the option of being 'de-briefed' about the birth of the baby, in recognition of the fact that the experience of childbirth can be impacted on in specific ways by the concealment process.

- Offer basic provisions to women who present unbooked in labour (such as personal care items and nightdresses for the woman and/or clothing for the baby) to alleviate some of the stresses this gives rise to.

The second set of recommendations designate lead responsibility to medical social worker(s) to liaise with colleagues of all relevant departments and brief them appropriately on specific issues relating to the woman's situation that will enhance their capacity to be empathetic and reassuring to the woman throughout her care in the hospital. Specifically medical social workers should:

- Liaise with the antenatal education department to ensure that an accelerated education and parenting programme, in keeping with that delivered to all women in antenatal care, is put in place.
- Liaise with administrative staff to advise them on procedures agreed with the woman for future communications between her and the hospital, as well as between the hospital and other health professionals, such as her GP or the public health nurse.
- Liaise with all relevant staff of the antenatal department to advise them of the woman's situation and any specific issues arising in her case that would better equip them to be sensitive and reassuring towards the woman.
- Liaise with midwifery and nursing staff of the maternity department as the woman reaches 36 weeks' gestation to advise them of her situation and any specific issues arising in her case that would better equip them to be sensitive and reassuring towards her in relation to childbirth, first contact with the baby, accommodation provision and room-in arrangements. Ensure the Maternity Department informs the medical social worker when the woman is admitted for delivery.
- Where a woman presents through the Accident and Emergency or another department in the hospital, staff there should be briefed on the woman's wishes regarding how they should respond to requests for information from companions.

11.4.4   Addressed to Antenatal Educators

An accelerated education and parenting programme, in keeping with that delivered to all women in antenatal care, should be put in place for women presenting late for antenatal care.

Women concealing their pregnancy should be offered the option of one-to-one intensive antenatal education sessions, in recognition of reticence expressed for group sessions. In addition, antenatal educators should assess whether younger, and/or single women might prefer group classes together. Consideration should also be given to delivering classes in the community in youth orientated settings.

Women concealing their pregnancy should be assessed for their need for specific interventions to prepare them for first contact with their baby, given women's accounts in the research of being unprepared for this. These interventions may even be required after delivery.

11.4.5   Addressed to Nurse Managers of maternity departments

A woman concealing a pregnancy who is admitted to the maternity department of a hospital will either have received some antenatal care in the same hospital or another hospital or will arrive unbooked. Staff should prioritise being empathetic and reassuring. Where the woman has been attending a medical social worker the information they provided during briefings to maternity staff on the woman's situation should be referred to. Medical social workers should be informed that the woman has been admitted at the earliest possible opportunity.

Where a woman is unaccompanied, the department should strive to offer her a team member who will act as a dedicated birthing partner to her during delivery. This staff member should be free to concentrate on supporting the woman, as opposed to having a role in assisting in the delivery. After the birth, the same member of staff should offer to de-brief the woman on the birth, in recognition that childbirth can be an even more stressful time for women who have concealed their pregnancy.

Women should be offered a range of options regarding accommodation, including a private room, group ward other than the post-natal ward or a post-natal group ward.

Women should be consulted regarding preference in relation to contact with the baby, including skin-to-skin contact immediately after delivery, rooming-in with the baby, placing baby in the care of staff with the intention of seeing him/her or placing baby in the care of staff without the intention of seeing him/her. They should also be offered counselling in preparation for first contact with the baby, in recognition of women's accounts of not being prepared for this event as a consequence of having concealed the pregnancy. The antenatal educator should be consulted on this.

Women should also be consulted regarding preference for feeding, including by bottle – using either infant formula or expressed breast milk – or feeding by breast.

11.5   Recommendations to Community/Adoption Agency Social Workers

Women in this study contemplating adoption highlighted a range of ways in which they found the approach of their social worker supportive and helpful to them in coming to a sound decision. The following recommendations reflect these:

– Women contemplating adoption should be given a full account of the adoption process from the outset. This should emphasise, in particular, procedures for direct and indirect means of contact between the woman and the child after placement.

– An on-going process of establishing women's consent should be engaged in, and women should be reassured that their decision is only final when the adoption order is made by the Adoption Board. Women should also be fully informed of the range of supports for mothers.

– Social workers should arrange for on-going contact between the woman, her child and the foster parents during the fostering process according to each woman's wishes. Women should be advised of the assistance this can be to her in coming to a decision. Women should be offered the option of being accompanied by her social worker at each visit.

– The social worker should strive to ensure the process of placement and adoption is as open as possible, in accordance with the woman's preference.

11.6   Recommendations to the Health Service Executive

11.6.1   Data information systems

Pregnancy denial and concealed pregnancies are not a thing of the past, they are very much of the moment, but a lack of rigorous data-collection and record-keeping to date has impeded the collation of data on concealed pregnancy. Procedures for systematically recording information on women presenting to hospital with a concealed pregnancy need to be devised. Medical social workers in maternity hospitals or departments represent the most reliable source of this information. The primary aim should be to generate prevalence data on concealed pregnancy at national level.

11.6.2   Resource GPs to screen for pregnancy

It is recommended above that GPs should be more proactive in the administration of pregnancy tests and adopt a principle of testing to screen for pregnancy rather than testing to confirm a pregnancy. To ensure that the cost of pregnancy test kits does not inhibit GPs in adopting such an approach it is recommended that the administration of all pregnancy tests should be provided on a universal, free basis funded under the General Medical Service, similar to the arrangements in place for Primary Childhood Immunisation. An alternative arrangement would be for the HSE to distribute a stock of pregnancy tests free of charge directly to all GPs for this purpose.

11.6.3   Resource increased coverage of social work services in antenatal/maternity settings

It is recommended that every antenatal/maternity hospital/department have at least one on-site social worker. It is further recommended that consideration should be given to making this service available on an on-call basis during out-of-hours periods. Implementing these recommendations will require additional resources from the HSE in many cases.

11.6.4   Review policy on fostering

This research demonstrated that concealed pregnancy can result in a woman giving birth without having engaged in a process of decision-making on her options regarding parenting or adoption. She may also have made no preparations for childbirth, meeting and caring for her child or introducing the child to her family and social network. These findings indicate a need to provide for the temporary care of the baby in such circumstances, to allow mothers the space to engage in such decision-making, planning and preparations at the post-natal stage. The system of foster care currently in place to care for the babies of women contemplating adoption could meet the needs of mothers during this time. We recommend that the criteria for placement in foster care be extended to include babies born following a concealed pregnancy where the mother requests it. A defined time-period for the provision of fostering of six weeks to three months would seem reasonable in such circumstances. Where women are contemplating adoption at the end of this time the baby could continue in foster care.

BIBLIOGRAPHY

Bonnet, C (1993) 'Adoption at birth: prevention against abandonment or neonaticide'. *Child Abuse & Neglect*, Vol. 17, 501–513.

Brezinka C, Huter O, Biebl W, Kinzl J (1994) 'Denial of pregnancy: obstetrical aspects'. *Journal of Psychosomatic Obstetrics & Gynaecology*, Vol. 15, 1–8.

Conlon, C. (2005) *Mixed Methods Research of Crisis Pregnancy Counselling and Support Services*. Crisis Pregnancy Agency, Dublin.

Craig, M (2004) 'Perinatal risk factors for neonaticide and infant homocide: can we identify those at risk?' In Journal of the Royal Society of Medicine, Vol.97, 57-61.

Crisis Pregnancy Agency (2005) *Crisis Pregnancy Agency Statistical Report 2005: Fertility and Crisis Pregnancy Indices*. Crisis Pregnancy Agency, Dublin.

Drescher-Burke, K., J. Krall and A. Penick (2004) 'Discarded Infants and Neonaticide. A review of the literature.' Berkeley, CA: National Abandoned Infants Assistance Resource Centre, School of Social Welfare, University of California at Berkeley.

Dulit, E. (2000) 'Girls who deny a pregnancy, girls who kill a neonate'. *Adolescent Psychiatry*, Vol. 25, 219-325.

Finnegan, P, E. McKinstry and G. Erlick Robinson (1982) 'Denial of Pregnancy and Childbirth.' In *Canadian Journal of Psychiatry*. Vol.27, December, 672-674.

Foster, J. E. and M. Jenkins (1987) 'A Schoolgirl with Onset of Anorexia Nervosa during a Concealed Pregnancy'. In *British Journal of Psychiatry*. Vol.150, 551-553.

Geary, M. (1997) 'Comparison of Liveborn and Stillborn Low Birth Weight Babies & Analysis of Aetiological Factors', *Irish Medical Journal*, Vol. 90 No. 7.

Gray, B. and L.Ryan (1997) '(Dis)locating 'Woman' and Woman in Representations of Irish Nationality.' In A. Byrne and M. Leonard (Eds) *Women and Irish Society. A Sociological Reader*. Blackstaff Press, Belfast.

Green, C.M. and Manohan, S. V. (1990) 'Neonaticide and Hysterical Denial of Pregnancy'. in *British Journal of Psychiatry*. Vol 156, 121-123

Guilbride, Alexis (2004) 'Infancticide; The Crime of Mothers.' In Kennedy, Patrica (Ed) *Motherhood in Ireland. Creation and Context*. Mercier Press, Dublin.

Haapasalo, J., Petaja, S. (1999) 'Mothers who killed or attempted to kill their child: life circumstances, childhood abuse, and types of killing'. *Violence and Victims*, Vol.14, 219–239

Hayes, J. (1985) *My Story*. Brandon Press, Kerry.

Inglis, Tom (2003) *Truth, Power and Lies. Irish Society and the Case of the Kerry Babies.'* University College Dublin Press, Dublin.

Kennedy, Patrica (Ed) (2004) *Motherhood in Ireland. Creation and Context*. Mercier Press, Dublin.

Mahon, E, Conlon, C. and Dillon, L. (1998) *Women and Crisis Pregnancy.* The Stationery Office, Government Publications, Dublin.

Maldonado-Duran, J.M., Lartigue, T. & Feintuch, (2000) 'Perinatal psychiatry: infant mental health interventions during pregnancy', *Bulletin of the Menninger Clinic*, Vol. 64 (3), 317-343.

McCafferty, N. (1985) *A woman to blame: the Kerry babies case.* Attic Press, Dublin.

Miller, LJ (2003) 'Denial of pregnancy'. In MG Spinelli. (Ed.), *Infanticide: Psychosocial and legal perspectives on mothers. who kill.* Washington, American Psychiatric Publishing.

Miller LJ (1991) 'Psychotic denial of pregnancy: phenomenology and clinical management'. *Hospital & Community Psychiatry*, Vol.41, 1233–1237.

Murphy-Lawless, J., Oaks, L. and Brady, C. (2004) *Understanding how sexually active women think about fertility, sex and motherhood.* Crisis Pregnancy Agency, Dublin.

National Maternity Hospital (2001) *Annual Clinical Report.* Dublin, National Maternity Hospital.

National Maternity Hospital (1999) *Annual Clinical Report.* Dublin, National Maternity Hospital.

O'Hare, A., Dean, G., Walsh, D., & McLoughlin, H. (1985). *Termination of pregnancy, England, 1984, Women from the Republic of Ireland.* Dublin: The Medico-Social Research Board.

Roussot, D. Buchmann, E.J., McIntyre, J.A. & Russell, J.M. (1998) 'Women who book late in pregnancy', *Journal of Cape Town Medical Association of South Africa*, Vol. 88, 905-908.

Sable, M., D. Wilkinson (2000) 'Impact of Perceived Stress, Major Life Events and Pregnancy Attitudes on Low Birth Weight.' In *Family Planning Perspectives.* Vol.32, No.6, 288-294.

Sadler, Catharine (2002) 'Mum's the word: research into what is believed to be the largest ever study of concealed pregnancy has been carried out in Lincolnshire'. *Nursing Standard* Vol 16/37; 29 May – 4 June, 14-15.

Saunders, E. (1989) 'Neonaticides Following "Secret" Pregnancies: Seven Case Reports', *Public Health Reports*, Vol. 104 (4), 368-72.

Spielvogel, A and H Hohener (1995) 'Denial of Pregnancy: A Review and Case

Reports.' In *Birth.* Vol. 22, No.4, 220-246.

Spillane, H., G. Khalil and M. Turner (1996) 'Babies Born Before Arrival at the Coombe Women's Hospital, Dublin.'

Spinelli, M (2001) 'A Systematic Investigation of 16 Cases of Neonaticide.' In American Journal of Psychiatry. Vol.158, 811-813.

Treacy, A., PJ Byrne and M.O'Donovan (2002) 'Perinatal Outcome in Unbooked Women at the Rotunda Hospital.' *Irish Medical Journal.* Vol.95, No.2.

Vallone, D and L. Hoffman (2003) 'Preventing the Tragedy of Neonaticide'. In *Holistic Nursing Practice*, Vol. 17, No.5, 223-230.

Wessel, J. and U.Buscher (2002b) 'Denial of pregnancy: population based study.' *British Medical Journal*. Vol. 324, 458.

Wessel, J., J. Endrikat and U.Buscher (2002a) 'Frequency of denial of pregnancy: results and epidemiological significance of a 1-year prospective study in Berlin.' In *Acta Obstetrica and Gynecologica Scandinavica*. Vol. 81, 1021-1027.

Wessel, J., J. Endrikat and U.Buscher (2003) 'Elevated risk for neonatal outcome following denial of pregnancy: results of a one-year prospective study compared with control groups.' In *Journal of Perinatal Medicine*. Vol 31, 29-35.

Appendix 1

Reports of discovery of body of newborn babies and abandoned live babies in the Irish Times 1996-2005

Table A:1

Reports of discovery of body of newborn babies in Irish Times 1996-2005

April 2005	Body of a baby found in a wheelie bin in Granard, Co. Longford. Reports indicate the mother had been taken to the Midland Regional Hospital in some distress, and after gardaí were contacted, the baby's body was discovered. Gardaí do not expect to bring charges against the mother.
March 2005	Body of baby found in a shallow grave on commonage in a rural Mayo village. News reports detailed that after some days a woman had been contacted and medical and counselling help had been offered to her.
November 2004	Body of a newborn baby discovered in a house in a housing estate in Donegal town. Reports indicated that one of the two women aged in their early 20s who were resident in the house was the mother of the baby.
January 2003	Body of newborn baby found on the roadside in Co.Antrim. Reports stated that a 22-year-old woman was arrested for questioning but released without charge.
July 2003	Dublin Coroners Court hears case of a baby's body found on a beach in Irishtown, Dublin 4. Date of death of the infant was recorded as July 2002. Reports indicated that the mother had not been contacted by Gardaí.
April 2002	Newborn baby found dead in a laneway in Co.Down. The body showed evidence of stab wounds and severe head injuries. Reports indicated that the mother had not been contacted by police.
July 2001	Body of a full-term baby found in a Limerick city suburb. Reports indicated that the mother had not been contacted by Gardaí.
March 2000	Body of a newborn baby found on wasteground in a rural townland of North Cork. The baby had been still born. Reports indicated that the mother had contacted Gardaí following an appeal.
August 2000	Body of a newborn baby found on a beach in Co.Kerry. No indication of whether the mother was contacted in news reports.
October 2000	Body of newborn baby found in a shallow grave on shore near Newtownards in Co.Down. A Coroner's court hearing ruled that the child had died from severe head injuries after suffering from considerable violence. One year later reports indicated that the

child's parents had not been contacted.

December 1999	Body of a newborn baby found in a field near town of Roscrea, Co.Tipperary on Christmas Eve. Reports indicated that the mother had not been contacted by Gardaí.
June 1999	Body of a newborn baby of premature age found in a shallow grave in boglands in rural townland on Inishowen peninsula in Co.Donegal. No indication of whether mother was contacted in news reports.
November 1998	An 18-year-old woman disclosed that she had given birth alone three weeks earlier in the house she shared with fellow students in Cavan town. She believed the child was stillborn and premature and placed it in a refuse bin. She made the disclosure to a friend who in turn told her parents who contacted the Gardaí. A Garda search was conducted of the town's landfill site for the body of the baby.
August 1997	Body a baby born at 36 weeks gestation found in the Wilton area of Cork city. Reports indicated that the mother had been contacted by the gardaí and they planned to interview her.
October 1997	Body of baby believed to have been stillborn found in Co.Antrim. No indication of whether mother was contacted.
October 1997	Body of baby believed to have been stillborn found in Co.Antrim. No indication of whether mother was contacted.

Table A:2

Reports of discovery of abandoned newborn babies in Irish Times 1996-2005

April 2004	Newborn baby wrapped in a blanket found outside a Church in Leixlip town, Co.Kildare. To date mother has not been contacted.
March 2004	Baby wrapped in tinfoil and placed in a bag at a bus stop in inner city Dublin found by pedestrian. To date mother has not been contacted.
October 2003	Newborn baby found on the grounds of South Infirmary hospital in Cork City. To date mother has not been contacted.
July 2001	Newborn baby found outside a GAA club in Ballymena, Co.Antrim. Mother came forward to police after an appeal guaranteeing her confidentiality.
December 1998	Newborn baby found at a golf club in north Belfast.
September 1997	Newborn baby found by the Fire Brigade in a telephone box in Dublin city following a 999 call from a woman informing the emergency services as to the baby's whereabouts.

Appendix 2

Case note template

Concealed pregnancy study template

Study group inclusion criteria

Presentation for antenatal care at 20 weeks' gestation or more and displaying either a denied pregnancy or a concealed pregnancy as defined below:

- **Denied pregnancy:**

  Where the woman has no subjective awareness of being pregnant throughout the majority of the gestational period or even up to a totally unexpected sudden delivery.

- **Concealed pregnancy:**

  Where the woman does know about her existing pregnant state, usually at a very early stage, but attempts by all means to prevent discovery of the pregnancy, at least from figures of authority in her life and from health care professionals. Wessel et al. describe how some young women in their study 'tried to forget' the pregnancy. At the most extreme form concealment means the woman has not disclosed the pregnancy to any of her social network. However, the definition for this study allows for some limited disclosure; e.g. telling her partner or a close friend who, as she may anticipate, then colludes with her and does not impel her to disclose the pregnancy further. A one-off contact with a health professional e.g GP or clinic nurse to perform a pregnancy test without any further contact is also within this definition.

Definition of 'casual' and 'long-term' relationship

In a casual relationship: Non-established relationship featuring irregular contact and/or no shared understanding of commitment.

In a long-term relationship: Established relationship of significance to woman featuring regular contact and/or shared understanding of commitment.

Guidance on completion of template:

- Please read section in full first before filling it in.
- Where multiple choices are given please tick as many as apply unless asked specifically for one.
- Don't hesitate to contact me at [TELEPHONE NUMBERS] if you are unclear about anything on the template.

ID CODE ____ ____ ____

Section 1: Information about the woman and her significant others

1.1   Information about the Woman

1.   Age at presentation: _____

2.   County of residence: _____

3.   Resident in a: City   ○   Town   ○
                           Village   ○   Rural area   ○

4.   Nationality: Irish   ○   Other   ○
                          Don't Know   ○   Other unknown   ○

5.   Ethnicity: White   ○   Traveller   ○   Don't Know   ○
                         Black   ○   Asian   ○

       Other ethnic origin (describe)   _____
       Mixed ethnic origin (describe)   _____

6.   Current marital status: Single   ○   Married   ○   Separated   ○
                                 Divorced   ○   Widowed   ○

       6b.   If married, is husband biological father?   Yes   ○   No   ○

7.   Current relationship status: Not in a relationship   ○
                                       In a casual relationship   ○
                                       In a long-term relationship ○

       7b.   If in relationship, is partner biological father?   Yes   ○   No   ○

8.   Has woman had a previous pregnancy   Yes   ○   No   ○

       8a.   Details of Previous Pregnancy Outcome(s) specify number:
              Miscarriage   ○   Adoption   ○
              Termination   ○   Parenting   ○

9.   Ages of Children (where applicable): ____ ____ ____ ____ ____ ____ ____

10.   Level of education to date specify highest attained:
       Primary education   ○   PLC Course   ○
       Some second level   ○   College Certificate/Diploma   ○
       Group/Inter/Junior Cert   ○   College Degree   ○
       Leaving Cert   ○   Postgraduate level   ○
       Other (please write in) _____

11.　Current Status: Please tick as many as apply

At School	○	Part-time Employed	○
At College	○	Unemployed	○
In Training	○	Working in the home	○
Full-time Employed	○		

In receipt of Benefits (e.g. OPFP, Back to Education, Disability etc)　○

12.　Current Occupation (if applicable):

13.　Accommodation details:

Living alone	○	Living with parent(s)	○
Living with partner/husband	○	Living with sibling	○
Living with friends	○	Other	○

1.2　Information about Biological Father

14.　Age:

Under 16	○	16-19	○	20-24	○
25-29	○	30-34	○	35-39	○
40-44	○	45-49	○	50 or over	○

15.　Nationality:

Irish	○	Other	○
Don't Know	○	Other Unknown	○

16.　Ethnicity:

White	○	Traveller	○	Don't Know	○
Black	○	Asian	○		

Other ethnic origin (describe)　＿＿＿＿＿＿＿＿＿＿＿＿＿

Mixed ethnic origin (describe)　＿＿＿＿＿＿＿＿＿＿＿＿＿

17.　Current marital status:

Single	○	Married	○	Separated	○
Divorced	○	Widowed	○		

18.　Current relationship status:

Not in a relationship	○
In a casual relationship	○
In a long-term relationship	○

19.　Family Status:　　No Children　○　　1 or more children　○

20.　Nature of relationship with Woman:

Once-off encounter	○
Casual relationship	○
Long-term relationship	○
Married	○

21.　Does woman anticipate support after birth:　Yes　○　　No　○

22.　What is woman's intention/decision on recording father's name on birth register?

Does not intend to record	○	Does intend to record	○
Did not record	○	Did record	○
Uncertain	○	Don't Know	○

23.　Will/Was father (be) present at birth?　　Yes　○　　No　○

If extra-marital conception

1.3   Information about Woman's Marital Partner

24.   Is husband aware of pregnancy: Yes ◯   No ◯

25.   Source of disclosure to husband:

Woman	◯	Woman's family	◯
Biological father	◯	Friend	◯
Relative	◯	GP	◯

Other _____

26.   At what stage was husband informed:

Before presentation for ante-natal care	◯
After presentation while still pregnant	◯
After delivery	◯

27.   Is support forthcoming from husband: Yes ◯   No ◯

28.   Is husband willing to share parenting: Yes ◯   No ◯

1.4   Information about Woman's Family of Origin

29.   Which of the following surviving relatives does the woman have:

Mother	◯	Father	◯
Sister(s)	◯	Brother(s)	◯

Number _____   _____

30.   Is she co-resident with any members of her family of origin:

Yes ◯   No ◯

If Yes, with whom:

Mother	◯	Father	◯
Sister(s)	◯	Brother(s)	◯

Section 2: Information about this pregnancy

2.1   Conception, Discovery and Concealment

31.   Circumstances of Conception

Please detail here any information recorded about the circumstances of conception e.g. non-consensual intercourse, contraceptive failure, under the influence of alcohol or drugs, planned pregnancy etc

_____
_____
_____
_____
_____
_____
_____

32.   Factors prompted discovery of pregnancy:

Missed Period	○	'Morning Sickness'	○
Foetal movement	○	Weight gain	○
Mother's prompt	○	Partner's prompt	○
Sister's prompt	○	Other's prompt	○
Friend's prompt	○	who _____	

33.   Circumstances of Discovery of Pregnancy:

Sought pregnancy test from GP	○
Sought pregnancy test from Women's Health Centre	○
Sought pregnancy test from Crisis Pregnancy Service	○
Done home pregnancy test alone	○
Done home pregnancy test with other	○
Presentation at GP with other complaint	○
Presentation at hospital with other complaint	○
Discovered during treatment for other condition	○
Discovered due to on-set of labour	○

Detail other circumstances or elaborate on circumstance indicated above if appropriate:

_____
_____
_____
_____
_____
_____
_____

34.   Stage of Gestation at confirmation of pregnancy: _____ weeks

35.   Describe woman's response when she confirmed the pregnancy:

_____
_____
_____
_____
_____
_____

36.   Reasons for Concealment (as per definition on front page):

| Not aware of pregnancy | ○ | In denial to self about pregnancy | ○ |
| To conceal pregnancy from others | ○ | | |

Detail other circumstances or elaborate on those indicated above:

_____
_____
_____
_____

37. Factors in concealment:
     Tick as many as apply   ◯
     Fear of rejection by biological father   ◯
     Fear of rejection by parents   ◯
     Fear of parents' reaction   ◯
     Fear of upsetting parents   ◯
     Fear of disappointing parents   ◯
     At behest of parents   ◯
     To avoid forming permanent link with biological father   ◯
     Pregnancy would threaten current relationship   ◯
     To conceal her sexual activity   ◯
     To conceal relationship with biological father   ◯
     To avoid stigma related to pregnancy   ◯
     To protect her family from stigma related to pregnancy   ◯
     To avoid others becoming involved in her decision   ◯
     To facilitate placing baby for adoption   ◯
     Detail other factors in concealment or elaborate on those indicated above

     _____
     _____
     _____
     _____
     _____
     _____
     _____
     _____

38. Options considered by woman for resolving pregnancy:

     Abortion ◯   Adoption ◯   Mothering ◯   Fostering ◯

2.2 Disclosure and Support

39. To which of the following did the woman disclose the pregnancy BEFORE
     attending for antenatal care:

     | Biological Father ◯ | Mother ◯ | Father ◯ | GP ◯ |
     | Partner ◯ | Sister(s) ◯ | Brother(s) ◯ | Counsellor ◯ |
     | Aunt ◯ | Grandmother ◯ | Grandfather ◯ | Youth Worker ◯ |
     | Uncle ◯ | Cousin ◯ | Friend ◯ | Teacher ◯ |

     Other _____

40. To which of the following did the woman disclose the pregnancy AFTER attending
     for antenatal care while STILL PREGNANT:

     | Biological Father ◯ | Mother ◯ | Father ◯ | GP ◯ |
     | Partner ◯ | Sister(s) ◯ | Brother(s) ◯ | Counsellor ◯ |
     | Aunt ◯ | Grandmother ◯ | Grandfather ◯ | Youth Worker ◯ |
     | Uncle ◯ | Cousin ◯ | Friend ◯ | Teacher ◯ |

     Other _____

41. To which of the following did the woman disclose the pregnancy AFTER DELIVERY:

Biological Father	○	Mother	○	Father	○	GP	○
Partner	○	Sister(s)	○	Brother(s)	○	Counsellor	○
Aunt	○	Grandmother	○	Grandfather	○	Youth Worker	○
Uncle	○	Cousin	○	Friend	○	Teacher	○

Other _____

42. Source of disclosure to Biological Father:

Woman	○	Sibling	○	Woman's Parent	○
Friend	○	GP	○	Hospital	○

Other _____

43. Source of disclosure to Parent(s):

Woman	○	Sibling	○	Woman's Parent	○
Friend	○	GP	○	Hospital	○

Other _____

44. Support While Pregnant:

44.a Is/was biological father supportive of woman: Yes ○   No ○   N/A
44.b Is/was partner (if different) supportive of woman: Yes ○   No ○   N/A
44.c Is/was mother supportive of woman: Yes ○   No ○   N/A
44.d Is/was father supportive of woman: Yes ○   No ○   N/A
44.e Is/was sister(s) supportive of woman: Yes ○   No ○   N/A
44.f Is/was brother(s) supportive of woman: Yes ○   No ○   N/A
44.g Is/was extended family supportive of woman: Yes ○   No ○   N/A
44.h Is/was friend supportive of woman: Yes ○   No ○   N/A
44.i Please detail any other source of support she received:

_____

45. Support Since Delivery:

45.a Is/was biological father supportive of woman: Yes ○   No ○   N/A
45.b Is/was partner (if different) supportive of woman: Yes ○   No ○   N/A
45.c Is/was mother supportive of woman: Yes ○   No ○   N/A
45.d Is/was father supportive of woman: Yes ○   No ○   N/A
45.e Is/was sister(s) supportive of woman: Yes ○   No ○   N/A
45.f Is/was brother(s) supportive of woman: Yes ○   No ○   N/A
45.g Is/was extended family supportive of woman: Yes ○   No ○   N/A
45.h Is/was friend supportive of woman: Yes ○   No ○   N/A
45.i Please detail any other source of support she received:

_____

46. Will/was any of the following (be) present at the birth:

Partner	○	Mother	○	Father	○
Sister(s)	○	Brother(s)	○	Grandmother	○
Grandfather	○	Aunt	○	Uncle	○
Cousin	○	Friend	○		

Other _____

2.3   Antenatal Care Record

47.   Presented to Hospital:
       For Antenatal Care ○   In Labour ○ Go to Q.67

48.   Source of Referral to Antenatal Clinic:
       GP   ○   Social Worker   ○   Crisis Pregnancy Agency   ○
       A & E ○   Other Hospital Dept. ○   Don't know   ○
       Other_____

49.   Week of Gestation at booking   _____ weeks

50.   No. of visits to hospital ante-natal clinic   _____

51.   Shared Care with GP: Yes ○   No ○   Don't Know ○

52.   No of Ante-natal classes attended (0-12)   _____

53.   Type of Ante-natal classes attended:
       a. Hospital group   ○   Private group   ○
       b. Hospital 1-to-1   ○   Private 1-to-1   ○

2.4   Contact with Hospital Social Worker/Crisis Pregnancy Counsellor

54.   Contact with Hospital/Crisis Pregnancy Social Worker: Yes ○   No ○

55.   Source of referral: _____

56.   Stage at first contact: _____ weeks   Post Natal   ○

57.   Number of each of the following contacts with SW:
       Individual interviews   ○
       Family meetings   ○
       Telephone Contacts   ○
       Visits while in-patient   ○

58.   Information supplied by SW:
       Adoption   ○   Supports for Parenting Alone ○
       Abortion   ○   Supports for Joint Parenting ○
       Birth Registration   ○   Custody/Access Issues   ○
       Family Mediation   ○   Guardianship   ○
       Grandparent support   ○   Partner support   ○
       Welfare entitlements   ○   Education supports   ○
       Employment supports   ○
       Other_____

59.   Was woman referred on to any of the following:
       External Crisis Pregnancy Agency   ○   Legal Service   ○
       Adoption Social Worker   ○   Family Support Service   ○
       Community Care   ○   Public Health Nurse   ○
       Other_____

2.5   Contact with Other Key Informants

60.   Did woman have contact with any of the following Other Crisis Pregnancy
       Services:

Cura	○	IFPA	○
Well Woman	○	Life Pregnancy Care	○
Mayo Crisis Pregnancy	○	Midland Health Board Crisis Pregnancy	○
One Family	○	PACT	○

61.   Did woman have contact with any of the following Key Informants about this
       pregnancy:

GP	○	Member of a Religious Community	○
Public Health Nurse	○	Youth Worker	○
Community Welfare Officer	○		

       Other_____

Section 3: Outcome of pregnancy

62.   Stage of Gestation at delivery: _____ weeks   _____ days

63.   Length of stay prior to delivery: _____ days

64.   Length of stay post-natally: _____ days

65.   State on Admission: _____

66.   Condition on Discharge: _____

67.   Outcome of Delivery:

Still-born Child	○	Single Live Child	○
Twin Live Children	○	Live Children	○

68.   Child's Birth Weight: _____ Kgs

69.   Child Feeding:

       Breast   ○   Bottle   ○

70.   Situation for Baby:

Rooming in with mum	○
Admission to SCBU for medical reasons	○
Admission to SCBU on mum's request	○
Transferred to specialised hospital	○

71.   Decision on Options at Point of Discharge:

Decided to parent	○
Decided on adoption	○
Still considering options and placed Baby in foster care	○
Still considering options and took Baby home	○

72.   If parenting, in what context:

Parenting alone	○
Joint parenting with biological father	○
Parenting with family of origin support	○
Joint parenting with current partner	○

73. Did contact with Social Worker/CPSS continue after discharge:
     Yes ○   No ○

74. Did women have contact with Other Support Services after discharge:

One Family	○	Family Support Service	○
Cura	○	IFPA	○
Well Woman	○	Life Pregnancy Care	○
Mayo Crisis Pregnancy	○	Midland Health Board Crisis Pregnancy	○
PACT	○	Other Adoption Agency	○
Don't Know	○		

     Other_____

75. Situation of woman and baby at time of coding for study:

Decided to parent	○
Decided on adoption	○
Still considering options and placed Baby in foster care	○
Still considering options and took Baby home	○

THANK YOU

Please Return to: Catherine Conlon, WERRC, Arts Annex, UCD, Belfield, Dublin 4

Appendix 3

Information sheet asking women to consent to details being released to researcher

Dear _____

Catherine Conlon is carrying out a study on the issues faced by women who come to antenatal care later than usual in their pregnancy – that is after 20 weeks. Catherine, who works with UCD, has done many studies about women and pregnancy. The aim of this study is to help women in the future who might need extra support. You can help by taking part in the study; you can give a real understanding of what kind of care and support is needed by women in similar circumstances.

In total Catherine wants 20 women (who came for antenatal care later than usual) to take part in the study – 10 from a Dublin hospital and 10 this from hospital.

Taking part in this study involves meeting with Catherine for about an hour-long interview that is just like a conversation. This can take place either in your home, a private room in the hospital, or in another place you might prefer. Your conversation with Catherine will be kept strictly confidential. No one in the hospital, or outside it, will know what you say. In the research report, all the information women give will be grouped together so that no one woman can be identified. All records of the interviews will be deleted 12 months after the study is completed.

There are 3 stages involved

1.   You tell me whether or not you agree to my giving Catherine your address and phone number so that she can contact you.

2.   The next stage will involve Catherine contacting you to talk with you some more about the study and ask if you are willing to take part. There is no obligation, and your decision will not affect your care in any way.

3.   The interview will be organised for a time and place of your choosing.

Catherine has been involved in research to do with pregnancy as well as women's health since 1996. She has a lot of experience of carrying out interviews with women in a sensitive and caring way. She is based in the Women's Education, Research and Resource Centre in University College Dublin. The study is being funded by the Western Health Board and the Crisis Pregnancy Agency.

If you have any questions about this study at any time please feel free to contact me

_____

Or

Catherine Conlon at WERRC, UCD, Belfield, Dublin 4, [TELEPHONE NUMBERS]

Your Consent

I have received an explanation of the study and agree to allowing _____
the Medical Social Worker to release my name and contact details to the researcher. I
understand that my participation in this study is strictly voluntary

Name _____   Date _____

Please keep a copy for yourself and return one signed copy in the Stamped-Addressed
Envelope Enclosed

Thank You For Your Help

Appendix 4

Concealed pregnancy study consent form

I am carrying out a study on the issues faced by women who attend antenatal care late in their pregnancy without having told anyone about being pregnant. I am seeking your permission to take part in an interview for this study, which will take about an hour of your time. I am also asking for your consent to tape-record the interview. Your participation in the study is completely voluntary. You are free to withdraw at any time and any information collected at that point will be destroyed. Your decision about whether or not to take part in the interview will not be discussed with your social worker and not affect your care in the hospital in any way. All information collected will be completely anonymous and confidential. The study has been approved by the Ethics Committee of the National Maternity Hospital, Holles Street, Dublin 2. A copy of this form will be given to you to keep.

The study aims to explore reasons for coming to antenatal care late in pregnancy, women's knowledge of antenatal care and the support women need from maternity and other services. The findings of the study will be used to design a package of services to meet the needs of women during pregnancy. In total 20 women will be interviewed for the study, 10 from the National Maternity Hospital in Holles Street, Dublin, and 10 from a hospital in the West of Ireland.

The interview is just like a conversation and will last about an hour. You may feel emotional or upset talking about your experiences during the pregnancy. The interview and the tape recorder can be stopped at any time if you wish to take a break. You do not have to answer any question you are not happy to.

I will be glad to answer any further questions you have at any time. Please feel free to contact me at any time: Catherine Conlon, WERRC, University College Dublin, 01 716 8550.

Your Consent

I have received an explanation of the study and agree to participate. I understand that my participation in this study is strictly voluntary.

Name _____   Date _____

_____   _____

Printed name of person obtaining consent   Signature of person obtaining consent

I agree for the interview to be tape-recorded.

Name _____   Date _____

Signature of Researcher

Catherine Conlon _____   Date _____

Appendix 5

Accounts of women in undetected pregnancy group

FINOLA

R: There was a virus going around which was vomiting, diarrhoea – the whole gruesome lot, so I had that for a while and went to my doctor eventually and the doctor gave me medication and said 'it's just a virus' and gave me a physical examination. So I went away and then Christmas came and very ill yet again over Christmas. In the New Year I went for a smear test and the nurse examined me and at that stage I would have been about 3½, 4 months pregnant, I think, and then I was still sick, which, stupidly enough, yes, it was morning sickness, but you don't [realise] when you weren't paying attention to it. So I went back to the doctor again and she tested me for diabetes, the thyroid glands and a couple of other things and all came back clear and she wanted me to come back again because she was kind of implying that there was something more sinister there but she didn't want to say anything until I came back and did more blood tests. So I had myself panicked that I had cancer or something and this lump was growing inside me and then I said, 'This is not cancer – this is a baby.' The head eventually got round it so.

I: How many times had you thought that before, or had you thought that before?

R: I had thought of it before Christmas and my partner, he was told when he was quite young that he would never be able to have kids so I told the doctor that just before Christmas and then I got a period over Christmas because my periods have always been irregular. So to skip one, two to four is nothing for me; I've always been doing it since I was about 17. So I told [my boyfriend], 'I think I'm pregnant' and he goes, 'You're not – you can't be' because himself and his last girlfriend never used protection and they were living together for two years. So I said, 'Ok. Well, I'm away with the fairies here,' and I agreed to go to a doctor, and then the smear test and a doctor again and then when I went back to the doctor the third time she told me I was pregnant. And I was like, 'Yeah, I know.' All I needed was to be told it but I knew it myself, about 2 weeks previously I confirmed it in my own head. Never actually went and bought a pregnancy test, which would be the sensible thing to do.

...

I: And this is on the third visit?

R: Yeah on the third visit.

I: [The doctor] did a pregnancy test?

R: Yes [the doctor] had never offered pregnancy tests beforehand and maybe that was silly on her part. She said to me, 'Do you think you are pregnant?' and I explained about my partner and that was it: the matter was kind of dropped. In hindsight that was a very silly thing to do but ... because when I said I had a period over Christmas she was happy with that and she goes, 'Was it a normal period?' and I said, 'For me, yeah,' and I think she was more worried about the way my periods have always been all my life that she, when they discovered I was pregnant, she goes, 'Well, at one stage I didn't want to tell you but I thought you'd never actually be able to conceive so in one way this is a godsend' and I was like, 'It might be to you but not for me!' That's how she had not even thought, entertained it ... As I said she had me seriously panicked that there was something wrong inside there and it was, I wouldn't say terminal, but it was serious. I didn't know what was going on and all she wanted me to do was come back for more tests and we had quite a few tests and they were all clear.

I: And in actually saying 'Ok I'm going to do a pregnancy test now', how did she introduce that idea?

R: She I came in and sat down and I told her I was still sick and worried from the last time I was in and she said 'Sure, why don't we try a pregnancy test?' but at that stage it was obvious by looking at me.

I: Right, and you had come to that conclusion?

R: Yes, I was fairly much, I was never big but it was starting to become fairly obvious; I was a bit square. It was fairly obvious at that stage. We wear fairly fitted clothes at work, so I went from work up to the doctor's. I said to the girls, 'I'm taking my lunch break and going up to the doctors' and came back pregnant.

I: And well into the pregnancy?

R: Thirty weeks.

...

R: It would be different if I'd never stepped inside a doctor's surgery, but to go in twice and a smear test ... the doctor did a physical examination on me both times prior to the third time and the first time I went in, I would have only been two and a half months pregnant and they said, 'I'll give you an examination' and that's fine – you let her away with that, but on the second time I went to see the doctor it was at, I'd say I was about five months pregnant when she did it, a physical, or no – four and half months pregnant when she did a physical examination.

[Finola]

GERALDINE

R: Well I was very late on when I found out. I was in hospital getting tests done on my heart for palpitations and fainting and dizziness and things like that and then they sent me down for an ultrasound about three days after I was admitted and it showed up that I was pregnant and then when they did a scan with more detail it showed up that I was 36 weeks gone ... I didn't realise how far 36 weeks was either so I was kind of, 'Right, 36 weeks, how far gone is that? Eight months? Oh my God.' So, like, four weeks you could say, 'Oh you're going to have a baby.'

...

R: We had been expecting all sorts. Like, I'd been told that I had a possible polycystic ovaries because all my hormone levels and everything were all over the place and a previous pregnancy test had shown up negative. Because I had been going to the doctor for about six months. This was in June I found out and I had been at the doctor since the January.*

* Months are changed to protect anonymity.

I: Which would have meant at that time you were what stage?

R: I was three months gone in January. So nothing was showing up then either, apart from that all my hormone levels were all over the place.

I: And doing pregnancy tests with the doctor never showed?

R: No, never showed up anything and I was supposed to be going for an MRI so that's why I was admitted to [the hospital] and then when they kept me in they did all the scans and it showed up. I didn't know what to be thinking – like what was wrong with me now? Because I wasn't showing; I didn't have a bump. You'd imagine you would know but I wasn't really showing at all.

…

I: So you had been going to the doctor feeling unwell?

R: Yeah, what happened was I was at work and I completely blacked out. My blood pressure was really low, so then when all the tests started it showed up there was some sort of an irregularity in my heart, but between going to the doctor and all this they had done all the tests and everything and they thought pregnancy and then it had been ruled out so I said, 'Right, that's grand. At least I'm not pregnant!' And then in June they were telling me, 'Right. You are going to have a baby in 4 weeks.'

…

R: Looking back, the signs were all there, but because I hadn't been told that I was pregnant I was putting it down to something else.

I: And your GP had done pregnancy tests?

R: Yeah.

I: And did you go back to that GP?

R: I'm still with him now. He was gob-smacked. He literally was gob-smacked, but [the hospital] had phoned me [to say] that it was possible for me to be pregnant and for it not to pick up because of different hormones, the different hormone levels, so he didn't feel as bad then when I told him that. I'd say he was more embarrassed than anything, but, like, he's still my GP because I have a newborn so I didn't bother changing him.

[Geraldine]

Appendix 6

Accounts of women in conscious denial group

PAULINE

R: I was kinda getting worried then and I said it to [my boyfriend] and he was just like, I was kinda making excuses for myself then: 'Oh maybe it's this, that and the other', and he was like, 'Oh yeah, whatever.' And then when I did a pregnancy test and I found out that I was pregnant I said it to him and he was really kinda negative. He turned around and he was like, 'Well it's nothing to do with me; I don't want anything to do with it.' So that's kinda how it started, then, that I didn't, that I got such a negative reaction off him that I didn't want to tell anyone else.

...

R: And, well, even before that I wasn't accepting it, like. I'd kinda think, 'Oh maybe it's because, you know, I'm out too much', or that sort of thing. It kinda didn't click.

...

I: Doing the pregnancy test, you were still early – you had only missed two periods at that stage, was it?

R: Yeah, it was. Well it still wasn't clicking even when I did the test, it was, kind of, I don't know. It's hard to explain but it just, it doesn't click. And even the other day, even though [my baby's] there now, it's still like, I can't believe that happened.

...

R: It doesn't sink in, like.

I: So what was it like? Was it just playing on your mind, or how?

R: Not really, I just kind of blocked it out ... It's kind of hard to think back now, but I mean, you know, if you had quiet times or at night time or something like that, or if something on TV would come up, you'd be kinda, you wouldn't know where to look, you'd be like, 'Oh God! I wonder if they can tell', if they could read your mind or whatever, anyone else in the room, stuff like that. You'd be kind of scared in case you'd get upset, but... I don't know, you'd just try and keep occupied so it doesn't, you don't start thinking of it.

I: And that you don't face up to it, was that part of it?

R: Yeah, that was basically it, like, I just couldn't.

...

I: And do you remember how you felt it was going to get sorted out, or were you able to think about that?

R: I wasn't, I was just trying to forget about it basically and hope it would go away.

I: Was it a day-to-day thing: that you were just living each day...?

R: Yeah, yeah, I think, like that. I wasn't really thinking, you know, what was going to happen a few months down the line and stuff like that. I was just kind of thinking, 'Oh it'll go away.'

...

R: It kind of got easier towards the end because I could see an end in sight. And I was like, 'Oh it will be over soon, and I noticed then as time went on, 'cos then my parents knew and my friends knew and stuff like that and even after a while it sunk in...

I: To you?

R: Yeah. I mean that wasn't until towards the very end, the last couple of weeks, around, when I think I realized, 'No. I am pregnant.' So in a way it was kind of like a short pregnancy for me because it was only really the last few weeks that I actually accepted it. And actually got used to being pregnant and everything.

...

R: Medically wise I mean everything was fine but it was just the fact that I concealed it for so long and the fact that, you know, what's the word, I was denying it as such, it was probably. Technically to me I was pregnant for about a month, that it actually was in my head, that I was.

...

R: You just try to think of other things, you just, I don't know, you can't really, you know, you're like, 'Oh God! This isn't me,' you know that sort of a way? You sort of think, 'God, that wouldn't happen to me,' you know. I don't know. It was strange 'cos even when you have a bump and everything like, I mean it's kinda hard to, you just go, 'Oh I'm getting fat,' or whatever. I mean you don't really, and even when it's kicking and everything, I don't know, it's just, it's strange. I don't know how you could explain, like, it's just, I mean you see life and everything going on around you and you're there like, you'd still be getting on with life, and so it was kind of strange in that kind of sense.

...

R: 'Cos I couldn't, like, imagine me with a child. 'Cos like my sister is what, [aged 10-14] now, so I mean, it's been a while since there's been baby things in the house and I was there trying to imagine, God, you know, I couldn't imagine a cot in my room, toys on the ground and stuff like that. And it was kind of strange, then. The whole normal thing: I mean my room would be covered in clothes and make-up and CDs and my life would be concerned with going out and going shopping and being with my friends and college and everything, so...it's kind of hard to imagine, you know, there'd be a baby thrown in the middle of that.

...

R: It's still kind of hard to imagine myself last year, though, you know, it's still, I don't know, it's kind of hard to think about it. I mean everything's okay now, but just kind of imagining myself in this position last year – it's still kind of strange to me. It's still kind of hard to believe that I was actually pregnant, do you know that sort of a way?

[Pauline]

MICHELLE

R: I think, I kept believing, I think I knew. I think I did. I knew I kept denying it because but I used to say, 'If I see a baby in a buggy it means I am pregnant,' and I'd walk around the corner and I'd see a baby in a buggy, and then I started looking at everything on television about babies, there was so many nappy ads. Why was there so many nappy ads on? Is someone trying to tell me something? Stupid things! The most ridiculous things went through my mind. Everything was about me being pregnant, I thought as well. There was, all I could think of was babies and I thought everyone was talking about babies constantly. I used to get mad with [my flatmate] – 'Oh turn that off you are always on about babies.' I knew, but I wasn't accepting it.

...

R: You can just walk around, you can accept it, if you want to have a baby and you find out you are pregnant, you are very accepting of it and you want to tell the world. If you don't want to have a baby, and you don't want to tell the world, then you don't want to accept it because the more you start to think and accept it the more you want to talk about it, the more you get involved and if you don't want to keep that baby you don't want to get involved in the whole being happy and rubbing your stomach and this and that so – that's what I found.

...

When you are so afraid of something that you think you are going to die if you tell someone you would rather pretend to yourself. Because if you have to think about it, it's like it's really true then, isn't it? And you have to deal with it, but if you don't think about it, it's not really true. It's not there; it's only this little thing inside you. At the back of your head, 'Maybe it is, maybe it isn't; it's not true don't be stupid. No, I wasn't sick that day, wait a minute how stupid am I? How could I think I was pregnant that day? That wasn't sick – that was only a cough.' It's so ridiculous.

...

R: Yeah, it was everything. So many times I was thinking wouldn't I love to be hit by a bus? Wouldn't it be great like if something happened me, and every time I'd see someone that got killed on television or something happened them, they got knocked down, 'Why doesn't that ever happen me?' And that's an awful way to think.

[Michelle]

AISLING

R: Well I didn't know until my period didn't come. I just didn't bother. I mentioned it to my sister, but she is a year or two younger than me. I didn't want to admit it, like, so I carried on; kept ignoring it and kept praying and cursing as you usually do that it would come, and I felt ashamed in myself. I didn't want to tell anyone so I ignored it, then, by working and going to college and I was grand.

I: Keeping yourself going?

R: Yeah. But after the Christmas when I started showing I was getting worse and I really did not want to say it. I don't know, then, how I did. It happened. It was in the middle of March after Paddy's day and I came home and I was talking to the brother and then eventually I just happened to tell him and of course he told all my other brothers and then he told mom and all that.

...

I wasn't even prepared for a child. I didn't even know what was happening to me. When I had the child I was sitting in the hospital and I was like, 'Ok, right, it's a baby.' I didn't even really know, and then she was down in intensive care and she wasn't with me then. So I'm sitting in the hospital: 'What am I doing here?' and then in another while I'd be, like, 'Oh my God – I have a baby.'

I: So it wasn't real because you weren't...

R: Yeah, because I hadn't, like, I didn't. I had told them here in March and nearly two months after I'd had her.

...

I'd go to bed and I was like, 'Oh my God', and I'd be telling myself that I am and then I'd start praying and cursing and whatever and you'd be saying if you were that you hope something will happen it – that it would go, get rid of it, or whatever, and then I'd be thinking, 'Will I put it up for adoption?' and then that was all the whole time. I'd have the day, then, that I wouldn't. I'd throw it out of my mind, that I wasn't, that there was something else wrong with me and then the next day I would be all down and out and different because you'd know that you were. I couldn't refuse it, like. And then to tell my brother. After that I was more relaxed, then, first when I told him, because you could talk to any of them and they knew what you were going through so there wasn't anything new said.

...

I: Do you think you were just denying and not entertaining the idea or was it that you were just hiding it? Which would you say?

R: I was definitely denying it, I definitely did not want it, nothing absolutely got to do with it or anything. I didn't want to even know ... I was always then afraid. You see I was thinking that I knew I was – I just didn't want to admit it, but I didn't want to actually go and ring in crisis because to have an abortion or whatever, because then I was admitting it and I didn't want to admit I was having it.

I: Right. So you couldn't get to that point of even looking for help?

R: No, because I didn't acknowledge I was ... I just went with the flow. I made out I wasn't pregnant and I just kept going. I kept that up that I wasn't and that there was no way I was and there was no way I was keeping it if I was or anything got to do with it. I had drummed it into my head at the earlier stage so I was just continuing on as if everything was all right and that I wasn't.

…

I was determined I wasn't but at the back of it all I still knew I was so I was trying to keep it all away but I still knew it was there and the odd time then you would be thinking it then.

I: Would that have changed gradually, would you have become more and more accepting of it or acknowledging it as being more real?

R: No, I don't think I ever came accepting of it never. No, because when I had told my brothers and then they all knew here I eventually, about a week or two after that then, the real end of March, I told my friends and they were all excited or whatever but I was just like, 'No, I hope it just dies', or whatever, that I certainly didn't want it.

…[When I went into labour] I was sitting there and the sweat was out through me and my back I thought was going to fall apart so I went down to my room and I told my sister and then she goes, "Will I get mom?" Now even at that stage I was like, 'No' because I was embarrassed. Then I just said, I was saying to myself 'Yeah. She knows. Just get her,' like. So my sister came up and got her and she came down and she told me that it was probably the baby turning because the week before prior to that I was in and the baby hadn't turned at all so she said it was probably the baby moving. That was grand and I got into the bed. I couldn't get used to it. I don't think labour even crossed my mind. I didn't have a clue. So she told me to go into bed and lie down, and that. But as soon as I jumped into the bed I jumped out the other side – I couldn't. So mom said, 'Do you want to go to [hospital]?' and I said, 'Yeah.'

I went in then and had [the baby]. They brought [baby] out and weighed and then they brought [baby] back, wrapped in a brown towel and she gave [baby] to me and I was holding [baby] like this and I was like, 'Ok [sister] do you want [baby]?' and I gave [baby] to my sister. Sure, I didn't know what I was up to … I was given [baby]. Sure, I didn't know what I was looking at, and then they brought [baby] off and they put her into the incubator and about an hour after they brought me down in the wheelchair to see [baby] and I was looking in and I could see this baby move about and I was like, 'Ok, sorry now, oh my god!' I'd wake up in the ward and I'd be looking around me and there'd be some women in with problems in their pregnancy beside me and there was some in and the babies roaring and I'd wake up and I'd be like, 'Right, why am I in here?' and then I'd be like, 'I have a baby downstairs.'

[Aisling]

Appendix 7

Accounts of women in concealment of pregnancy group

IMELDA

R: I tried on a pair of jeans one day and I couldn't fit them. I said yeah, I'd put on weight, next thing I thought then, maybe, I'd missed [my period] and I said how would I cope again. And then I put it out of me mind that day. So anyway, that was grand anyway and went on for another few weeks and I said, 'No, I couldn't be pregnant now.' I couldn't say anything. I said, 'I'll say nothing,' went in to buy a pregnancy test.

I: And you were only thinking this to yourself, you never said it?

R: Yeah, I never said it. I kept on going on anyway and made myself fit into the trousers and all this crack, made sure I put on a jumper and made sure I pulled it out a good bit, and put on coats. Anyway, summer came and it was grand, there wasn't a bother on me, until I realized in September I was getting sick and everything – terrible. I'd sit down on a chair and I just fell asleep. I was getting violently sick then, and I thought 'It's probably a tummy bug', and everything, and then I said, 'What'll I do? Go to the doctor?' and I said, 'No. What am I going to do now?' The shock, how'll I cope, you know?

...

 I thought [my partner] was looking at me at one stage too, a few times, and I was dealing with problems with him – he was drinking a lot and, you know what I mean, he was putting more pressure on me. I didn't know what to do. He was getting aggressive and everything, and I said this is putting more pressure on me, drinking and coming home here drunk ... So I said, 'No – I can't have another one now.' So I went into work the following week and I just cried, like. I said to myself, 'I can't cope with this.'

...

R: So I went to the doctor one day [I felt unwell], out of work.

I: A lady doctor that you just picked?

R: She's some of the family's doctor, but I said it might be easier to talk to her, so I went in. I made an appointment and went down from work and she called me in and I said to her about the pain in me lungs. I said nothing, now, at this stage about being pregnant. Next thing, I start crying. And she says to me, 'What's wrong?' and I said, 'I'm pregnant,' and she said, 'How far are you gone?' and I said, 'About 35 weeks.'

...

R: She said, 'I'll do your blood pressure,' and all that, and she said, 'Your blood pressure is sky high,' and she said, 'I want you to go to [the hospital]'. So that was grand anyway. I went back up to work. 'I'll give you a cert,' she said, 'if you want to go home or anything...'

I: And how did you feel after telling her, Imelda?

R: I felt the bubble had burst, the big one anyway had burst, but there was still one there and I had to go home and tell him. You know what I mean – me mother didn't even know, no one knew, [workplace] didn't even know. I went back up to the [workplace], she gave me a cert anyway for work, medical reasons, and she gave me a letter for [the hospital], as I said. I came home here after being at the doctor and I sat down and I said, 'I've just been at the hospital after dinner, for blood, they're doing blood counts on me and things like that, me blood pressure was sky high and [the doctor] is referring me to [the hospital]' and I said no more.

...

R: So, I rang a taxi for next morning to bring me [to hospital] and I got down there then around 12 o'clock and met the nurses. I was in straight away, I didn't go into the Outpatients or anything, I just went up straight to the Maternity Ward and in there I went, and I just said to the Nurse, 'Can I speak to you privately,' I said. She said, 'Come in here.' I told her the situation, that I hadn't told me partner I was pregnant or nothing, me kids, no one knew ... So I filled a form so, to go into a private room, which I thought was brilliant ... They brought down the social worker. So I met her anyway, and telling her about finances and the way it happened and all this, and she was saying, 'Don't be worrying; try and tell your partner.' And I said I couldn't, and then we went through the options for me, to give up the child for adoption or fostering, so then she said she was going to contact the [Health Board] for fostering, you know, a couple would foster the child. And they asked me did I want to know the sex of the child and I said no, because this child was, in my head, going up for adoption. And I said, 'Look, could you deliver early for me, section me and get out and get home and there'd be nothing?'

...

Tuesday, I started getting the pain. Of course I said nothing again. He was gone down town for a few drinks and came back that day around 2 o'clock and the pain was getting worse and worse and worse that day. The kids were off then on the Wednesday, Thursday and Friday. I thought if I could get down now and have this child and say nothing I'd be alright. So the next thing he came home that Tuesday evening and I was sitting at the end of the table having a cup of tea and I had covered myself up I was getting darts of pains in me back, contractions....

I: And you knew that's what it was?

R: I knew straight away, I was timing them. Every 5 minutes, I thought, and then I thought they were every 2 minutes, I thought, 'Oh no.' ... So he came in the door around six, next thing I just burst it out. And he said, 'Why didn't you tell me?' and I said I couldn't, and he said 'Tell me?' and I said 'No', and he said, 'Sure, I'd still stand by you,' he said. And I said, 'The way you've been behaving is brutal: you're out drinking and getting me to cover for everything, then,' I said. He said to me, 'When are you due?' and I said 'I'm 37 weeks gone', which I would have been, or 38. I said, 'I've to go back to [hospital] on Thursday.' I said, 'I think I'll be going in tonight with the pains in me back.' ... So that night anyway, he went out again, and he went to a neighbour and he said to her, 'Will you go out to Imelda, she's upset over something.' Now he didn't say anything to her, and I said, God forgive me, I said, 'You're going out again now,' I said, 'more drink', I said. I was sitting here. So, the neighbour came over and she says to me, 'What's wrong?' she said. '[Your partner] came to the door and told me you were upset,' and I said, 'No I'm fine,' I said, you know, passing her off, so I said, 'Come in for a minute anyway and have a cup of tea and we'll have a chat.' ... So I told her I was pregnant and she says, 'When are you due?' and I said, 'I think I'll be going in tonight', I said, 'with the pains in my back,' and she said, 'Why didn't you tell me?' and I said, '[name], I couldn't tell no one. I didn't even tell him there till half an hour ago,' and she says, 'He's out again.' I said, 'Yeah.' See, she knew what he was like, you know, in and out, in and out, in and out, and you'd never hear from him again, come home here into bed and back out again, and d'you know, that sort of thing.

I: So no relationship?

R: No relationship. I'd be gone to bed before he'd come home, with the two kids, 'cos I didn't want, I wanted peace. Go to bed and there'd be no arguments, nothing wrong, no nothing then, and no violence. Anyway he'd never....he never got a chance to do anything like that, thank God.

[Imelda]

LIZ

R: When you're living at home and whatever and not married and, its hard, well, I found it very hard to tell my mother. I was just gone 7 months when I did tell her and plus I was getting big at the time so I said, 'It's now or never.' Like, I had to tell her. I told her and it was such a relief when she did know, but two of my friends knew before my family knew. My friend's mother knew. But when I told [my mother] it was grand. Shocked. But you would get that, everyone would. But once the dam was opened it was grand – I could go to the doctor. Mam said we better go to the doctor or whatever so we went anyway and from there to [the hospital] then.

I: Was that your local GP that you had gone to for everything?

R: Yes, so we went from there then from where my GP is to [the hospital] for the first scan. It was grand then and they said [the due date] I knew it would be January anyway, mid January.*

I: You knew your dates yourself?

R: Well there could be a day or two in it but I was judging all along the 15th and [the baby] was born on the 17th .

...

I: And when did you get the first symptoms yourself that you were pregnant?

R: I knew all along. Well I missed a period, say, and I just copped on straight away.

...

• Month here is changed to protect anonymity

R: Well I was reminding myself about it.

I: Were you?

R: Yes.

I: Was it playing on your mind?

R: Yes.

I: What were you thinking about it?

R: I was thinking about the future, kind of, afraid to tell mammy or what's it going to be like once they knew. They were shocked but they were grand.

...

I: Were you denying it or just trying to ignore it, or how would you describe that?

R: I knew all along that I was [pregnant].

I: So you weren't denying it to yourself?

R: No, and I kept reminding me that I am pregnant and it was really just to tell the family at home that was the hardest thing.

...

R: Afterwards [disclosing] it was great – you could go out and buy the clothes or whatever and bring them home and you wouldn't be hiding them in the bags, going off to the room.

I: Had you been doing that on your own?

R: Well, not really, but we were looking at clothes, or whatever. Everyone thought it would be a girl and it was all pink clothes then yellow.

I: So all the time you were getting yourself prepared for it?

R: Yeah. If I was off looking at the Argos catalogue I'd bring it into the sitting room and I'd be looking at the toys, or whatever, or the teddy bears and as soon as I heard mammy coming in then, or anyone, I'd shut the page over to the jewellery or something.

[Liz]

SARAH

R: It was two weeks after I missed my period and I was going frantic. I was tearing my hair out and I got one pregnancy test and it came up negative, so I was delighted with myself. I left it again for nearly six weeks and I did another one just for the sake of it because I didn't know if it was stress of the whole first one maybe it put my period off, and I said I'd do it anyway and it came up positive. So I went into hiding for two weeks. At this stage I was in [the City] because I was working there for the summer and I was going back to school then, so I went back for a couple of weeks and then I realised this is no good. So I moved to [the city] with my brother and one of his friends and I kept working because I said if I am I want to be able to support myself; I want to go ahead with it. So I had a fairly good head on my shoulders, like, at the time, but it went downhill from there almost.

...

R: So everything was going great and then I got awful back pains. I couldn't, I didn't know what was going on at the time. Mam would say something to me at home and I'd start crying and she could not make it out at all. So it just came to the stage where I had to do something so I went to the doctor.

...

I had an appointment in the hospital. Now at this stage I was panicking because I had to go to the hospital nearer to home here. I knew I wasn't going to be staying in [the city]. I had no support because my brother had moved out at this stage so I had no support in [the city] so I decided I'd go, I'd pick [the hospital local to home]. So I was going, 'There's going to be people down there that's going to know me and its going to get back.' I went to the first one and that's how it got back to my parents. Someone knew me and it got back to my parents in a pub on a Saturday night.

...

I: How far down the road were you towards telling [your parents] do you think?

R: I don't know if I would have ever told them. I think I'd have taken off. It had come to the stage where I just didn't want to let them down. I'd have taken off, I think.

I: Do you think you would have?

R: I think I would have.

I: Did you make any plans?

R: I'd rang a friend in England I hadn't spoke to in two years but I unconsciously did that, but now when I think back to that, I would have, yeah.

[Sarah]

MADELINE

Madeline was a migrant worker living in Ireland for over two years. Her family network were all in her home country but she had established a close network of friends from her home country who represented her closest support network in Ireland. Her employer also acted as an important part of her support network while in Ireland. Because of the stigma attaching to non-marital pregnancy in her country of origin the pregnancy represented a crisis to her from the start. Also, she could not envisage raising a child alone while apart from her support network.

She disclosed the pregnancy to her partner and they both agreed that adoption was her only option representing a means by which she could maintain concealment even after birth. She contacted a support service that included the option of adoption and from there was referred to a maternity hospital for ante-natal care. Her unfamiliarity with the Irish health system meant she did not attend a GP before this time.

She concealed the pregnancy from her family at home and her compatriot friends in Ireland throughout the entire gestation of the pregnancy. At seven months pregnant she visited her family at home and maintained the concealment. At eight months pregnant her employer asked her if she was pregnant and she disclosed the pregnancy to her. The employer was supportive and presented arguments in favour of Madeline being able to keep her child and encouraged her to do so.

After the baby was born she took it home for three days while awaiting the appointment of a foster family. She found relinquishing the baby to foster care and the prospect of adoption very difficult. While fostered, she visited the baby weekly. After three months she decided not to pursue adoption and took the baby home. She described feeling guilty that those who were hoping to adopt her baby would be disappointed and anticipated negative judgements against her among the community. She found a private childcare place and continued to work. Her partner did provide help and support but his input was limited by the fact that they lived two hours apart.

She only disclosed the pregnancy and baby to her network of compatriot friends when the child was returned to her from foster care at three months. Her sister came on a pre-arranged visit to Ireland when the child was four months of age. She disclosed the birth of her child to her sister when she arrived at her apartment and met the baby. This represented her first disclosure to her family. Her sister expressed feelings of hurt and disappointment they she had not confided in her during her pregnancy. She agreed to undertake the process of disclosing the pregnancy to the rest of her family when she returned home over a period of months in consultation with Madeline.

JACKIE

Jackie acknowledged her pregnancy from early on, was happy to be pregnant and always anticipated motherhood. She determined to keep her pregnancy concealed from her family throughout gestation because she anticipated they would not accept the pregnancy. She believed her parents would be resistant to the prospect of her becoming a mother because they felt she would find it hard to cope, despite her own desire to do so. She also anticipated that they would want her to pursue her career over her wish to become a mother. She feared they may pressurise her into abortion or adoption as had occurred when she became pregnant once before.

She did disclose the pregnancy to her partner and to close friends she expected would be supportive and began buying clothes and equipment in preparation for the birth of the baby. She embarked on putting in place the practical arrangements she would need to care for the baby in her own living environment. She also presented for antenatal care at a maternity hospital from twelve weeks' gestation and attended all of her recommended antenatal check-ups and care. She made it clear to staff in the hospital that she was concealing the pregnancy from her family and sought support to enable her prepare for motherhood without the anticipated support of family.

When the baby was born she called her family from hospital and told them. They were shocked but sought to give her the practical help she needed while in hospital. It was agreed she would go to stay in a married sibling's family home when discharged. As she anticipated her family were strongly in favour of her placing the baby for adoption. They advocated arranging for an intra-family adoption where her child would be placed with a married sibling. She was very disappointed about this and would not agree, resulting in tensions and a breakdown of relations. She reverted to relying on support services to assist her return home with her child, and she succeeded in doing so. As time passed the differences between herself and her family were being slowly resolved but she felt that while practical help was forthcoming she was not getting their support.

Appendix 8

Structured interview schedule for focus groups and one-to-one interviews with health professionals.

1. What challenges are presented to your Department and team when a woman presents at an advanced stage in pregnancy up to the point of delivery without having disclosed the pregnancy to her social network?

2. Thinking back to those cases of concealed pregnancy you have encountered in your years of experience in your profession, can you describe any specific steps you have taken in responding to a woman presenting with a concealed pregnancy that go beyond the usual practices in antenatal/maternity care?

   In particular here we are looking for a description of procedures that have developed 'organically' over the years in your care setting as well as examples of specific innovative steps you may have taken in particular case(s).

3. A key objective of this research is to formulate a set of recommendations representing a national framework for the management of concealed pregnancy to apply across the range of services, from antenatal care to other support services. What particular recommendations would you like to see as part of that framework?

Notes

Notes

Notes